The French Political System

The French Political System

Suzanne Berger
Massachusetts Institute of Technology

Foreword by **Samuel H. Beer**

Part 3 of *Patterns of Government*, Third Edition,
Samuel H. Beer and **Adam B. Ulam,** General Editors

Random House, New York

Reprinted from *Patterns of Government,* Third Edition

Berger, Suzanne
The French political system.

Rev. ed. of pt. 3 of Patterns of government, 3d ed., edited by S. H. Beer and A. B. Ulam.
Bibliography: p.
1. France—Politics and government—1958–
2. France—Politics and government. I. Beer, Samuel Hutchison, 1911–   ed.   Patterns of government.
II. Title.
JN2594.2.B45   320.9′44′083   74–795
ISBN 0–394–31818–8

Foreword

This volume is a paperbound edition of Part 3 of the third edition of *Patterns of Government: The Major Political Systems of Europe*. The larger work includes sections on Britain, France, Germany, and Soviet Russia and an introductory part on modern political development—all now available as separate paperbacks.

The five parts of *Patterns of Government* are integrated by the common theme of modernization. But each country account is also written so as to be suitable for study either separately or in conjunction with other countries not considered in *Patterns*. In the latter connection one attractive possibility would be a combination that would include the United States; for in each of the country accounts of *Patterns* a comparison with America, seen as a typical modern polity, is never far in the background of the analysis. Whatever one's preference, the present publication of the introduction and the country accounts as separate books provides the necessary flexibility.

A word about the general approach of *Patterns*: After a brief eclipse, history is making a strong comeback in political science, largely under such headings as "modernization" and "development." A period of neglect was healthy, since it obliged political scientists to decide what use they really wanted to make of history. In the third as in the previous editions of *Patterns*, a leading characteristic of the methodology is the use of both theory and history in the study of contemporary politics. The authors hold that patterns of political behavior in the present can be best explained if we have an understanding of how they originated and what traits they displayed in the past. In taking this view, the authors follow the example of some of the leading figures in modern political science, from Montesquieu to Weber, who used history to enlarge the body of empirical political theory and then used that theory to analyze and explain the historical process as it flows from the past through the present into the future.

Each country is examined as an example of a highly developed modern polity. This approach has two implications. First, it means emphasizing certain features the countries have in common. Second, it means treating these common features as the issue of a course of historical development moved by similar forces, passing through similar phases, and culminating in similar problems. But the stress on the common features of modernity does not lead the authors to overlook the crucial differences that distinguish the four systems. Quite the contrary. To show what is common helps them to bring out the differences more sharply. As a specialist in the country he is writing about, each author is accordingly concerned not only with its common modernity, but also with the traits and tensions that are unique to it.

Harvard University   SAMUEL H. BEER

Contents

Appendixes

Select Bibliography

Index

The French Political System

One

The Tradition of Modernity in France

France was the first modern state. Secularization and political democracy may have appeared earlier in the United States, national bureaucracy and rationalized central administration may have been accomplished earlier in Prussia, and national political integration may have proceeded furthest in Britain. But it was in France that these processes of political modernization first coincided at the end of the eighteenth century to produce a state unlike any that Europe had ever known. The Revolution of 1789 was in this sense a modernizing revolution. It did not create the nation or the bureaucracy or even the urge to secularism and democracy—these had all existed in some form before the Revolution, as they had existed in the other European states. What the Revolution accomplished was to build a political system in which all these processes of modernization could be institutionally expressed and organized. What was new was not the values themselves, but the creation of a state to enforce them for the entire society. In the years of political struggle to restore the political system of the Revolution, the parties that contended understood that the battle over the legacy of the Revolution was the battle between political traditionalism and political modernity. Now, almost two hundred years after the Revolution, the values embodied in the Revolution have themselves become a tradition. Both Left and Right of the Fifth Republic draw on this legacy. And if in Britain contemporary politics show the modernity of tradition, French politics today represent the tradition of modernity.

France, Britain, the United States—all modern states—have developed different political institutions, values, and problems. If the processes of political modernization destroyed and eliminated the old political system and created a wholly new one in its place, we would expect all modern states to be more or less identical. But in fact, political modernization does not clear the political terrain of all vestiges of the past and raise a new house on bare earth. Rather, modern states have been built on top of and with the half-collapsed, half-standing institutions of the past. States differ, however, in *how much* and *what* they preserve of the past. In the United States, for example, the legacy of the nation's beginnings is liberal, individualistic, and participant. In France the past is the society and politics of the "old regime": traditional, hierarchical, and static. With different pasts to build on, France and the United States, both modern industrial societies, developed political systems that are and most likely will continue to be very different.

Modern states differ not only because they build on different bases, but also because they make different choices about how much of the past to preserve in the modern political system. The French political elites, confronted with the issues of modern politics, made decisions that did not radically eliminate the old political values and institutions, but rather embodied them in the new order. France modernized by fusing elements of traditional and modern political systems into the state. In France, therefore, political modernity and political traditionalism coexist. The result is a state with certain great strengths and capacities. France, better than many other industrial nations, has been able to accommodate great social and economic change while protecting the fabric of society. The notions of social prestige, the values of social conservatism and familism, and the class structure that modern France inherited from the old regime all worked to slow down the process of industrialization and to ward off some of its harshest consequences for the social groups that in other countries suffered most. At the same time, the coexistence of competing values and institutions in politics has been the source of major strains and disruptions.

To understand why the French elites systematically preferred a solution that preserved significant parts of the traditional state and society, we would have to examine the social situation and aspirations of the elites themselves. But here we are primarily concerned not with why the elites chose to maintain traditional values and structures, but with the consequences of those decisions.

The decisions of the elites about how to integrate the remnants of the old polity and society into modern France—about how to modernize state and society—covered a wide range of different issues. The passionate debates over state subsidies to Church-run schools were in reality debates over the place of the Catholic church in a modern state. Legislative argument over the inheritance laws and laws governing corporations turned on different appreciations of the values of the family and the needs of modern industry. The political battles over agricultural tariffs were in fact battles over whether the state should protect a traditional sector of the economy even at the expense of industry. As the Radical party declared in 1934 in favor of preserving the traditional countryside in modern society:

> Though the economic function of agriculture is important, some people have contested the utility of maintaining it because of its high costs. It is pointless to pose the problem in economic terms. The social benefits that the peasantry provides the nation are vital to national life and irreplaceable: no matter what their cost is, it must be paid.[1]

The choices that were made in all these cases where the stakes were the mix of traditionalism and modernity that the state would authorize have been profoundly important, for they have determined the major problems of contemporary French politics. The decisions of the elites about how to achieve national political integration are particularly important in this respect, for they relate directly to the two major weaknesses of the French state today: the contested legitimacy of government and the crisis of relations between citizens and the state.

The goal of national political integration is in certain respects imposed on all modern political systems, but there are more ways than one to organize power territorially, to integrate the national economy, and to create a political community. The French political elites had available to them several possible courses of action for achieving territorial integration, economic integration, and a certain integration of the political values of the national population. The alternatives they chose were decisive for the future of the state.

Territorial Integration

The territorial definition of France was a matter solved before the other problems of modernization moved onto the agenda of national politics. Through centuries of annexation, conquest, and royal marriages, the French monarchs had carved out a nation whose boundaries were by and large fixed at the beginning of the eighteenth century. After a period of rapid territorial expansion and contraction during the Revolutionary and Napoleonic wars, the Second Peace of Paris (November 20, 1815) defined the territory of France and settled Frenchmen within boundaries that they acknowledged as the legitimate confines of France. By the time when mass political participation and political parties were developing, the French generally agreed on who was and who should be French. The only out-

---

[1] Cited in Serge Mallet, *Les Paysans contre le passé* (Paris: Seuil, 1962), p. 15.

standing territorial problem was the annexation by Germany of two provinces, Alsace and Lorraine, in the settlement of the Franco-Prussian War (1870–1871). Though this amputation of French territory generated different ideas about foreign policy and military preparation, it did not provide a basis for fundamental political alignments. Unlike Germany, where territorial questions provided a major axis of political division in the modern political system, France rarely experienced serious domestic political conflict over the territorial dimension of national power. The single major exception was the dissension over Algeria. In the conflicts that divided the French political elites over granting independence to Algeria, the Algérie-Française group opposed independence on the grounds that Algeria was not a colony but, rather, an integral part of French territory. Despite the bitterness and violence of the controversy, once Algerian independence was granted, in 1962, the political groups that had mobilized around this territorial issue disappeared quickly.

Even after the territory over which the state should extend its authority was determined, the distribution of the state's power in this territory was still open for decision. The question of territorial integration involves a resolution of the question of how a state will exercise political power in the nation as a whole: how it will divide power and authority between the center and local and regional governments. By choosing a particular blend of centralization and decentralization, the state shapes the outcomes to three other political questions: How much political liberty will there be in the state? What kind of political participation will citizens experience? How will the barriers to political community that derive from the diversity of local situations, needs, and desires be overcome?

The relevance of the territorial organization of power to political freedom has been one of the recurrent themes of modern political theory. The writers of the American constitution were deeply concerned with this issue, and they believed that the federal system they adopted would best protect the freedom of individuals and groups, even though they recognized that federalism might not maximize the efficiency and effectiveness of the state. In France the theorist most concerned with this issue was Alexis de Tocqueville (1805–1859), whose studies of the Revolution of 1789 and notes on the Revolution of 1848 were reflections on the problems of freedom in a democratic society. Tocqueville observed that the process of democratization at work in France in the nineteenth century had as its principal outcome the destruction of intermediary groups between the individual citizen and the state. In the aristocratic old regime these intermediary groups were formed on the basis of birth and privilege, and they exercised many functions that today are considered political. The administration of justice, the levying and collection of taxes, and police functions were in the hands of private individuals or corporations, acting not as agents of the state, but rather, as the privileged wielders of rights that they had inherited or purchased. The central state could neither hire nor fire these secondary political actors; it could control them only by dispossessing them: only by "nationalizing" the power and authority exercised by these private groups. The centralizing monarchs had throughout the eighteenth century attempted to gain control of these autonomous centers of power, for example, by revoking the charters of autonomous municipal corporations. But the greatest pressure for the destruction of these intermediary groups came from the forces that sought a greater democratization of society and, therefore, tried to destroy aristocratic distinctions. The leveling of political privileges based on class and birth concentrated political power in the hands of the central government, which gradually became the sole repository of power and authority in the nation. As Tocqueville commented:

> The State has everywhere resumed to itself alone these natural attributes of sovereign power. In all matters of government the State tolerates no intermediate agent between itself and the people . . . all these various rights, which have been successively wrested, in our time, from classes, corporations, and individuals, have not served to raise new secondary powers on a more democratic basis, but have uniformly been concentrated in the hands of the sovereign. Everywhere the State acquires more and more direct control over the humblest members of the community, and a more exclusive power of governing each of them in his smallest concerns.[2]

The state intervenes more and more in spheres of life once regulated autonomously by the individual or for the individual by some other group —family or class or corporation. This expansion of the central government into the sphere of personal liberty goes virtually unchecked, Tocqueville argued. The only effective obstacle to the extension of power is the resistance of another power, and in France democratization has removed those groups which once checked the power of the central state: the aristocracy and the feudal guilds and corporations. In Tocqueville's words:

> The circumstance which most contributed to secure the independence of private persons in aristocratic ages, was, that the supreme power did not affect to take upon itself alone the government and administration of the community; those functions were necessarily partially left to the members of the aristocracy: so that as the supreme power was always divided, it never weighed with its whole weight and in the same manner on each individual. Not only did the government not perform everything by its immediate agency; but as most of the agents who discharged its duties derived their power not from the State, but from the circumstance of their birth, they were not perpetually under its control. The

---

[2]Alexis de Tocqueville, *Democracy in America* (New York: Schocken, 1961), Vol. II, pp. 363–364.

government could not make or unmake them in an instant, at pleasure, nor bend them in strict uniformity to its slightest caprice—this was an additional guarantee of private independence.[3]

Tocqueville recognized that it would be impossible for an aristocracy to serve this role in a democracy, but he argued that there are functional equivalents to an aristocracy that a democratic nation might use. Freedom, he suggested, can be preserved in a democracy only by organizing separate, autonomous, and therefore competitive centers of political power. On his travels in America he had observed that voluntary associations of like-minded citizens, an independent judiciary, the press, and state and local governments were performing essentially the same function in checking the central government that the aristocracy had played in France during the old regime. What Tocqueville hoped for in France was the development of independent local institutions that would both provide citizens with political experience at the local level that they would carry over into participation in the state and, at the same time, check the powers of the central government.

There have been many in France to challenge the premise of Tocqueville's thesis that the chief danger to freedom lies in the action of the central government and that the most important way to increase an individual's freedom is to expand the sphere in which he is not touched by the state. To the contrary, it has been argued that a strong state is the best guarantee of individual liberty and that action of the state may increase freedom and state inactivity reduce it. In France, the idea that centralization and liberty are directly related is best expressed in the Jacobin tradition. The Jacobins were a radical, activist faction that formed during the French Revolution, under the leadership of Maximilien Robespierre and Louis de Saint-Just. While other political factions saw the loosening of the grip of the central state in the wake of the Revolution as an opportunity for enlarging the liberties of local and provincial governments, the Jacobins sought to strengthen the authority of the central state. In the initiatives and independence of local centers of power, the Jacobins saw threats to the unity of the nation. And on this unity depended the freedom of the individual citizen. For the Jacobins justice required that the republic be one and indivisible. Laws must be the same for every citizen in every part of the nation. And if substantial discretion and autonomy were left to local authorities, this result would not be achieved. The citizen who lived in Lozère would be obeying laws different from those that governed the citizens of another department. The Jacobin conception of political justice implied, therefore, that only the central government should legislate.

---

[3] *Ibid.*, pp. 386–387.

Centralization receives political support in France not only from the Jacobin Left but also from an important section of the Right, which continues the legacy of the centralizing monarchs. Indeed, centralization has become a key tenet in the tradition of modernity shared by both Left and Right in contemporary France. In the recent debate over the creation of regional governments, the Communists referred to this tradition when they charged that dismantling the state would open France up to the greed of foreign monopolies and concluded that "to organize the region must not mean creating fiefs as was done in the past for barons. Political power can only be national and the law can only be the same for all Frenchmen, whether Bretons or Alsatians."[4] A Gaullist deputy, attacking the same regionalization proposals, wondered rhetorically whether the government should not put the regional advocates on trial for treason ("atteinte à la sûreté de l'Etat") and appealed to Frenchmen of the Left and Right to defend the nation—"the sole political entity."[5] The Gaullist parliamentary group discussed regionalization and resolved: "In restoring the State, General de Gaulle gave strength back to the nation. We consider therefore that any attempt to disaggregate the State would lead to disaggregation of the nation."[6] At the heart of the conflict among French political elites about how to organize power in the nation lies the profound disagreement about freedom in a modern state that is expressed in the conflict between the Jacobin thesis that centralization supports and increases the political liberty of citizens and Tocqueville's thesis that only decentralization of power can preserve freedom in a democracy.

The second issue at stake in decisions about the division of power between central government and local and regional governments is political participation. One of the principal concerns of contemporary political science has been the impact on the state of different patterns of civic participation. Whether citizens participate, how much, and in which kinds of organizations are all questions of critical importance for the state. The recruitment of new political leadership draws in large measure on the network of secondary political groups. The capacity of the state to manage the problems of society requires a chain of intermediary organizations capable of channeling social needs, desires, and information up to national centers of power and carrying back state policy. And finally, the stability of the political system as a whole depends on maintaining a delicate equilibrium whereby participation is neither so intense that the fate of the state hangs constantly in the balance nor so weak that the mass of citizens

---

[4] *Le Monde,* January 6, 1971.

[5] *Le Monde,* December 8, 1970.

[6] *Le Monde,* January 8, 1971.

remains apathetic, passive, and uninvolved in politics and the regime can find no popular support.

The relationship between participation and the organization of the state is not, however, one-way. Participation does shape national politics, but at the same time national politics shapes the kind of participation that is possible and likely in a given state. In this regard the decisions on centralization are critical, for the degree to which power has been concentrated at a single central point or dispersed through the nation determines whether there will be participation, how it will be organized, and when it will occur. In France, for example, the Ministry of Education makes virtually all decisions about education everywhere in France, down to the scheduling of subjects in each school day. With power concentrated in Paris, what sense does it make for parents in a town to band together in a P.T.A. to try to influence local educators? Why participate in local voluntary educational associations when the power to change the school is not located on the local level? Why form local civic associations when the municipality has so little discretion in the use of its funds that virtually all matters must proceed through the prefecture, the departmental headquarters of the central government? Why belong to a local historical sites association when it is the Fine Arts bureaucracy in Paris that will decide what kind of tile must be used to roof an old church? Why participate at all in local groups when the questions that matter most to a community are by and large decided in Paris, far beyond the reach of local groups and local participants?

When local or regional governments have the political power and fiscal resources to resolve certain of their own problems, they provide targets for citizens who find opportunities within their reach for influencing politics. In France the pattern of centralization has made such opportunities scarce. The weakness of participation at the local level that results from this has two important consequences. Democratic politics requires that the political system provide experiences of conflict and compromise, discipline for group ends, and leadership and followership—in sum, a political education, both for political activists and for the interested but less active citizenry. This education, as well as the more specific skills of administration and planning that are the prerequisites of effective intervention in contemporary politics, can only take place through actual participation. By limiting the possibilities for participation, the French state has reduced the reservoir of civic experience and left only a small pool of political militants from which the state may draw to replenish its ranks. By controlling or eliminating the possibilities for local initiative, the state does limit the risk of having incompetent or corrupt local officials, but at the same time it stunts the growth of responsible local leadership by depriving men at the local level of the resources for attaining their goals. By centralizing power at the top, the "republic one and indivisible" assures that the rules are the same everywhere. But this means that there is little chance that the rules can ever be changed.

The difficulty of bringing about political change is, indeed, the second consequence of the scarcity of opportunities for participation at the local level. The virtual impossibility of bringing about any significant change on local or middle levels of the system engenders frustration and apathy about politics and support for political ideologies and parties that aim at a total capture of the state and total transformation of the social system. Civic passivity and revolutionary politics are in a sense two sides of the same coin in France. Men feel either that change is impossible, and they become cynical and apathetic, or else they come to feel that the only way to change anything at all is to change everything: to capture the central government. If to influence local school policies, one must reach out and change the Ministry of Education in Paris, then the logical instrument of political action is the political party with a global political strategy, not the limited-purpose interest group. The centralization of France has, therefore, provided a permanent incentive for organization in ideological political parties with plans to transform the state and society and a permanent disincentive for groups with more limited and, potentially, more parochial concerns.

The decisions that the French made about the distribution of power in the nation have had a third set of consequences for politics. The division of power between the center and local or regional authorities is a matter that affects not only the liberty of citizens and their opportunities to participate but also how the country will be governed. It is difficult to imagine any country so simple and homogeneous that all decisions could be made in the capital. The diversity of needs and situations always requires that some discretion be left to men on the spot to appraise and act on the problems of the locality. As societies become modern, their complexity and diversity increase, so it becomes more difficult to concentrate power at any single point in the system.

As the modern state has assumed responsibility for the regulation of social and economic problems once left to the initiative of private groups, it has discovered the need for more information and for a kind of information that cannot simply be channeled up to the top. If the problem were only one of transmitting facts, advances in the field of computer technology might promise to make a completely centralized state possible. The fact is, however, that managing a modern economy requires not a set of discrete decisions but, rather, a process of decision making during which modification and adaptation of policies is continuously taking place in response to feedback from earlier decisions. Examples are easy to find, both in the economy and society. The development of a prototype aircraft, for example, like the setting up and administration of a welfare program, involves a series of complex decisions requiring judgments by persons directly in contact with the problem. Whenever such matters have to be referred to higher authority, the results are technological stagnation in the first case and tensions and pressure for self-rule and community power in the second. As the goals that are pursued through political institutions multiply, excessive centralization of power is more likely to paralyze the state than to increase efficiency.

While it is not possible for a modern state to govern society from the capital, there are more ways than one of moving political decision making closer to the problems. One method is decentralization: to give the authority for making a decision and the resources to carry it out to a body that is independent of the central government. In the United States, for example, decisions on education are ordinarily taken by state or local authorities and financed by their own fiscal resources. The independence of these subnational bodies is ensured in two ways. The state or local official has his own political base, for he has been directly elected and is not appointed by or responsible to the national government. And whereas in France, a local official can be recalled by the national government, the American President and Congress have no authority to remove a mayor or governor. The independence of American local government is the result, moreover, of its independent fiscal resources. State and local governments have the authority to levy taxes, within limits that they set for themselves and that are outside the purview of the national government. Just how different France is and the consequences of the differences will be discussed in Chapter 5. Here we intend only to suggest that moving power and authority closer to the problems, which in the United States (and in Britain and Germany to a lesser extent) is achieved by a decentralization of political power, in France is accomplished by another method: deconcentration. Deconcentration is the delegation of the power of the central government to one of its agents, who exercises this power in the region or locality. Rather than making local decisions in Paris or giving local officials the authority and resources to make their own decisions—the decentralized solution—the national government delegates its authority to one of its own representatives in the locality. In the words of one of Napoleon III's ministers, "Deconcentration means striking with the same hammer, after shortening the handle."

There have been three ways of shortening the handle in France, three different agents of the center who make decisions in the localities: the prefect, the representative of the government ministry, and the mayor. The most powerful of these is the prefect, who is the direct arm of the state, representing both the government and the Ministry of the Interior. Between the communes and the national government there is only one other governmental level: the department. There are ninety-five departments in

France; in each of them executive power is exercised by a prefect. While the prefect formally shares power with an elected departmental council *(conseil général),* his legal prerogatives as well as the department's financial dependence on the central government give the prefect the real power in the department. The second set of state agents are the representatives sent out to the departments by the government ministries. They report both to the prefect, who is supposed to coordinate their local activities, and also back to their ministries in Paris. The third representative of the state is the mayor, who is the local agent of the Ministry of the Interior and thereby directly responsible to the prefect. Mayors are elected, but their dual role limits their independence; many of their decisions have to be approved by the prefect, who may, in fact, revoke them. As in the case of the departmental council, the power of the mayor is severely constrained by the limited possibilities of obtaining financial resources, except by recourse to the state.

The consequences of administering the country with deconcentrated rather than decentralized authorities are important. There are obvious advantages, the most important of which are associated with the uniformity that such a system can ensure. The common education and outlook of the prefects, as well as their common dependence on central authority, tend to produce the same kinds of decisions in all parts of the country. In France situations like those that arose in the United States when Southern governors defied the rulings of the Supreme Court on school desegregation would be inconceivable. The checks and controls with which the central government surrounds local officials also make municipal corruption of the kind that is common in the United States a rare occurrence in France.

At the same time, however, the reliance on deconcentration instead of decentralization has heavy costs. In terms of its impact on citizen participation, deconcentration has much the same effect as the centralization of power. It limits the field for local initiative and deprives local leaders of political experiences that might prepare them for national politics. With respect to the quality of decisions, the reliance on a restricted set of state agents makes innovation difficult, for in areas where prefects or mayors lack expertise, they must fall back on formal rulings and precedent. A decentralized system, in contrast, is much less restricted to a given set of formal authorities; according to the needs of the situation, local authorities may create new bodies to deal with new problems. The diversification of urban problems in the United States has thus produced a multiplication of new governmental bodies: model-city boards, metropolitan districts, commissions, interstate commissions, port authorities, and so forth. In France, in contrast, there has been little institutional innovation because of the limits set by the hierarchical system in which authority is exercised. The institutional rigidity of the system makes it difficult to cope with new problems.

Economic Integration

Compared with her European neighbors, France attained a high measure of economic integration at an early stage in the process of political modernization. In contrast to Germany, where well into the nineteenth century a multitude of autonomous jurisdictions and sovereign powers posed barriers to trade, in France, the Revolution of 1789 tore down the last legal barriers to free exchange throughout the nation. Indeed, the obstacles to intranational trade had been severely weakened even before the Revolution, and the Revolution provided the final push that cleared the ground of the privileges with which provinces and cities, guilds, and corporations had protected monopoly rights.

The problem of establishing national markets for labor and capital and a set of national prices for goods is not solved merely by destroying the legal and political obstacles to exchange, however. To create a free flow of men and goods through the nation, an infrastructure of transportation and communication networks must be set into place. Despite the political turmoil of the half-century after the Revolution, the successive regimes carried out a vast program of building highways, secondary roads, and canals. Though regions at the periphery continued to experience difficulties in reaching urban markets, nonetheless the situation of the outlying provinces of France was far from that of the isolated regions of Italy, for example. In Italy, even after national unification, the differences between the traditional economy of the South and the modern industrial economy of the North survived, indeed increased, so that today economists often consider these two parts of the nation as separate economies in order to analyze the Italian economic system. In sum, national unification may be a necessary, but is not a sufficient, condition of economic integration.

France by the middle of the nineteenth century had achieved economic integration, but she had done so in a way that left two problems outstanding. First, the pattern of industrialization in France left intact many of the institutions of the traditional economy. These "feudal remnants" not only survived industrialization but were often reinforced by it. The case of agriculture is revealing. The modernization of farming with the use of machines, fertilizers, and scientific methods of cultivation and the appearance of large capitalist farms in the Paris Basin did not eliminate the large numbers of small and medium-sized peasant farms. Instead, the peasant farmers used modern technology to support their traditional enterprises. When fertilizers increased farm yields, the peasants used the new surpluses to maintain a large population on the family farm. When machines became available, the farmer who was losing his workers to the cities could continue to run his farm in much the same way as before, by simply replacing the farm laborer-turned-factory worker by a tractor or thresher. The modernization of agriculture was a process that did not rule out the survival of a large peasantry. Economics and technology, in short, left open several alternative solutions for the countryside. What was decisive were the policies of the French state, which encouraged the preservation of a large traditional peasantry.

The price of this choice was high. In order to permit the peasant on a small, inefficient farm to survive, the government supported agricultural prices at a high level. The state had to abstain from programs of modernization of farm structures, because the immediate result of policies to increase average farm size or encourage crop specialization by the more productive farmers would have been to reduce the number of farms. A fundamental transformation of the agricultural system that would have made French agriculture more productive would have sacrificed the traditional peasantry. This the state refused to do, and as a result, the price of food remained relatively high in France, perhaps slowing the rate of industrial growth.

Why did France choose to maintain the peasantry? More generally—for the cases of small commerce and business are like agriculture—why were traditional sectors of the economy preserved in the process of economic integration and modernization? The answers to these questions are political. The elites of France believed that the preservation of traditional structures alongside modern industrial structures was necessary for the political stability of the nation. The political equilibrium on which the governments of the Third and Fourth Republics were based was one in which industrial interests shared power with the representatives of the traditional sectors of the economy. In order to support this political balance, the economy could not be dominated by the interests and values of the modern industrial sector alone. Indeed modern industry itself, having grown up in the protective fold of a system that muted competition and rewarded values other than those of economic rationality, was not eager to eliminate traditional firms. These considerations were strengthened by the realization that dismantling the traditional countryside, for example, would trade peasant electors for working-class electors, thereby increasing the clientele of the socialist parties.

What are the consequences of the decision to maintain the traditional sectors of the economy alongside the modern sectors? The problems that France faces today in adjusting her economy to the competition of the other members of the European Common Market are in large measure a result of these political decisions of the past century. The family businesses of France are no match for the foreign firm that can draw on outside capital to finance its investments and on the expertise of trained managers to run the business. The small French farms have trouble competing with modern Dutch agriculture. The solutions that the state once developed for the economic integration of the traditional sectors of the economy become less and less viable as France is opened up to the competition of other producers. In the last decade in France there has been a new awareness of the costs of maintaining the less productive sectors of the economy, resulting in series of proposals for modernizing the most important of them: the nationalized industries, agriculture, and the railroads. Aside from the economic problems that such proposals raise, there remains the political dilemma: Can the regime afford to diminish the reservoir of traditional voters, from whom it draws support? The question of how to modernize the French economy without destabilizing the political system thus remains one of the most important issues in French politics today.

The historic pattern of economic integration has left another serious problem on the agenda of contemporary politics: regional disparities in economic development. The communication and transportation networks that made economic integration possible serve certain regions of France far better than others. The western periphery—Brittany and the Vendée—the Massif Central, and the departments in the Southeast are regions whose contacts with the rest of France are difficult. Highways and railroad lines are not only less densely distributed in these regions, relative to the rest of France, but they are also less modern. The same is true of telephones: In the region around Paris, 21 percent of the population have telephones, while in the Breton department of Côtes-du-Nord, for example, only 5 percent have.[7]

The problem of the "French desert," however, is a product not only of poor infrastructure but chiefly of the centralization of economic activity in a few regions and the underdevelopment of the rest of France. There are two comparisons that reveal the magnitude of regional disparities in France today: the contrast between Paris and the rest of France, and the contrast between the rich, industrial France northeast of a line from Mont-Saint-Michel to Arles and the poor, more traditional France southwest of it.[8] Political centralization in France is paralleled by a concentration of economic control and of working population in and around Paris. Over half the head offices of important firms in 1962 were located in that area—a degree of economic control out of proportion to the total amount of economic activity in the region, since only a third of the working population was located there. In contrast, the industrial region around Lyons, which has a work force half as large as that of Paris, has only one-seventh as many very large firms based in the area. As Kevin Allen and M. C. MacLennan concluded from their study of French regions: "The effects of this concentration in economic, social, administrative and political terms is observably large and as a result the area of influence of the Paris region

---

[7]Yves Durrieu, *Régionaliser la France* (Paris: Mercure de France, 1969), p. 124.

[8]Kevin Allen and M. C. MacLennan, *Regional Problems and Policies in Italy and France* (Beverly Hills, Calif.: Sage, 1970), p. 125.

is vastly superior to that of any other urban centre in France."[9] One measure of this predominance is the difference between family incomes in Paris as compared with the rest of the country. Household incomes (excluding social security benefits) in 1962 in Paris were 50 percent higher than anywhere else in the country. Wages and salaries in industry, agriculture, and services are highest in the Paris regions, while in the West, Southwest, and Massif Central they often do not reach even half the Paris level. Indeed, these three regions lag behind the rest of France on virtually all measures of standard of living, industrial strength, and modernization.

The differentials between "rich" France and "poor" France pose both economic and political problems. Because of the concentration of economic activity in the area around Paris and the facilities for easy communication and transportation, businesses prefer to locate there, rather than in regions like Brittany, where the traditional basis of the economy, agriculture, is in crisis and industrial jobs are badly needed, but where industry is weak and infrastructure poor. Industry continues to expand in Paris, creating problems of housing, schools, and urban transport, while in the provinces the people leaving the farms find no jobs in their own region and are forced to migrate to the big city. As Paris and a few other modern, industrial regions grow, the disadvantaged regions lose traditional sources of employment and find no new industries to replace them.

Regional disparities are not new in France, but political awareness of them is. Problems become political issues only when groups mobilize around them, define them in terms that relate to the other issues on board, and introduce them into the process of political decision making. The groups that might have picked up the problem of regional disparities and challenged the economic policies creating and reinforcing such disparities were the opposition political parties. But in France opposition to the economic policies of the government has been organized by left-wing parties whose doctrines focus on class, not on region. The Socialists and Communists have been sensitive to the impact of state economic decisions on the fortunes of given social classes. In legislative debates on the national Plan, for example, the Communists examine proposals for their effect on workers and present analyses of their opponents' position and their own in class terms. The impact of state decisions on regional differentials has been a question in which no major political group has been interested. As a result, regional problems have not surfaced as political issues.

This has begun to change, however, in the last few years. The awakening of political interest in regional problems has a variety of causes: increased desire for participation in local and regional affairs, an exacerbation of the economic difficulties of the underdeveloped regions as agriculture and

---

[9] *Ibid.*, pp. 143–144.

traditional industries decline, and a new concern with domestic problems now that France's colonial involvements have come to an end. Whatever the outcome of the recent discussions of reform proposals to create regional governments and whatever the effects of the increased level of demands for national assistance to backward regions, the significant facts are that the region has become a political issue and that political groups are beginning to align themselves on positions of support and opposition with respect to various regional projects. One political party, the Radicals, made regionalization the banner of its platform in a recent campaign before municipal elections. And groups advocating regional platforms are springing into life in the provinces. The problems of the regional distribution of economic activity and of the place of traditional sectors in the economy are political problems that derive above all from the policies the government pursued to achieve economic integration and growth. The process of economic integration, like that of territorial integration, required choices on the part of the French state. The pattern of these choices has in significant measure determined the agenda of contemporary French politics.

Integration of Political Values

Economically and territorially, France was more integrated than many other European states at comparable stages of political modernization. In one critical respect, however, France was profoundly divided. Despite the new ties that the economy created among Frenchmen in all parts of the nation, despite the new possibilities for communication and social intercourse, the area of political consensus in France was apparently diminishing and not expanding at the beginning of the twentieth century. The French in this period were deeply divided over the values and goals of the political system. It seems as if the increasing awareness of the importance of the state that social and economic integration fostered led to less agreement than had existed before about the purposes that the state should support.

The politicization of the French population proceeded through the nineteenth century in two broad stages. First, wide sections of the population became increasingly conscious of the significance of the state in affairs of everyday life. For millions of peasants, isolated from the centers of national power, the decisions of the state to tax or to conscript or to interfere in the running of the parish church were the first demonstrations of the importance of the state for private life. Once individuals blamed their troubles on private failings or on the decisions of local elites. Now, increasingly, they perceived the central government—Paris—either as the source of the problem or as capable of providing a remedy for it. The links between private, everyday life and the state became more and more visible.

As individuals all over France became aware of the impact of the state on local and personal affairs, the politicization of the population moved into a second stage. Common, national perceptions of what the major political issues were began to emerge, and people in all parts of the country began to see themselves as allies or enemies in a common cause. The development of a set of political issues that people in all regions regard as salient and central is a gradual process and one that is neither unilinear nor irreversible. Political modernization tends to promote the emergence of issues that carry the same political meaning and weight throughout the nation, but in even the most developed countries there are issues more important for certain regions or groups than for others. In the United States, for example, despite a very high degree of political modernization—however measured—it is only recently that the "nationalization" of political issues has proceeded to a point where racial questions begin to have the same political salience in North and South.

The organization of national political life around common issues in no way assures a greater measure of political integration. Indeed, political conflicts and tensions that were scattered and defused by their uneven relevance for different groups and regions may become embittered when they are perceived in the same terms in all parts of the country. Apparently this is what happened in France. As all sections of the country began to see the principal issue at stake in politics as the Church-state issue, the measure of political consensus that had already been achieved was undermined by new polarization over secularism. Politicization of the French coincided with the emergence of the Church-state issue, and this was to have profound consequences for modern France.

The Church-state issue involved three distinct relationships between the Catholic church and the French government: institutional and social, international, and ideological—relating to the control of the beliefs and loyalties of Frenchmen. The institutional aspect of the problem was by and large resolved by the Revolution of 1789. In the social system of the old regime, the Church was one of the feudal orders. It possessed important political, fiscal, and judicial privileges. It had independent economic resources from the tithe and from its own rural and urban land holdings. The clergy paid no taxes but, rather, voted subsidies to the state. The higher clergy were secular lords; in 1789 all of them were of noble birth. The local priests were in effect the local governmental officials, since they kept parish records, conducted marriages, ran the schools, and organized poor relief. On the institutional level, the Church suffered the expropriation in the Revolution that was the fate of the other feudal orders. Indeed, the priests' initial enthusiasm for the Revolution led them to encourage the notables and the higher clergy to renounce voluntarily their feudal privileges. It was the Bishop of Autun—later known as Talleyrand—who proposed that the state take over Church land in exchange for paying the priests a salary and assuming the expenses of the Church. By the end of 1789 the Church had lost all the institutional privileges that it had enjoyed as a feudal order.

In its international aspect the Church-state problem centered on the relations of an external sovereign power—the pope—with Catholic clergy and believers who were French nationals. The conflict had its origins in the struggles between monarchs and popes over the control of the Church in France, and it revived with new violence after the revolutionary assemblies attempted to integrate the Church into the republic by making priests subject to elections and requiring them to swear oaths of allegiance to the state. To the French Republicans, the Catholics appeared to be the agents of a foreign and hostile power that, in the hope of restoring the monarchy, sided with the countries that attacked France. However, not only Republicans regarded the hold of the pope on French citizens with deep misgivings. None of the regimes after the Revolution—neither Napoleon nor the restored monarchs—ever agreed to restore to the Church the autonomy it had enjoyed before the Revolution. The Napoleonic Concordat did recognize the Catholic church as the religion of France, subsidized churches, and allowed priests to resume teaching in primary schools—since the state in any event did not have enough teachers. But in matters that Napoleon considered critical to the state, like higher education, he refused to let the Church intervene, declaring that "priests do not have that national spirit, the independence of opinion that teachers of a great nation need." The battle over which rights the Catholic church was entitled to exercise in France continued through the nineteenth century, focusing on the activities of certain orders, like the Jesuit order, that were particularly associated with the pope, and on control of educational institutions. These struggles led to the 1906 decision of the Chamber of Deputies, against the bitter opposition of French Catholics and the Pope, to separate Church and state. The state would no longer recognize Catholicism as the state religion, pay the salaries of priests, or subsidize Church schools. Church buildings, which had been the property of the state, were to be turned over to lay Catholic groups.

The violent reaction of the Church to this "expropriation" was the culminating point in a long attack on the Third Republic. In the course of the nineteenth century the Church had become the mainstay of all the elements that wished to overthrow the republic and reinstate the old regime. The other groups of the old regime—the king and the nobles— were too weak and too divided to organize effective opposition to the republic. The monarchists after 1830 could not agree on candidates for the throne. Moreover, while the monarchy ruled it had not needed and had not built a base of popular support, so that once universal manhood suffrage was instituted the monarchists had increasingly to rely on the Church for mobilizing support. The Church, in short, was left holding the bag of reaction. On a succession of issues that were the life crises of the Third Republic—the attempted coup d'état of General Boulanger, the Dreyfus case—the Church lined up with the enemies and attackers of the republic, even when no direct interest of the Church was at stake. By the end of the nineteenth century the defense of the Catholic church had become inextricably tied up with the defense of all the conservative, old regime interests.

The highest Church officials publicly denounced the republic; local priests actively worked to elect antirepublican candidates. One priest declared before the 1901 elections,

> In the next election, from one end of this land to the next there will be only two candidates: Jesus Christ and Barabbas; Jesus Christ in the person of the Catholics, or as a second choice, of those candidates who will defend Christian freedoms; and Barabbas under different names: Barabbas, the anti-clerical, Barabbas, the Freemason, Barabbas, the revolutionary, Barabbas, the anarchist, Barabbas, the communard. Are you going to vote for Barabbas? . . . To battle under the shield of Saint Michael, the guardian angel of the country, the enemy of the Revolution. He conquered the revolution in heaven by defeating the chief revolutionary: Satan! Forward with Saint Michael against the Revolution!

The republicans responded in kind. Emile Combes, a Radical premier, declared during a legislative debate in 1903 on whether priests should be allowed to teach:

> It is the spirit of olden days, the spirit of reaction, which makes these religious orders rise up out of the debris of the old society like a living negation of the fundamental principles of modern society. The spirit of modern society, the spirit of the Revolution must relegate them forever to a past definitively condemned by the doctrines and morality of democracy.

Pope Leo XIII finally recognized that the Third Republic was not likely to collapse under the Church's attack and that the interests of Catholics would be protected best by participation within the framework of the system. The acceptance of the republic (1892) did not, however, mean that the Church-state crisis was resolved, for in its third aspect the problem remained as acute as before. The issue that remained was that of the control of belief. In the old regime virtually no conflicts arose between the monarchy and the Church over men's loyalties. The monarchy neither required nor could have tolerated popular participation: it needed subjects not citizens. The attitudes, beliefs, and opinions that men held on political matters were a matter of little concern to the state. Since the state did not need citizens as participants, it did not need to educate them in a particular set of beliefs.

The passive, apolitical conduct, the parochial loyalties, and familistic attachments of average Frenchmen were, one might say, the political culture of the old regime. Whether or not the Church controlled education, then, was largely a matter of indifference to the state, since the state did not need to use the schools to inculcate a set of civic beliefs and allegiances. Modern states have important interests at stake in the educational process, both because it turns out citizens and because it provides the skilled personnel needed for the government and for the economy. The monarchy needed neither of these products, and so the clergy's exclusive control of the institutions in which beliefs and loyalties were transmitted went unchallenged by the state.

The Revolution of 1789 brought about a radical change in the conception of the authority of the state, and as a result, the Church's monopoly on Frenchmen's beliefs came under mortal attack. The new state of the French Revolution depended on the active political participation of a nation of citizens. To make men citizens they had to be educated in a new set of civic virtues and sentiments. As Robespierre and the Jacobins understood well, the survival of the republic and of the new system of politics depended on the political commitment of common men who would participate in politics not only or primarily for self-interested reasons but also because of a desire to serve the public good. The revolutionaries saw that citizenship requires an understanding of the state not only as a mechanism for dispensing goods to individuals but also as the basis of the good life. The state is the instrument with which to implement values in society. As Jean Jacques Rousseau had argued before them, men can be good only when they live in a good state, and, conversely, to build a good political community requires a high degree of moral commitment from citizens. Once political leaders reasoned this way, the morality and beliefs of private individuals became a matter of the greatest importance for the state. What the state sought from its subjects was no longer limited, as under the monarchy, to passive, obedient conduct; it required the active, willing, moral commitment of the citizen. The purpose of legislation, declared Robespierre before the Convention, should be the reinforcement of all those values on which the republic is based:

> Everything that stirs up love of country, that purifies morals, that elevates the spirit, *everything that guides the passions of the human heart towards the public interest* should be voted or established by you. Everything that tends to focus feelings on narrow personal matters, or to arouse a fascination with the trivial and a disdain for what is important, such things should be rejected or repressed by you. *In the system of the French Revolution, all that is immoral is impolitic, all that is corrupting is counter-revolutionary.* [Italics added.]

In other words, the attitudes, beliefs, and "passions of the human heart" have become critical for the state. The state can no longer afford to ignore the ideas and feelings of men. Rather, the government must legislate in such a way as to produce in men the attitudes and beliefs that will make them good citizens and make the state a good state.

What can the state do to foster civic virtues in its citizens? Robespierre, like Rousseau before him and the school teachers of the Third Republic after him, believed that what was needed was a kind of "civil religion," a set of beliefs that would attach men to the notions of justice, brother-hood, and equality with the same conviction and fervor with which they had once held religious beliefs. The principal institution for accomplishing this end was public education. As Robespierre explained in a 1794 speech,

> Public education must be stamped with high aims, corresponding to the nature of our government and the sublimeness of the destinies of our Republic. You realize the necessity to make education common and equal for all Frenchmen. We are no longer going to educate "gentlemen" but citizens. Only the nation has the right to raise its children.

The new values, conception of citizenship, and radically expanded scope of state authority all required that the monopoly control of belief that the Church had held until the Revolution should be "nationalized" by the state. Where once the Church had formed the beliefs and world view of men, now the state needed to do so in order to make citizens.

In the conflict that ensued between Church and state over the loyalties of Frenchmen, the chief battlefield was the school. Through the first half of the nineteenth century the Catholics tried to reestablish their right to run secondary schools. After the establishment of the Third Republic they were beaten back to a defense of their position in primary education. And in 1906 when the separation of Church and state was voted by the Cham-ber of Deputies, the state finally ended all support to Church schools.

The political passions over the "school question" fed into a political system that was already polarizing into two camps, indeed into two Frances: secular republican France and Catholic France. The political groups that stood for a secular republican France identified themselves by a common set of ideological ancestors, a common set of ideas, and a common institution: the public school. The revered ancestors of republi-can France were the Jacobins, the revolutionaries of 1830 and 1848, and the founders of the Third Republic. As for a common enemy, in the words of Léon Gambetta, one of the fathers of the Third Republic: "Clericalism, there's the enemy!" At the core of republican political doctrines was a philosophy about the character and purpose of public education, ex-pressed in the term "laïcité." In English laïcité would have to be translated as neutrality or secularism, but the operational sense of the term in France was the exclusive control of education by public institutions. Indeed the defenders of laïcité argued that the public school should not and could not be simply neutral in its teachings on Catholicism and the old regime, for example, since these latter were false beliefs and evil institutions.

The camp of Catholic France was organized around different values and different institutions. The values were those of authority, hierarchy, and order; the institutions were family, Church, and the Catholic school. In the view of the Catholics, the values, beliefs and minds of the young ought to be shaped by the Church. Even a neutral school—and the Catholics denied that the *laïque* school was neutral—is in principle bad, for in their view, life itself is not neutral but pervaded by values that a child should be taught to recognize and respect. As Pope Leo XIII declared—and Catholic France concurred—"The school is the battlefield where it is decided whether or not society will remain Christian."

By Catholics here we mean political Catholics: those individuals and groups who were politicized by the range of conflicts that arose between Church and state and who were mobilized by these conflicts on the side of the Church. In the religious sense, of course, the vast majority of all Frenchmen were Catholics—born, married, and buried in the Church. Not only the defenders of Catholic schools but also the Radical politicians of the Third Republic baptized, confirmed, and married off their children in the Church. The Catholics, politically defined, were a subset of religious Catholics who were made aware of the impact of politics on their lives principally through the impact of state decisions on the religious institutions to which they belonged and whose response to this impact was to line up on the side of the Church. Whether or not there *are* Catholics in this sense in a given country depends on the course of political development in the state—on whether there is political mobilization around the Church-state issue. It is not a simple function of religious practice.

Mass political participation, then, developed in France at a time when the burning questions in politics turned on the issue of which values and beliefs were so important to society and the state that the state should be able to mold them and which values and attitudes were primarily religious and thus fell into the province of the Church. The political issue that first politicized the French was secularization. The violence of the conflict and the irreconcilability of the opposing positions led to a polarization of the political system into the two camps that have been described above as republican France and Catholic France. The parties and coalitions of Left and Right were organized within these camps. Between the two camps there was no shared ground, or at least, during the height of the conflict at the turn of the century political groups behaved as if there were none. The ideological character of the issue at stake meant that conflict on this one issue extended to a wide range of other phenomena.

What occurred in France at the turn of the century was a hardening up of the lines of fissure in the system and a division of the parties into a Left camp and a Right camp, each defined primarily by its position on the Church. These political allegiances and alignments have proved remarkably resistant to subsequent changes in French society. As Chapter 3 on the party system will describe, various axes of political division have been created alongside the Church-state axis, but the latter continues to exert a significant influence on contemporary political life in France.

The political choices that were made when the central issue in politics was conflict over the values of the national community have willed a difficult legacy to modern France. Like the solutions that the state developed to integrate the nation economically and territorially, the policies of political integration created new problems and left others unresolved. The ideological character of politics, the contested legitimacy of the Constitution, the challenge of protest that is not only antigovernment but antiregime—these and many other problems on the agenda of France today derive directly from decisions made along the route to political modernity.

Two

Political Legitimacy and the Constitutional Order

The government and institutions of the French political system today are called the Fifth Republic, because the constitution under which the French have lived since General de Gaulle's return to power in 1958 is the fifth of the republican constitutions that have been tried in France. France since the Revolution of 1789 has been governed by two monarchical systems (the Bourbon and Orleanist) and two imperial systems (those of Napoleons I and III), as well as by the four republics that preceded the Fifth Republic: the First, Second, Third, and Fourth Republics of 1793–1799, 1848–1852, 1870–1940, and 1946–1958. Why have there been so many fundamental changes in the organization of the French state? Why have the French been unable to define neutral "rules of the game" that all participants in the political process could accept? Under what conditions might the French finally agree on a constitutional framework within which all political groups could pursue their goals? Does the constitutional settlement of the Fifth Republic have wide enough support so that political groups will turn from challenging the regime to working within it? The unstable and often violent history of French politics since the Revolution of 1789 suggests that these are the questions on which the future of France depends.

A constitution is a set of fundamental rules defining the scope, distribution, and exercise of political authority in a society. In every stable political system, there exists some general agreement on the extent of state power, on who ought to wield the power of the state, and on which constraints ought to limit the state. These national decisions on the rules of the political game are constitutional decisions, and they may be embodied in a formal constitutional document, as in the United States, or simply understood and agreed upon, as in Britain. The problems that arise in a state about the legitimate use of power are so numerous and complex that no single constitutional law could possibly settle all points in controversy. What constitutions do attempt to resolve are the *fundamental* rules of the political game—the basic framework within which political action and conflict will take place.

The history of even such relatively stable states as the United States and Britain shows that what is constitutional is never decided once and for all in a nation. Political values change, and the constitution, too, is forced to adapt, insofar as the national consensus it once represented has been modified. Such constitutional adjustments are easy when there is general national agreement on new rules for the political game, as, for example, in the recent United States decision to admit eighteen-year-olds to full participation in politics. But the same question of who has a right to share in political power was far less simply resolved on previous occasions in American constitutional history, when other groups demanded a change in the framework of the state. The civil rights of women and of black Americans were not generally acknowledged, and the struggle to amend the Constitution to recognize their rights to full citizenship was a long one.

In France, however, the basic problem has not been the constitution's responsiveness to changing political values but, rather, the inability to find a constitutional settlement that could reconcile the conflicting and mutually exclusive sets of political values held by the major participants in the political process. Frenchmen have held different views on the fundamental questions of politics: In which spheres of private and social life may the state legitimately intervene? What should be left to the initiative of individuals and groups? What rights does the individual have, even against the state? What can the state demand of citizens? On matters that are subject to authoritative decision, who in the state has the right to act? local or national officials? bureaucrats or politicians? Parliament or President? How should these various authorities be related? And when political authority does act, what are the means and procedures that should be employed? These are the issues that constitutions try to resolve so that within an agreed-upon set of rules, citizens and groups can pursue their goals without at each point challenging and endangering the very existence of the state. Each of the French constitutions has embodied a certain set of answers to the above constitutional questions, but in every case significant opposition to the constitution has persisted and weakened the stability of the system.

The fault lay not with the men who wrote the constitutions but with the politicians, who failed to create a national consensus on the organization and exercise of political power. In stable political systems the area of constitutional agreement is broader than the constitution. In the United States, for example, the country's sense of what is constitutional includes not only the document bearing that title but also the Supreme Court's interpretations of the document. In Britain there is no single written constitutional document; what is referred to as the constitution are all the laws and political conventions regarded as basic for the political system. In contrast, the problem in France has been the persistence of profound disagreements over what the state should be and how state power should be exercised along with the absence of an area of constitutional consensus wide enough to accommodate the major political forces of the nation. In this broad sense, despite almost a dozen constitutional documents, France has always lacked a constitution.

Constitutional Traditions in Conflict

The search for a constitutional framework acceptable to the major political groups of the nation has been a central problem of contemporary French politics. One of the principal obstacles has been the profound mistrust that permeates the political community. The intensity of the political conflicts over secularism, over socialism, and over Gaullism created camps of permanent enemies in politics (see Chapter 3). No group was willing to contemplate the possibility of its mortal enemies taking power, and so each one took advantage of its periods in power to refashion the constitution in such a way as to reduce its opponents' chances in politics. The laws on elections were prime targets of such maneuvers, each side trying to write an electoral law that would maximize its chances and diminish those of its rivals. The parties with strong national organizations always tried to obtain elections with proportional representation; the parties based on local notables always tried to use single-member districts. The Gaullists upon their return to power in 1958 restored the latter system and were richly rewarded for their pains: In the 1958 legislative elections the Gaullist party, with less than 18 percent of the vote, won 40 percent of the seats in the National Assembly, while the Communists, who received 19 percent of the vote, won only 2 percent of the seats. The electoral system is only one case of many in which legal arrangements have been used by the political parties in order to increase their power at the expense of opponents. The constitutional questions of whether to have a second house in the legislature, whether to strengthen the presidency, and how to distribute power between central and local governmental authorities have been treated by the political groups in the same way: as potential weapons in political battle. The constitution, far from limiting the terms of political conflict, has been simply one prize among others of political warfare.

Chapter 3 describes the issues dividing the political parties and suggests some of the reasons why the nature of partisan conflict in France has made it impossible to define any set of rules of the political game that appear neutral and fair to all participants. Here we shall consider the political values that figure in controversies that are directly related to the constitution. The different conceptions of authority that divide French political groups have been expressed in two opposing constitutional traditions, each with its own institutions, personnel, and typical political practices. These two constitutional models are the parliamentary and the presidential. In the parliamentary constitutions like those of the Third and Fourth Republics, the legislative assembly is the sole representative of national sovereignty, and governments are formed and changed at the will of this body. Those groups in French history who have supported parliamentarism have had in common the belief that political institutions should be structured, above all else, to maximize the values of representative democracy. Representative democracy has meant different things to different political groups in France. For the Jacobins and those who followed in their ideological footsteps, those institutions were best in which there was the most direct democracy and the least delegation of authority. The people were sovereign, and the best representative assembly was one that most closely reflected and expressed the will of the people. For other groups, like the conservative republicans of the Third Republic, the best system was one in which the system of representation allowed the people to choose a legislature whose collective will was the sovereign expression of France. The Parliament itself embodied national sovereignty. As Paul Reynaud, a former Prime Minister, declared in the National Assembly in 1962, "Here and nowhere else is France."

In what we will call presidential constitutions, the chief of state derives his effective power and authority from sources independent of the legislature. The chief executive—whether President in the Fifth Republic, head of state in the Vichy regime, or emperor in the Second Empire—is not responsible to the legislative assembly, and the assembly itself is in significant measure dominated by him. The most important value associated with this constitutional tradition is that of the political unity of the nation. Beyond the reach of political parties, contending interest groups, and opposing ideologies, above the forces that divide France, the chief of state defends the unity of the nation. According to the supporters of presidential constitutions, only a strong and unitary executive can develop coherent policy for the country; only he can bring the nation intact through periods of crisis. Government should not be entrusted to an assembly, for this would only transmit the divisions in the society and the conflicts among political groups into the state and thus make any stable political authority impossible. Political order is the prerequisite of all other political values, and in France the only way to assure political order is to organize the power of the state in a system that provides a strong executive, the supporters of presidential government believe.

On paper, most French constitutions have been mixed constitutions and have attempted to incorporate some elements of both models. The Constitution of the Fifth Republic, for example, has many features of a parliamentary regime. But in practice the mixed constitutions have always served to establish the predominance of either Parliament or head of state, and there is no precedent in French political history for the effective sharing of powers between the legislature and the President that characterizes American political practice. The failure to reconcile the competing ideals of authority of these two constitutional traditions has meant that a parliamentary regime seems illegitimate to the supporters of strong executive power and, conversely, that a presidential system like that of the Fifth Republic is unacceptable to the proponents of government by legislative assembly.

Parliamentary Democracy

A parliamentary constitution is, quite simply, one that uses a representative assembly to produce a government out of the assembly, to check and control the government, and to change it. Who holds executive power, how this power will be exercised, and when it will change hands are all decided by the legislature. As rapid comparison shows, a parliamentary system organizes the state very differently from a presidential system in all three respects. In a presidential system like that of the United States, the legislature has no say on who is to hold executive power, for this is settled by direct popular elections. In checking and controlling government, the Congress has a large but not exclusive role, for the Supreme Court, too, shares this function. Moreover, in a presidential system the checking of power is a two-way street: The Congress may amend or reject the President's bill, but he may veto theirs. In determining when and how the government changes hands, the legislative assembly in a presidential system plays no role at all; executive power is regulated by fixed terms of office. The Prime Minister of the French Third Republic could fall from power any day; the presidency of the United States changes hands only at regular four-year intervals.

In parliamentary systems, governments are created, checked, and changed by the legislative assembly. *How* this happens varies greatly from country to country. In Britain since the thirties the electoral system and the strength of the two major parties combine to produce legislatures in which one of the parties has always been strong enough to form the government alone. In the French Third and Fourth Republics, in contrast, governments were produced not by the clear mandate of election results but by parliamentary coalitions. The two principal reasons for this were the multiplicity of political parties and the effects of the electoral system (see Chapter 3). No single party in the Third and Fourth Republics ever won a majority of seats in the National Assembly, so in order to form any government at all, several parties had to ally. The governments lasted only as long as the parliamentary coalitions on which they were based, and in France this was on the average a very short period. From the first government under the Constitution of the Third Republic to the last government under the Fourth Republic (1876–1958) France was ruled by 119 governments.[1] The average life of a government was eight months. Weeks might pass between the time one government was voted out and a new government could be formed, and, in fact, for almost three months out of the last year of the Fourth Republic France was without a government.

There is no reason why parliamentary coalitions cannot produce stable and long-lived governments. Though governments based on a single party are inherently more cohesive, the examples of Sweden, where the Socialist and Center parties ruled together for many years, of West Germany, where the Social Democrats and Christian Democrats formed a government that lasted three years, and of other European parliamentary democracies show that governmental instability is not the inevitable product of multiparty coalitions. Therefore, to understand why the French parliamentary system in the Third and Fourth Republics was unable to create stable governments, we must look for factors other than the multiplicity of parties.

If the French political system is compared with the political systems of those European countries where the parliamentary system has produced strong, stable governments, two important differences stand out. First, coalition governments are stable when the parties composing them are able to discipline their members. In France, however, the parties of the Third and Fourth Republics that participated most often in governmental coalitions were the parties with the weakest party discipline. The parties that were reservoirs of the *ministrables,* the deputies most eligible for ministerial careers, were loosely knit groups of local political notables, banded together in a national party whose structure was shadowy and control over its members nonexistent. The governmental parties of the Fourth Republic (the Socialists, the M.R.P., the Radicals, and various Center parties) were more disciplined than the typical governmental parties of the Third (the Radicals, Radical-Socialists, moderate Republicans, Left Republicans, and Center parties), but nonetheless, in every crisis of the Fourth Republic, the Prime Minister had always to worry first about whether he could carry his own party along with him as well as whether he could satisfy the other parties of the coalition. The Prime Minister often

---

[1]François Goguel and Alfred Grosser, *La Politique en France* (Paris: Seuil, 1970), p. 36.

could not control the policies of Cabinet ministers of his own party, for in the absence of any effective party discipline, he could discipline a member of the Cabinet only by threatening to dissolve the government. The weakness of party discipline contributed even more directly to governmental instability by making it possible and indeed profitable for members of the government to abandon it at an opportune moment in order to be "eligible" for participation in the next government. The minister who defected was not often punished by his party, and he was frequently rewarded by the system for having known when to jump off a bandwagon that had run out of steam in order to jump onto the next one.

The second point of difference between the parliamentary systems successful in creating stable governments and the French system is the set of attitudes and expectations regarding executive power that have developed in political culture and political practice. In Britain parliamentary tradition and political culture support a strong executive. Although the government is ultimately dependent on and responsible to Parliament, Parliament acknowledges and accepts the authority of the government and the desirability of according it substantial powers. In radical contrast, French political culture and parliamentary tradition are deeply antagonistic to the notion of strong and autonomous executive authority. One of the strongest themes of French political culture is profound mistrust of the state and hostility toward the exercise of power. As François Goguel and Alfred Grosser have written, the French

> look at their participation in politics as a way of weakening the State, rather than reforming it or getting it to serve their interests and preferences. It is this hostility towards the State, this tendency not to understand its role and to distrust those who work for it which is the clearest evidence today of the traditional political behavior of Frenchmen.[2]

A survey carried out in 1970 on the attitudes of a representative sample of Frenchmen discovered that attitudes about the state are a mixture of resentment and expectation.[3] Almost half of those interviewed believed that the state defends the rich rather than the poor; a third found it unjust. Most described the state as an organizational labyrinth, impossible to understand or to influence unless one is an expert (73 percent of the sample). Each felt that he was powerless in dealings with the bureaucracy and that "others" were receiving special favors that were denied to him. But at the same time that the citizen distrusts the state, he expects much from it. For 64 percent of those surveyed the most important function of the state is to provide economic and social security. The state should

---

[2] *Ibid.,* p. 26.

[3] *Le Monde,* October 10, 1970.

protect the citizen against the risks of unemployment, inflation, old age, sickness, and dislocation due to transformation of the economy. Only after this cardinal demand for state protection did the group interviewed mention demands for state action to maintain public order, to regulate economic activity, to assist underprivileged groups in society, and to defend France in the international arena.

Both for public opinion and for the political elites many of the ambivalent feelings about the exercise of state authority are centered on the role of the executive. When Frenchmen were asked "What is it that for you best symbolizes the state?" the largest number (25 percent) answered "the President of the republic"; the second largest group (23 percent) replied "the government." It is not surprising, therefore, that in the parliamentary republics the general societal mistrust of political authority combines with the doctrine of parliamentary sovereignty to focus hostility on the executive. Where the British Member of Parliament expects to support the policies and, more generally, the authority of a government formed by his party, the French deputy regards with suspicion even a government for which he has voted and jealously watches for any encroachment of the executive on the assembly's sovereign prerogatives. The notion that Parliament should consider its main function as blocking and checking the executive, rather than collaborating with him, was best expressed in the political ideas of Alain, the penname of Emile Chartier, who commented on the politics of the Third Republic. As Alain saw it, the principal problem of politics is to defend individual liberty against forces that constantly seek to exploit and enslave men. In modern society these forces are the great economic and social powers; the political elites are nothing but the political arm of these oligarchies. Power, like wealth and status, corrupts those who possess it: "No elite is worth anything, for it is destined to exercise power and therefore destined to be corrupted by the use of power."[4] Even when the rulers are elected by the ruled, the latter end up being exploited by the men they have chosen. As Alain wrote:

> Universal suffrage does not really create democracy . . . A tyrant can be elected by universal suffrage and that does not make him any less a tyrant. What matters is not the origin of power, but the continuous and effective control that the ruled exercise over government.
>
> . . .
>
> In every constitution there are monarchic, oligarchic, and democratic elements, more or less in balance. The executive is inherently monarchic. In action one man must always command, for everything can not be decided beforehand . . . The legislating function, which includes the administrative, is inherently oligarchic, for in order to run an organization, scientists, lawyers are needed

---

[4]Alain, *Elements d'une doctrine radicale* (Paris: Gallimard, 1933), p. 11.

. . . What then is Democracy if not the third element that I call the Controller? It amounts to the power, always in vigor, to depose the Kings and the Specialists immediately, if they do not serve the interest of the majority. For many years this power was exercised through revolutions and barricades. Today it works through Parliamentary Motions of Confidence. Democracy is in this sense a perpetual struggle by the ruled against abuses of power.[5]

There is something new in politics these days, democracy, which is nothing other than the organization of resistance against these formidable powers, against the rulers. A representative assembly can neither substitute itself for these powers, nor choose them, but in the name of the people, it can refuse to obey them.[6]

The deep suspicion of executive power that found expression in Alain's conception of resistance—putting obstacles in the path of executive action —as the proper function of the legislature was an important element in the political culture and parliamentary practices of the Third and Fourth Republics. Political personalities who seemed likely to become strong executives were feared and resented by the deputies, and they were systematically kept out of governments—until, of course, a crisis arose that could not be handled by the usual parade of ministers. The long periods of political "exile" of Georges Clemenceau, who later served as Prime Minister during World War I, of Pierre Mendès-France, to whom the National Assembly finally had to have recourse to extricate France from the Indochinese war, and of Charles de Gaulle, whom the Assembly called back only when civil war seemed imminent, exemplify the fate of strong leaders in a political system hostile to executive authority.

Even when the Assembly was willing to elect a Prime Minister, it had an armory of weapons with which it could prevent him from carrying out his program. The parliamentary commissions that considered a bill before it was voted on in the Parliament could amend the government's project in any respect, so that the bill Parliament debated was no longer the government's, but the commission's draft. Even the budget could be amended by the deputies. Though various rules were adopted that prohib- ited amendments increasing public expenditures, in fact the deputies found ways to circumvent these limitations on parliamentary sovereignty. The Parliament, moreover, set its own agenda, so that the timing of debates on issues the government considered critical was at the discretion of the legislative assembly, not the government. The ultimate weapon was the threat to vote down the government. Despite the various attempts (particu- larly in the Constitution of the Fourth Republic) to tie the assembly's hands

---

[5] *Ibid.,* p. 152.

[6] Alain, *Propos de politique* (Paris: Rieder, 1934), p. 183.

by prescribing more stringent requirements for defeating a government, these provisions, which might have strengthened governments by increasing their longevity, remained dead letters. Neither the Third nor the Fourth Republic was ever able to accommodate stable and effective government and the exercise of parliamentary democracy. Unwilling to live with strong governments, the French Parliaments denied the state the means required to act on the great problems of contemporary societies. The backlog of unresolved problems and the social tensions and frustrations they engendered burdened weak governments, which sought to evade making decisions for fear of falling from power.

The counterpart of the weak governments of ordinary times were the "savior" governments of times of crisis. When domestic pressures or problems in the international arena became too insistent to be handled by inaction, Parliament abdicated power into the hands of the executive. The "savior" governments of Clemenceau, who stepped in to organize France for war, of Raymond Poincaré, who rescued the economy in the interwar crisis, of Henri Pétain, called to head the government after the military collapse of 1940, and of de Gaulle in 1958 were the necessary concomitant of a parliamentary system that deprived governments of the authority necessary to rule the state.

Another way of stating the problem of French parliamentarism is to say that the three functions carried out by the legislative assembly—creating, checking, and changing the government—were so confused that governments were never able to acquire sufficient authority so that the checking and controlling of the Parliament did not amount to sabotaging the minimal life requirements of government. In France the normal mode of checking a government was changing it. Ministerial crises, followed by a rotation in the personnel of the government, not popular elections, were the dominant mechanism for changing the wielders of power. Ministerial instability as a mode of political change depends on the existence of a broad spectrum of political groups from which new governments can be drawn. In the Third and Fourth Republics the size of the pool of Cabinet-eligibles was always limited by the existence at both ends of the political spectrum of antiregime parties. The parties of the extreme Left and extreme Right were not an Opposition, in the British sense, for the political alternatives they proposed were not only a different set of policies from those of the government in power but also a different constitutional framework. What the monarchists and the Communists in the Third Republic or the Gaullists in the Fourth Republic challenged was the regime itself. They offered not alternative governments but alternative states. In face of this threat to the political status quo, the other political parties, despite great differences among themselves, could usually agree on a strategy toward the antiregime parties. They were to be isolated in their political "ghettos," and all means were good that avoided increasing their numbers. This meant avoiding recourse to elections, for the citizens might return more of the extremes, thus making it more difficult to form governments.

Ministerial instability as a mode of regulating political change worked reasonably well in France as long as the Center that provided the personnel of power remained broad and solid. When all political change takes place by shifts among the Center groups and by varying the weights of these groups in different governments, the political system becomes rigid and unworkable if the Center is reduced by the growth of the extremes. This is what happened in France at the end of the Third Republic. The old formulas for making governments failed because they depended on a broad Center that no longer existed.

Ministerial instability as the mechanism of political change had certain advantages for a country as profoundly divided as France was in the Third and Fourth Republics, for it made government possible. By making non-electoral change the dominant mode of change in the system, the government was insulated against popular pressures, which in some periods at least were so intense and so polarized that no government could have satisfied them. The price of such protection was very high. Isolating the process of political change from the pressures of the electorate and the threats of the extreme parties cut Parliament off from the nation and tended to make it a closed arena. The walls that defended Parliament against the outside world, that made it, in Nathan Leites' phrase, a "house without windows," kept out the stones and the burglars, but they also kept out the winds of change in the country.

All institutions tend to acquire a life of their own: to develop a system of values and a set of roles that define the social system of the institution. In some degree all institutions socialize their members by making acceptance of the "rules of the game" the prerequisite of success within the system. And as has been observed in many legislative assemblies in various countries, one of the roles that a deputy plays is that of member of the parliamentary social system, among such other roles as member of his party, representative of his constituency, representative of particular interest groups, and so forth. What is striking in the French parliamentary system is that the values and roles associated with membership in the legislature have been so powerful as to rival, if not outweigh, all other allegiances. The behavior of the French deputy has been heavily conditioned by the single role of member of Parliament, and he has often been willing to sacrifice the goals of party or constituency in the service of parliamentary goals. As Robert de Jouvenel ironically put it, two deputies, one revolutionary, the other reactionary, have more in common than two revolutionaries, one of whom is a deputy and the other not.

Changes in governments and shifts in parliamentary alliances thus often reflected not conflicts over issues and interests, but maneuvers aimed at increasing the participants' success within the parliamentary arena. Ministerial instability can be explained in part as a product of the internal politics of the legislative social system. Deputies were eager to vote down a government because that opened new possibilities for entrance into the next government. The governments themselves resigned too easily, for each minister was already thinking of his place in a future government. The rewards of the system—Cabinet posts—were reserved for deputies with certain talents: flexibility, a capacity to arrange compromises and avoid divisive choices, and weak allegiance to party. The qualities that made for success in the parliamentary arena were not, however, characteristics that produced national political leaders. Indeed those deputies who tried to use their position in the legislature as a base for appeal to the nation or, conversely, who tried to mobilize popular support in order to maximize their strength in Parliament were punished—deprived of possibilities of participation in governments—by the rules of the parliamentary game.

To many in the nation, Parliament seemed a system in which internal maneuver and success mattered more than output and in which the friction of the machine consumed all energy. A large part of the electorate came to hold the entire parliamentary world in contempt. Cutting the Parliament off from political pressures had simply displaced the locus of political conflict. Peasants, policemen, industrial workers, and others protested in the streets. Growing frustration about the difficulties of reaching across the barriers that shielded Parliament from public pressure and about the ineffectiveness of the institution fed extremist parties that remained outside the cozy parliamentary world. In the Third and Fourth Republics antiparliamentarism was an important theme not only for the antiregime parties but also for broad sectors of public opinion.

Diagnoses and Remedies

Why did parliamentarism work in Britain to produce both representation and expression for the major social groups and stable political authority while it failed in France? There are three approaches to this problem, each diagnosing a different disease and prescribing a different medicine for France. One explanation focuses on the role of the parliamentary institutions themselves. Those who hold this view believe that the principal determinant of governmental stability and effectiveness is political structure, so that one set of institutions may produce instability in a country where another set of arrangements would promote effective government. Some defenders of the parliamentary model argue that the institutions of the Fourth Republic might have worked if the deputies had actually observed the rules. The Constitution of the Fourth Republic contained, for example, a number of requirements for special majorities to defeat governments, but these stipulations were never followed, and governments continued to fall on simple majorities in ordinary debates. Similarly, the deputies themselves voted to limit their powers to amend budgets, but these provisions, too, were often disregarded. If not the parliamentary structures of the Third or Fourth Republics, then another set of parliamentary institutions can be devised to produce representative and effective political authority. Such is the view of Mendès-France, who rejects the presidential model of the Fifth Republic and urges a return to a reformed parliamentary system with guarantees both for more effective links between the electorate and the Parliament and for stronger executive power.[7]

Attributing the same crucial role to institutions, the critics of the parliamentary model charge that the weakness and instability of the Third and Fourth Republics were due to inherent defects of parliamentary institutions. Michel Debré, the major author of de Gaulle's constitution, wrote a book during the Fourth Republic on the failures of the regime, *The Princes Who Govern Us (Ces princes qui nous gouvernent).* He asked rhetorically whether the troubles of the system were simply reflections of the troubles of the nation and then proceeded to argue that the political divisions of France were created by the parliamentary system. Parliament is not the legitimate expression of the nation, he noted, but only the product of a particular electoral system and of a constitution approved by only one-third of the electorate, of which one-half were Communists. Neither Britain nor the United States are any more united than the French, Debré argued. If their governments are more stable, it is because they have known better than to build their divisions into their governments. To achieve unity, a strong executive, a state with authority, France needed new institutions. Debré's critiques of the parliamentary regime were blueprints for the Constitution of the Fifth Republic, in which he at last had the opportunity to give France the institutions that he believed would produce strong government.

There are other observers of French politics who believe that the weakness of the parliamentary state reflected not so much bad institutions as the existence of profound political divisions in the country. The rigidity of class distinctions in France, the low level of civic education, the ideological quality of political conflict, the burden of the problems the state faced— these were some of the causes that have been suggested for the breakdown of the parliamentary regimes. As Philip Williams explained the fall of the Fourth Republic:

> The personal and factional intrigues of the deputies merely aggravated a far more serious situation: it was the lack of a majority in Parliament (because there was none in the country) which made unstable government inevitable. As if this were not enough, France was the only country which had both a great empire and a strong Communist party. Without the Communists the shrivelled democratic Left and progressive Centre could not muster a majority for decolonization; but

---

[7]Pierre Mendès-France, *A Modern French Republic* (New York: Hill & Wang, 1963).

with Communist support came fears for domestic stability and international tranquillity which alienated Centre votes and in turn made it impossible to find a majority.[8]

The parliamentary regimes of France were weakened by the range, depth, and concurrence of the problems they had to solve. The combined weights of economic reconstruction, rearmament, and decolonization were an intolerable burden for a state whose very legitimacy was contested by substantial political groups. Are there any constitutional arrangements that could produce strong and representative government in a country where a substantial proportion of the electorate supports antiregime parties? Would institutional changes attenuate the ideological conflicts that make political compromise so difficult in France? According to this analysis France needed social and economic reforms and also a reform of the political system as conceived in the largest sense: more civic participation, internal restructuring of the political parties, and decentralization. To change only the organization of power at the national level would simply not get at the roots of France's political troubles.

The future of parliamentary institutions in France may, however, depend on considerations quite different from those on which the institutionalists and the political reformers have focused. The significant question may be whether Parliaments, no matter how organized, are competent to deal with the typical problems of modern politics. As long as the main substance of parliamentary work was the production of legislation of a general, regulatory nature, legislative assemblies seemed to be adequate instruments for the conception and control of policy. Before World War II the political elites of the governmental parties rarely conceived of law as an instrument for transforming and developing society and economy or as an instrument for reducing inequality. Both the liberals and the Jacobins believed that the law should have an equal impact on citizens and that so long as discrimination was not deliberately legislated, it would. After the war this conception of the task of the state changed drastically. Demands arose from all sectors of society for the state to play a more active role in the economy in order to control fluctuations in economic activity and in order to encourage economic growth by selectively supporting certain industries and by promoting investment and innovation. A broad segment of public opinion demanded that the state intervene to reduce the inequalities of French society: inequalities among different individuals and social groups, among backward and advanced regions, among different sectors of the economy. The policies of economic planning and the social legislation that responded to these demands required very different political skills from those possessed by the deputy. No special expertise had been re-

---

[8]Philip Williams, *The French Parliament (1958–1967)* (London: Allen & Unwin, 1968), p. 17.

quired for decisions on periods of conscription, for example, or on state aid to Church schools, or on subsidies for winegrowers—typical parliamentary issues of the Third Republic. Nor had the casual, ad hoc, piecemeal intervention of the state in the economy before the war required coherent long-term legislation. When the work of government became more technical and complex, the deputies had difficulty understanding the problems before them, let alone proposing effective means for dealing with them.

As the tasks assumed by the modern state have multiplied in number and complexity, power has shifted from the hands of parliamentarians to experts in the administration, to the "technocrats." Not only in France, where the parliamentary system worked badly, but also in Britain where it worked well, the locus of decision-making moved from parliamentary arenas into the ministries. The specialists, the bureaucrats, and the representatives of special interest groups have come to play a more important part in making policy, and the politicians a less important part. Not only in France, where Parliament has few resources for obtaining the information and the expertise necessary for presenting alternatives to the government's proposals, but even in the United States where Congress has organized specialized committees, hearings, and technical assistance for the legislator, the President's access to expertise and to an organization inherently better suited to the conduct of such state business as foreign affairs has apparently given the executive and the administration an insuperable advantage over the legislature. The question is whether in any modern state a legislative assembly will be able to carry on the work of government in a way that was possible when the problems of politics required less specialized knowledge, technical competence, and long-term planning and organization to resolve them.

Presidential Democracy

The Constitution of the Fifth Republic was written in reaction against the constitutional pattern of the parliamentary system.* When General Charles de Gaulle agreed to form a government in May 1958, after a revolt of the French settler colony in Algeria and the disobedience of army units had sapped the authority of the government in office, the parliamentary system appeared to have confirmed the worst prognostics of its critics. Cabinet instability had increased as the problems of decolonization in Algeria became meshed with the internal divisions of the political parties, and for long periods in the last year of the Fourth Republic, no government could

---

*For the Constitution of the Fifth Republic see Appendix A, p. 153.

be formed and the country's affairs were left in the hands of caretaker governments. Every day turned up new evidence of the government's inability to control the army and the bureaucracy. While governments stood by impotently, Paris police demonstrated against Parliament; colonial administrators conspired with the French community in Algeria to ignore orders from Paris and to carry out their own policies; and the army in Algeria supported insurrectionist projects of civilians opposed to decolonization. The parliamentary system appeared incapable of creating a government with enough cohesion to formulate an Algerian policy and enough authority to oblige the army and the bureaucracy to carry it out. As a condition of his forming a government, de Gaulle demanded that the parties agree to a vote on a new constitution. Pressured by the collapse of the authority of the state and the rapidly deteriorating state of affairs in Algeria as well as by a loss of confidence in their own capacity to reestablish order and preserve the republic, the party leaders acceded to de Gaulle's conditions. De Gaulle was at last free to write the constitution with the strong executive power that he had always advocated for France and to get rid of the parliamentary system of the Fourth Republic, which he had attacked from the beginning.

The Constitution of the Fifth Republic was drafted by a small circle of de Gaulle's trusted political associates, with Michel Debré, the future Prime Minister, in charge; then submitted to a Constitutional Advisory Committee, composed primarily of members of Parliament; then presented in a national referendum to the French. In all essential respects the document embodied the constitutional system that de Gaulle had been urging on the French since the war. Indeed, one of de Gaulle's early postwar speeches, at Bayeux in 1946, presented a virtual blueprint of the Constitution of the Fifth Republic. De Gaulle declared in 1946:

> It is obvious that executive power should not depend on the Parliament, based on two houses and wielding legislative power, or else there will be a confusion of responsibilities in which the Government will become nothing more than a cluster of [party] delegations. . . . The unity, cohesion, and internal discipline of the Government of France must be sacred objects, or else the country's leadership will rapidly become impotent and invalid. How can such unity, cohesion, and discipline be preserved if the executive power emanates from another body, with which it must be balanced, and if each member of a Government which is collectively responsible before the national representative body is but the emissary of his party? The executive power should, therefore, be embodied in a Chief of State, placed above the parties, elected by a body that includes the Parliament but is larger than it . . .
>
> It is the role of the Chief of State to consider the general interest in his choice of men, while taking into account the orientation of the Parliament. It is his role to name ministers, and first of all, the Prime Minister, who will direct the policy

and work of the Government. It is his role to promulgate laws and make decrees, for they obligate the citizens to the State as a whole. It is his task to preside over the Cabinet and, there, to defend the essential national continuity. It is his function to serve as an arbiter, placed above the political circumstances of the day, and to carry out this function ordinarily in the Cabinet, or, in moments of great confusion, by asking the nation to deliver its sovereign decision through elections. It is his role, should the nation ever be in danger, to assume the duty of guaranteeing national independence and the treaties agreed to by France . . .

The main points of the Bayeux speech were themes that drew on an old constitutional tradition that was based on a strong executive. Like other critics of the parliamentary model before him, de Gaulle denounced government by legislative assembly as destructive of national unity and strength. According to antiparliamentary analysis, government by assembly meant government by the political parties. Instead of creating a mechanism for representing and defending the public interest, government by the parties meant perpetual conflict among partial and partisan interests. The authority of the state was destroyed in these contests. The executive was a weak creature, dependent on the will of changing assembly votes. In ordinary times the government was so dependent on the interest groups and political parties that it was incapable of any independent initiative. In times of crisis, the government was so weak that the country was likely to fall into the hands of authoritarian rulers (as had the First, Second, and Third Republics, de Gaulle pointed out in the Bayeux speech). It was with a view to overcoming these political weaknesses, problems that according to the Gaullists derived from the parliamentary system, that the Constitution of the Fifth Republic was conceived.

The constitution established three fundamental political authorities: the President, the government (Prime Minister and Cabinet), and the Parliament (National Assembly and Senate). In theory, the constitution sets up a mixed parliamentary-presidential system, for the government remains responsible before the legislative assembly (unlike a pure presidential model), while the chief of state has substantial powers that are not subject to parliamentary control (unlike a pure parliamentary model). In fact, the political practices that have developed on the basis of the constitution in the past decade have produced a presidential system in which Parliament plays a secondary role. Though the powerful personality of de Gaulle, the first man to hold the presidency, may account in part for the predominance of the President in the system, the experience of the second President of the Fifth Republic, Georges Pompidou, shows that levers of power that the constitution provides to the presidential officeholder allow even a less forceful individual than de Gaulle to dominate the political system.

The Parliament

If the President has emerged as the central political figure of the Fifth Republic, it is in large measure due to the changed role of the National Assembly and the Senate in the political system. The curtailment of the power of these two legislatures (together called the Parliament) has made it possible for the President of the republic and the government to enlarge the substantial grants of authority that they are given by the constitution and to establish a position of predominance in the state. In the parliamentary regimes of the Third and Fourth Republics, Parliament chose governments, controlled them by controlling their legislative programs, and changed them. In the Fifth Republic, Parliament still participates in carrying out these three functions, but it must share its power with President and government. The powers it continues to exercise are clearly circumscribed by the constitution.

Forming a government, once the exclusive prerogative of the Parliament, has now become one of the powers of the President of the republic. The President names the Prime Minister and on his suggestion chooses the ministers. The constitution does not require the Prime Minister to present his program to the National Assembly for a vote of confidence, and though some of the governments of the Fifth Republic have done so, others have not. The role of the Assembly in the choice of the government has thus been reduced to a right to defeat the government by passing a motion of censure. Even this possibility has been sharply decreased. The new constitutional rules require that a motion of censure initiated by the Assembly first receive the signatures of one-tenth of the members of the Assembly; that the vote on the motion be delayed for forty-eight hours; and then that the motion receive a majority of all members of the Assembly (not only of those voting) in order to pass.

In a second respect as well the National Assembly has lost power in the formation of the government. The governments of the parliamentary republics were composed of members of the legislature, and when the governments fell, the ex-ministers resumed their jobs as deputies. The Constitution of the Fifth Republic, in contrast, requires a deputy who enters the government to give up his parliamentary mandate. Every deputy now stands for election with a "substitute," who takes the Assembly seat of a deputy named to the government. When the minister leaves the government he cannot resume his Assembly seat. The intention behind this new rule was to prevent ministers from resigning from governments with the hope of bringing them down in order to serve in new ones—one of the practices of the parliamentary regimes that, in the view of the framers of the Constitution of 1958, had contributed to Cabinet instability. The ex-ministers of the Fifth Republic have sometimes circumvented the requirements of the new rules by having their substitutes resign so that a by-election can be held and the ex-minister can run for his seat again. The violation of the spirit of the new requirement has not, however, revived the old patterns of ministerial indiscipline. In addition to the constitutional rules that sever the members of the government from the Assembly, a new political practice has contributed to weakening the influence of the Assembly on the government. In violation of the unwritten rules of the parliamentary system, de Gaulle named men to the government who had never been deputies at all. Some were high civil servants; others had experience in the private sector. The most prominent of these "technicians" was Georges Pompidou, now President of the republic, who was a bank director in 1962 when he was named Prime Minister by de Gaulle. This trend was reversed in the latter years of de Gaulle's presidency, and the members of the governments chosen by Pompidou in the first legislature of his presidency were all deputies. But in April 1973 Pompidou named three non-parliamentarians to important posts in the government that included the Ministry of Foreign Affairs.

Of all the functions that Parliament had performed in the Third and Fourth Republics, that of controlling the legislative process was the one most profoundly modified by the Fifth Republic. Where the parliamentary constitutions were silent, the legislature was free to act. The Constitution of 1958, in contrast, describes and delimits with considerable detail the part that the legislature may play in the legislative process, and the Parliament may not exceed the grants of power specifically accorded it by the constitution. The main feature of the new division of power between Parliament and Government in the legislative process is a distinction between "laws" and "regulations" (Articles 34 and 37). The Parliament is entitled to deliberate and vote only on laws, a category described in the constitution as including legislation concerning civil liberties, political rights, crimes, taxes, elections, and nationalization of industry. Into the category of law also fall the "basic principles," though not the detailed provisions, of legislation on defense, local government, education, property, work, and social security. The subjects which are the object of law and to be deliberated and voted on by Parliament are thus strictly delimited, and all other subjects are constitutionally defined as the objects of regulations, which are proclaimed by the government without the participation of Parliament. In cases of dispute over whether a bill falls into the domain of law or the domain of regulation, the Constitutional Council decides. The constitution also allows the government to request authorization from Parliament to make by ordinance decisions that would normally fall into the domain of law (Article 38). According to the constitution, these ordinances must be ratified by Parliament, but in practice the government has used this power to handle politically touchy matters, like the licenses of liquor distillers, and often has either delayed for long periods before obtaining parliamentary ratification or has failed to obtain it. Finally, the constitution limits the role of the Parliament in the budgetary process by specifying that only the government may introduce a bill that would increase public expenditures or decrease public revenues.

The first consequence of these limitations on the domain of Parliament has been to reduce the burden of parliamentary work. Nine-tenths of the bills introduced in the last year of the Fourth Republic would be considered regulations by the new rules and would never appear before the Parliament at all. In principle, the Parliament can devote more of its time to consideration of the most important pieces of legislation, instead of dispersing its efforts on minor bills. In fact, the Parliament often finds itself in much the same rush as before. The constitution fixes the dates of the parliamentary sessions, allowing the Parliament to meet only six months a year, far less than the average session of the parliamentary regimes. The constitution also specifies that the Parliament may spend no more than seventy days on the budget, or else the Government may enact the budget by decree.

Even more important has been the impact of the constitutional limitations of the Parliament's role on the relationship between Parliament and government. Parliament has been weakened not only by having had its business strictly defined, but also by having had spelled out in the constitution how its business is to be conducted. Bills go first to committees of the National Assembly or Senate for discussion and possible amendment and then are reported out for discussion and vote. In the Third and Fourth Republics the committees were powerful actors in the legislative process; the bill that reached the Assembly was not the bill that had originally been introduced but the bill as amended by the committee. The government had no power to require the Assembly to consider the original governmental proposal. In the Fourth Republic, there were nineteen committees, each one closely associated with one or more ministries. Deputies representing particular economic interests served on the committees linked up with the ministry most directly concerned with those interests, and from this network of interests, pressures, and influence a governmental bill often came out mutilated. In order to prevent this collusion between the interest groups, the committees, and the ministries, the framers of the Constitution of 1958 specified that there would be only six standing committees in the Assembly, each having jurisdiction over a broad range of different subject matters. Since every member of Parliament serves on a committee, the committees have become for the most part unwieldy bodies from which it is unlikely that a common outlook could emerge and which would be unlikely to unite and present a solid front against a governmental project. The deputies are distributed among the committees in such a way that the political parties are represented in each committee in proportion to their strength in the legislature. The constitution also provides for setting up special committees to consider a single bill, and this has been done occasionally. The experience with these special committees showed, however, that since they were composed of deputies with a strong interest in a particular measure, the committee was able to formulate a common position and resist government propositions far better than the large all-purpose standing committees could. The special committees, in short, turned out too much like the old regular committees of the Fourth Republic, and the government now tends to avoid creating them.

After the committee reports out the bill, it moves to the National Assembly for debate and vote. The government decides the order in which bills will be presented, and so the Parliament is no longer "master of its agenda," as the expression of the parliamentary regimes put it. The organization of parliamentary time is now determined by the government's legislative priorities. A private member's bill must in effect be accepted by the government if it is to be discussed at all. The only time in the parliamentary schedule that the government does not control is oral question day, one session per week that the constitution sets aside for questioning of the government by the deputies. In the parliamentary republics, questions followed by a vote of confidence on the government's reply were one of the great weapons of the Parliament against the government. But in the Fifth Republic, the Constitutional Council has ruled that votes on motions introduced in question sessions are unconstitutional, and so the government is protected against the harassment of any votes of confidence it does not itself initiate, with the exception, of course, of the motion of censure.

In debate on the floor the government enjoys a kind of constitutional protection against its adversaries that gives it great tactical advantages. First, the timing of the debate is at the government's discretion. The text of the bill that the legislature discusses is the government's, with only those committee amendments that the government has chosen to accept. The government's program no longer suffers the fate of the government bills of the Third and Fourth Republics, which often emerged from committee in a form unacceptable to their original authors, who had no recourse against the committee except to get a deputy to introduce amendments to the committee product on the floor in order to restore the original bill. Once the debate is in process, the government may reject consideration of any amendment that was not presented before the committee. The penultimate weapon of the government is the right to demand that the legislature vote on the whole bill and not vote separately on individual clauses and amendments. The "package vote" allows the government to force the legislature to agree to a bill whose general purposes they accept, even when particular provisions would be rejected if ordinary legislative procedure were used.

Finally, the government can force the legislature to accept a bill by declaring its passage a matter of confidence. In such a case the bill passes unless the opposition can present and pass a motion of censure. This means that the bill on which the government has staked its existence passes unless an absolute majority of the assembly opposes it. Since a motion of censure requires a vote of the majority of all members of the National Assembly, those who abstain or are absent in effect count for the government. The opposition has been able to muster the necessary majority to defeat the government only once in the course of the Fifth Republic. In October 1962 the government of Georges Pompidou was censured after de Gaulle proposed a referendum on a constitutional amendment for the direct popular election of the President of the republic. De Gaulle had bypassed the Parliament, which according to the Constitution of 1958 (Article 89) must vote on proposed constitutional amendments before they are submitted to referendum. After the vote of censure, Pompidou resigned; de Gaulle dissolved the Assembly; called new elections; and the new legislature gave a vote of confidence to the new Pompidou government.

The third major function of the legislative assembly in the parliamentary system was to change governments. In the Fifth Republic, the National Assembly still exercises this function, but in a fashion that is circumscribed by the constitution. Although the President names the Prime Minister, he cannot recall him. He can only accept his resignation. Only the National Assembly can oblige the government to resign by defeating it on a motion of censure or on a vote of confidence initiated by the government itself. The result has been continuity in the office of Prime Minister. As of January 1974 only five men have served as Prime Minister in the Fifth Republic: Michel Debré, Georges Pompidou, Maurice Couve de Murville, Jacques Chaban-Delmas, and Pierre Messmer. The phenomenon of ministerial instability has not, however, disappeared. Even in the absence of effective parliamentary pressures to change the composition of governments, the government has felt it necessary to change its politics by changing its personnel. The Ministries of Agriculture and Education, for example, have each had three different ministers over the past five years.

The constitution has modified not only the functions performed by the Parliament but also the relationship between the two houses, the National Assembly and the Senate. The National Assembly, with 487 deputies, is essentially the same body as the Assembly of the Fourth Republic. The Senate (283 senators), however, replaces the second chamber of the Fourth Republic, the Council of the Republic, and has more power than its predecessor, which could amend or defeat a bill the Assembly had voted only by an absolute majority. Senators are elected by indirect suffrage—the representatives of local and departmental governments elect them—and they serve nine-year terms. The role of the Senate in the legislative process depends on the government's decision. If the government does not intervene, both the National Assembly and the Senate play the same part in the passage of legislation. Bills must pass both houses; any differences between the houses have to be ironed out in a conference committee composed of members of each house and then submitted to both chambers for final vote. However, when the Senate and the National Assembly do not agree, the government has the option of sending the bill to the National Assembly for final determination. The Senate then does not participate in the decision. In other words, the Senate cannot oppose the National Assembly effectively, if the government supports the Assembly. The Senate is clearly secondary to the National Assembly in other respects as well. Only the National Assembly may defeat the government with a motion of censure, and Prime Ministers have presented their programs for votes of confidence only in the Assembly. The Senate thus plays no part in the formation or defeat of governments.

The Senate has been losing power throughout the course of the Fifth Republic. After a constitutional amendment providing for direct election of the President was passed in 1962, the Senate was left as the only national political authority that did not emanate directly from national popular elections. The Senate's electorate of local officials is disproportionately rural, small-town, and provincial; and the senators are in large numbers men who were once the deputies of the Fourth and even Third Republics. Particularly in the early years of the Fifth Republic, the senators were the most active opponents of the government's programs and, as mentioned above, the government frequently had recourse to the National Assembly to overrule the Senate. The Senate was discredited in the eyes of the Left as an inadequately representative body; it was discredited in the eyes of the Gaullists as an obstructionist stronghold of the political forces opposed to the Fifth Republic.

It was therefore a great surprise when in April 1969 a national referendum defeated General de Gaulle's proposal that the Senate be replaced by a body that would include representatives of economic and social groups as well as of territorial units. The Economic and Social Council would essentially have been merged with the Senate, and delegates from the professions, the unions, business, commerce, and family associations would have sat in the new assembly alongside the representatives of local governments. The reform would have changed not only the composition of the body, but its powers as well. The new Senate would have had the right to present an opinion on laws, but not to vote on them. The transformation of the Senate was tied to a project establishing regional authorities throughout France. The authors of the reform intended that the new governmental bodies be organized in such a way that they could not be used by the political parties or the traditional political elites as bases of power from which to challenge the government. The mode of selection of the members was supposed to ensure that the "real" forces of the nation, the economic and social groups, presumably less partisan and more concerned with finding solutions to problems within the framework of the existing system, would dominate in the new assemblies at the regional and national levels. Political groups that had been in favor of decentralization and regionalization all along were not enthusiastic about the government's proposal, because they found it inadequate, and they pointed out that it would probably allow the old local notables to take control of the new regional authorities. On the other side, the traditional political elites also opposed the reform, for they felt it endangered their position in local politics. The great opponent of the reform was the Senate, whose members fanned out into the country to lead a campaign to vote no in the referendum. De Gaulle announced before the referendum that if the vote were negative, he would resign his office.

Despite the transformation of the regional referendum into a vote of confidence for de Gaulle, 53 percent of the voters cast their ballots against the proposal, defeating it. It would be impossible to conclude that this vote measures popular support for the Senate, because a variety of other factors clearly influenced the outcome, most important of which were dissatisfaction with the regional aspects of the reform and the widespread feeling that since there was a likely successor to the presidency (Pompidou), de Gaulle's ultimatum could be ignored without imperiling the stability of the regime. From a comparison of voters who supported de Gaulle in the 1962 referendum (on direct election of the President) with the supporters in 1969, it appears that the groups defecting were drawn heavily from the traditional sectors of French society. Though the role of the Senate may be "altogether secondary" (de Gaulle's phrase) and the institution itself may appear to groups from the modern, urban centers as a dead weight from the past, for a significant part of the country the Senate represents "a certain France." The groups who feel this way are still strong enough to protect the institution.

The Government

The government includes the Prime Minister, ministers he names to the Cabinet, and state secretaries. In a certain sense, the President of the republic is also a member of the government, since he presides by right over the meetings of the Council of Ministers. Anyone who read only the sections on the government in the Constitution of 1958 would have a hard time predicting the role the government has actually played in the Fifth Republic. The constitution states that "the Government determines and conducts the policies of the Nation. It disposes of the administration and armed forces" (Article 20). "The Prime Minister directs the action of the Government. He is responsible for national defense. He assures the execution of the laws" (Article 21). These rather vague descriptions of the role of the government and the Prime Minister left open the most important question: Would the executive power be exercised primarily by the Prime Minister and government or by the President? The history of the Fifth

Republic has answered the question in favor of the President. The Prime Ministers have been the trusted and hand-picked associates of the Presidents. Major policy decisions under Pompidou as well as de Gaulle have been made by the President and carried out by the Prime Minister.

Historical circumstances, rather than the structures laid out in the constitution, explain the development of the political system in a direction that strengthens the President and weakens the Prime Minister. Charles de Gaulle, the first President of the Fifth Republic, was an exceptional figure, whose role in French history conferred an extraordinary prestige and authority on his person. (See the section "The President" in this chapter.) Both because of his personal authority and because of his own conception of the presidency, de Gaulle was bound to dominate the relationships with his Prime Ministers. Though Debré chafed in the role when he was obliged to carry out Algerian policies with which he was hardly in agreement and Pompidou apparently did not espouse some of the policies he had to present after May–June 1968, neither of the two men ever challenged the President's right to make the major policy decisions.

De Gaulle's power and prestige were so great that he might have dominated all state policy. In noncrisis periods, however, he concerned himself primarily with foreign policy. Here de Gaulle made decisions alone, often announcing his policies only after the fact to the Council of Ministers. Sometimes he did not even trouble to do that, and the government learned of the decision from the newspapers, as on the occasion when he came out for independence for Quebec while on a trip to Canada. De Gaulle's exclusive control of foreign affairs supported the development of an extra-constitutional distinction between a "reserved sphere" in which the President may act and a residual parliamentary and governmental sphere. Into the President's sphere, as defined by de Gaulle's interests, fell foreign policy, defense, and constitutional matters. "All the rest" he ordinarily left to the government. The distinction had the effect of shearing the Prime Minister of powers that according to the constitution were his, if not to exercise alone, at least to share with the President. The constitution does not give the President a monopoly of the conduct of foreign policy, though it does grant him the right to "negotiate and ratify treaties." Nor does it give the President a predominant role in amending the constitution. On the contrary, the constitution specifies that constitutional amendments must be initiated by the President and the Prime Minister together and voted by both houses of the Parliament. Because of de Gaulle's exceptional authority, the President was acknowledged to have an exclusive right of decision on these questions that is nowhere recognized by the constitution. With the passing of the presidency from de Gaulle to Pompidou, the boundaries between the reserved sphere and the rest have become blurred. Nonetheless, the distinction has not altogether disappeared. It was revealing in this regard that Pompidou, not Chaban-Delmas, met Edward Heath, the British

Prime Minister, to discuss British entry into the Common Market and, more generally, that it is Pompidou who makes foreign policy decisions.

The third historical circumstance that worked to make the Prime Minister a less powerful figure than the letter of the constitution might suggest was the strength of the Gaullist party in the legislature. At least in the early years of the Fifth Republic, this factor of Gaullist party dominance, like the development of a reserved presidential sphere, depended on the extraordinary esteem in which de Gaulle was held by the French electorate. A vote for the U.N.R., the Gaullist party, was in the minds of the voters a vote for de Gaulle. The significance of this for the role of the Prime Minister was that his majority was in fact a majority held together by the President. The Prime Minister had no power base independent of the President, and had he attempted to challenge the President, he would not have been able to rally his parliamentary majority behind him. This phenomenon has two components: The Prime Minister is weakened because his party has a double allegiance, to him and to the President, and even further weakened because, in the final analysis, his party supports him *because* he is the President's candidate.

It might have been anticipated that after de Gaulle, the tight embrace between the party and the President would loosen up and that in a more fluid situation the Prime Minister would be able to liberate himself from dependence on the President and to develop more autonomous relations with the legislative party majority. In fact this has not happened. Even a man like Pompidou, with none of de Gaulle's charismatic relationship to the French and with no glorious historic role to recommend him, has been able to take hold of the party and to keep the Prime Minister in almost the same dependent role as that which Pompidou himself had experienced during his terms as Prime Minister. Only six weeks after Chaban-Delmas had received a large vote of confidence from the National Assembly, Pompidou requested his resignation (July 1972), once again demonstrating where the real power in the regime lies. Perhaps a man less popular with the U.N.R. than Pompidou might not have the same authority with the majority in the legislature, but it seems more likely that in modern states all those factors that focus attention on a single leader—elections, television, press—will work to make the President and not the Prime Minister the real leader of the majority.

What if the Prime Minister were of a different party than the President? If the legislative elections returned a National Assembly whose party composition was such that the President could only name a Prime Minister of a party other than his own, what powers might the Prime Minister exercise by virtue of functions assigned him in the constitution? The constitution grants the Prime Minister several important powers that he may use even without the agreement of the President. The most important of these is the right to make policy and enact decrees on any subject except those specifically assigned by the constitution to the Parliament. When a bill falls into the category of regulations, not law, the government may act without the approval of Parliament or President. Moreover, in many of the laws that do require the consent of Parliament there is provision for enabling legislation, and this is prepared by the government and cannot be rejected by Parliament. The constitution also grants the Prime Minister important weapons for controlling his own government and for dealing with Parliament. Because it is the Prime Minister who is empowered to enact regulations, he may refuse to sign the decrees prepared by his ministers. The Prime Minister may summon Parliament to meet in special session. The decision to convene a conference committee of deputies and senators to resolve differences over the passage of a bill is his. With few and rather unimportant exceptions the other powers of the government can only be exercised together with the President.

The President

The constitutional document of 1958 did not create a presidential system. Indeed, most observers of the French political scene described it as a modified parliamentary system, which would revert to traditional parliamentary practices once de Gaulle left the presidency. The Constitution of 1958 places the President in much the same position as the Prime Minister: with few powers that he might exercise without the agreement of either government or Parliament. Those powers are, however, extremely important. The President may dissolve the National Assembly and call new elections at any time, except if he has already done so within the year. If the legislative elections return a National Assembly whose political composition makes it impossible to form a government, if a government pursues policies he disapproves, or if the Assembly refuses the Prime Minister he has named, then the President may appeal to the electorate. The risk he runs is that, like the first President of the Third Republic, Marshal Marie de MacMahon, who dissolved a chamber he found too republican only to have the electorate return more of the same, he may find himself obliged to give in or resign. The one dissolution of the Fifth Republic followed the 1962 censure of the Pompidou government, and it did serve the President's cause, for new elections brought back an Assembly with more loyal Gaullists.

The second major set of presidential powers are the emergency powers he may exercise ''when the institutions of the Republic, national independence, the integrity of national territory or the application of international commitments are threatened in a serious and immediate fashion and the normal functioning of public institutions is interrupted'' (Article 16). In such circumstances the constitution authorizes the President to take whatever measures he deems necessary to meet the emergency. The only checks

on the very broad grant of powers extended by Article 16 are the requirement that the President consult with the Prime Minister, the Presidents of
the two houses of Parliament, and the Constitutional Council and the
provision that Parliament remain in session during the period of exercise
of these special powers. In the final analysis, these checks do not constitute
an obstacle to the President's exercising his own judgment both as to
whether an emergency exists, which requires the use of the special powers
of Article 16, or as to what ought to be done during the emergency. Indeed
the only formal limitation on the vast powers implied by the phrase "whatever measures circumstances require" is the qualification that the President's decisions must be motivated by the intention to allow the basic
public institutions to operate as soon as possible.

Article 16 was invoked once during the Fifth Republic—in April 1961,
when French generals in revolt against a policy leading to Algerian independence threatened to invade the French mainland and take over the
government. De Gaulle declared a state of emergency. Even though the
Military *Putsch* was defeated a few days after Article 16 had gone into
effect, de Gaulle continued to exercise the special powers of Article 16 for
another five months.

In other respects as well, de Gaulle interpreted his own powers under
Article 16 broadly and the checks that other groups might exercise, restric-
tively. Parliament, as the constitution required, met during the period of
special powers, but de Gaulle refused to allow them to legislate. On
another occasion, when Parliament in 1960 had tried to defeat the government over a bill creating an independent nuclear force, de Gaulle was
apparently willing to contemplate using Article 16 if the motion of censure
passed, though whether a parliamentary veto on nuclear armaments
would have created a state of emergency was highly debatable, to say the
least. The constitution provides no effective check on a President who
would choose to use Article 16 in an arbitrary or dictatorial fashion, and
the only real controls are the President's own respect for democratic
process and the possibilities of extra-constitutional resistance to the President's special powers by other public bodies.

The third set of powers that the President may exercise alone—without
the agreement of government or Parliament—concern the administration
of justice. The President names three of the nine regular members of the
Constitutional Council; and he has the right of pardon.

Beyond these powers the President can act only in collaboration with
other political bodies. Even to call a referendum, which the President alone
may do, requires that either the government or the Parliament propose it
to him. Since 1958 the referendum has played a very important role in
strengthening the presidency. De Gaulle used it when he critically needed
support for a decision disputed by parts of the political elite, at such times
calling a referendum and declaring that he would resign unless the sover-

eign will of the people confirmed his policy. Referendums were held in September 1958 on the new constitution; in January 1961 to approve the policy of self-determination for Algeria; in April 1962 to approve the Evian agreements that ended the Algerian war; in October 1962 to ratify a constitutional amendment for the direct election of the President; and in April 1969 to decide on regional governments and reform of the Senate. Pompidou in April 1972 called a referendum to approve adding new countries to the European Economic Community.

The device of the referendum allows the President to present an issue to the public in terms that often simplify complex matters by demanding a yes or no answer from the voter. By staking his office on the outcome of the referendum and threatening the public that without him the political system would return to the disorders of the Fourth Republic, de Gaulle was able to win massive public approval in the referendums. In each case except the last one, de Gaulle was supported by a large majority of the electorate, and he was able to push through policies that powerful groups in the political elite opposed. Once the President had behind him a successful referendum vote, it was—and will be—virtually impossible for any of the other branches of government to block his projects, for the expression of public sentiment in the referendum has the weight of popular sovereignty. For example, when the President of the Senate requested that the Constitutional Council rule on the constitutionality of the 1962 amendment for direct election of the President, a change that had been ratified by referendum but not previously approved by the Parliament, the Council refused to consider the case. The Council argued that while it had the right to judge the constitutionality of laws voted by Parliament, it should not consider those passed by referendum, since such decisions are "the direct expression of national sovereignty."

All other acts of the presidency can be taken only in close cooperation with the government. Since this is the case, why has the Fifth Republic developed into a presidential and not a parliamentary system? The reasons for the predominance of the President in the Fifth Republic derive not from the letter of the constitution but from two other sources: de Gaulle's conception of the presidency and the constitutional amendment providing direct election for the President. The political system of the Fifth Republic is in many respects the creation of a single man, Charles de Gaulle. De Gaulle came to power in 1958 supported not only by overwhelming public approval of the constitution he proposed, but also by widespread and profound public respect for the historic role and political figure that de Gaulle represented. For Frenchmen, de Gaulle was the man whose refusal to accept defeat in 1940 had preserved French honor and the integrity of the French nation for the future. De Gaulle had saved France once, by leaving France for England in 1940 and organizing armed forces that served with the Allies and aided in the liberation of France in 1944. He saved the country a second time, when he agreed to form a government in 1958 to avert civil war. In his own mind, as well as for what may have been a majority of Frenchmen, de Gaulle had a double legitimacy: not only the legitimacy that election conferred, but a legitimacy that flowed from a historic destiny in which de Gaulle had embodied and defended France.[9] De Gaulle commanded a kind of religious respect and admiration from his closest political associates as well as from the public. Without understanding this, it would be impossible to understand how, with a constitution that gave as many levers of power to the Prime Minister and government as to the President, de Gaulle was able to impose his will on the entire political system and to orient according to his own ideas not only the content of policy but the institutional development of the regime. Few jurists would have accepted de Gaulle's interpretation of the constitution when he declared in 1964 that "the indivisible authority of the state is entirely entrusted to the President by the people who have elected him and all other authority, whether ministerial, civil, military, judicial is conferred and maintained by him." But the political practice of the Fifth Republic proceeded as if the constitutional system were indeed such as de Gaulle described it.

The place of the presidency in the political system bears the stamp of de Gaulle's conceptions of how the French state ought to be organized if France is to play the great role that is her rightful part in world affairs. Already in his Bayeux speech, de Gaulle had shown a clear preference for a political system in which the President would be dominant. Political unity, he argued then, can be preserved only when the executive power of the state is in the hands of a single authority, responsible before no group but the nation itself. The Constitution of 1958 assigned functions to the President that seemed substantially less broad than those de Gaulle had outlined at Bayeux. In part de Gaulle may have felt it necessary to reassure the traditional political elites about the democratic and republican character of the constitution he was proposing by limiting the powers of the presidency. And he may also have felt certain of being able to accomplish what was necessary by force of his own authority, even with a constitutional grant of power that fell beneath his ultimate hopes. De Gaulle's experience in office confirmed that his own prestige and authority gave the presidency the preeminent role in the system that he felt necessary to political stability. The problem was whether his eventual successors, who would not bring the same authority with them to the office, would be able to govern with the same set of constitutional powers. The question became a pressing one after an assassination attempt. And when de Gaulle decided on the 1962 referendum to ratify the constitutional amendment for direct

---

[9]Maurice Duverger, *Institutions politiques et droit constitutionnel* (Paris: Presses Universitaires de France, 1970), p. 741.

election of the President, it was not because his own authority in the office was insufficient for his purposes but, rather, to strengthen future Presidents.

The direct election of the President has fundamentally changed the nature of the constitutional system. In the Constitution of 1958 only the National Assembly depended directly on universal suffrage, and this legitimated a claim to supremacy over Senate and President, both of which were chosen by indirect suffrage. The President was elected by an electoral college that resembled the Senate's: local and provincial officials, deputies, and other high officials in the state. The President was thus dependent on the traditional political elites for election. In an age of mass politics, direct elections confer a democratic legitimacy to authority that no other method of selection or election can. The President of the Constitution of 1958 could appeal to the national electorate only by the referendum or by dissolving the National Assembly and calling new legislative elections. Both these methods could be used in only rather limited circumstances; neither of them provided the President with the kind of national confirmation of his authority that direct election of a man confers. By changing the mode of election, then, de Gaulle was able to provide the President with a claim to represent national sovereignty that, except for its lack of tradition, was as strong as the National Assembly's claim.

The result is a mixed system of authority in which, as long as President and government are of the same party, the presidential elements are likely to dominate. As Pompidou described the system in 1964:

> France has now chosen a system midway between the American presidential regime and the British parliamentary regime, where the chief of state, who formulates general policy, has the basis of his authority in universal suffrage but can only exercise his functions with a government that he may have chosen and named, but which in order to survive, must maintain the confidence of the Assembly.

Despite the predominance of the President, the system will work only when the President and the government can work together, for each one has sufficient powers to block the functioning of the state. For this collaboration between Parliament and President, the majorities that elect each of the two ought to be as close as possible. This may be better assured in the future if Pompidou's recent proposal to amend the constitution to reduce the presidential term of office from seven years to five, like the deputies' term, is passed.

The Constitutional Council

Until recently, the Constitutional Council would not have merited more than a mention in a description of the functioning of the Fifth Republic.

Though the powers granted the Council in the constitution seemed to lay out a role as broad as that exercised by the American Supreme Court in determining the constitutionality of legislation, the history of the Constitutional Council has justified none of the expectations (or fears) of strong judicial authority. The very composition of the court assured that the government would find a very sympathetic hearing in it. Three of the nine regular judges are named by the President, three by the President of the Assembly, and three by the President of the Senate; the nine judges serve nine-year terms. Former Presidents of the republic serve as lifetime members. The main substance of the court's activity has been settling conflicts between the Parliament and executive over the boundaries of law and regulation (see the section "The Parliament" in this chapter) and deciding the outcomes of disputed elections. In virtually all important decisions, the Constitutional Council upheld the authority of the executive. It refused to determine the constitutionality of the 1962 referendum vote on direct election of the President; nor would it decide whether Parliament should have the right to present a motion of censure when meeting in special session during the exercise of the special powers of Article 16 (1961).

The Constitutional Council seemed so compliant an auxiliary of executive authority that no one could have anticipated its ruling against the government in July 1971 on the constitutionality of a law regulating voluntary associations. The government had presented a bill to Parliament that modified the 1901 law on the freedom to form associations. The 1901 law automatically granted legal recognition to any group requesting it. In 1936 when the activities of right-wing and fascist groups had threatened the republic, legislation had been passed that gave the government the right, subject to judicial review, to dissolve groups whose acts endangered the state. After the May–June 1968 student and worker strikes, the 1936 legislation had been used rather freely by the Minister of the Interior to close down left-wing associations and ban their newspapers. Now the government was requesting legislation that would allow it to refuse the right to form an association to any group that was considered to be simply a revival of an organization previously dissolved. Such a change would have amounted to prior censorship and, as such, a serious limitation of the freedom of association guaranteed by the 1901 law. The National Assembly passed the bill, but the Senate refused it, and the government used its right to return the bill to the Assembly for final deliberation. The President of the Senate then requested that the Constitutional Council determine the constitutionality of the bill. The Council accepted the case and declared parts of the law unconstitutional because they limited freedom of association, a right protected by the preamble to the Constitution of 1958. This case of judicial protection of civil liberties against the executive has hardly established a precedent for wide use of the powers of judicial review by the court. What is important about the case is that in a political system with few effective checks on the power of the executive when President and government agree, the court may be the only institution that can defend fundamental liberties. One question is whether the court would be willing to play this role, and here it would be premature to draw conclusions from a single case. The other, and more fundamental, issue is whether such an exercise of judicial authority would be considered legitimate in a political system where authority that does not derive from popular sovereignty has little sanction in republican political tradition.

Three

The Development of the Party System

For anyone raised in a country with a two-party system, the multiplicity of French political parties seems both unnecessary and unsuited to the purposes of modern politics. Why are there six major parties when a simplification of the party system to two or three would better serve the functions of governing and organizing opposition? Why are parties with interests and programs as close as those of the Radical-Socialists and the Center parties or as those of the two Socialist parties unable to unite or even to form stable coalitions? How do parties formed at the time of the passionate conflicts between partisans of Church and state survive even when the issue that created them has almost vanished from the political scene? And even more difficult to fathom, what shifts in French society or changes in the policies of the state might promote the emergence of a new party system?

First, how can we explain the multiplicity of parties and account for the particular parties that occupy the political arena in France today? There are several explanations of why a country develops either a two-party or a multiparty system. One theory emphasizes the importance of electoral systems. The single-member district, one round of balloting, winner-take-all elections of the United States and Britain apparently disadvantage third parties, which receive far fewer legislative seats than the number to which they would be entitled were their share of the national assembly calculated as a proportion of the total national vote. Instead of being added up nationally, however, votes in the United States and Britain are counted in single-member districts, in each of which the third (or fourth) party is most likely to be swamped by the two big parties. In France, on the other hand, the two rounds of balloting, multimember large districts, and proportional representation that have been used in various combinations at different times allow smaller parties a better chance for representation and survival, for these parties can add up their votes over a wider territory. When, for example, elections are held in single-member districts, a party that wins one-third of the votes in several constituencies wins no representatives at all. If, as has often been the case in French elections, these small constituencies were combined into larger, multimember electoral districts, then such a party would have won one-third of the seats at stake.

France has experimented with several electoral systems, and each one has apparently strengthened and weakened different parties. In 1951 a reform of the method of calculating proportional representation provided incentives for the Center parties to ally and reduced the representation of the parties of the extreme Right and Left. In order to weaken the parties at both ends of the political spectrum, General de Gaulle when he came to power in 1958 returned to a single-member district system, with no proportional representation. This system, with two rounds of balloting, is the one used today in French legislative elections. American and British electoral rules have never been tried in French elections, so one can only speculate about whether their adoption would reduce the number of parties. The procedure adopted in 1965 for electing the President of the republic does force the voters to choose between the candidates of two parties on the second ballot. The two presidential elections that have been held with this system (1965 and 1969) apparently strengthened the largest parties and weakened the smaller ones, but it is still premature to draw conclusions about the impact of this electoral constraint on the French party system.

Other explanations of the multiparty system have identified ideology as the cause of the proliferation of political parties in France. Ideological stakes, or values, are less susceptible to compromise and accommodation than are economic stakes. While it is possible to negotiate political agreements that partially satisfy each of several groups' claims to a larger share of the national pie, it is difficult to imagine a political agreement that divides up absolute values. Workers seeking wage increases of 15 percent may be satisfied with a settlement that gives them 10 percent; but workers who want nationalization of the factory they work in must be either entirely satisfied or wholly dissatisfied, for a factory cannot be half-nationalized.

In spheres involving other values than economic ones, the point is even clearer: What compromise could satisfy both those who want the state to recognize Catholicism as the state religion and those who want a secular state? In sum, in countries where men find it more important to express and defend certain values than to obtain satisfaction of material interests, political compromises may be difficult to arrange. Considerations of political effectiveness and the hope of winning partial victories, which lead some groups to ally or to coalesce in larger, stronger, though less homogeneous organizations, weigh much less heavily in the calculations of political groups that are primarily concerned with defending ideological values. Ideological groups have fewer incentives to ally and many more reasons to protect jealously their independence and autonomy—for only in so doing can they continue to express the values for which they were founded. The strength of ideological factors in French politics may keep alive numerous political groups, even though the economic and social interests they represent are neither widely divergent nor irreconcilable.

Whatever the explanation of the multiplicity of French parties, however, it cannot account for the particular parties that have emerged in France. Despite changes in labels, splits, and regroupings, there has been a remarkable continuity in the major party organizations over the twenty-five years since World War II. Six political formations—Communist, Socialist, Radical, Christian Democratic, Independent, and Gaullist—have managed since the early years of the Fourth Republic to weather the vicissitudes of electoral swings, the arrival of new generations in politics, and even changes of regime to survive into the seventies.

Why this should be so is difficult to understand. One possibility is that each of the six parties represents a distinct social group, cluster of interests, or class and that the particularities of the party reflect the special characteristics of the group it defends. If such a theory were true, we could explain why these six political parties emerged and continue to exist and could predict that these parties would change when the interests of the social group they represented changed. Unfortunately, this answer does not help decipher much of the French political puzzle. Examination of the social bases of support of the political parties shows that each of them draws significant support from various social groups. The Socialist party in 1965 got 33 percent of its vote from blue-collar workers, but also 15 percent from peasants, 19 percent from white-collar workers, and 10 percent from businessmen and members of the liberal professions (see Table 1). The Independent Republicans, whose politics are at the other end of the political spectrum from the Socialists, had virtually the same pattern of electoral support. Even the Communist party must appeal to various classes: Only half of its votes come from workers. The characteristics of the social groups that provide supporters for a party may explain some aspects of the party's physiognomy and program, but the mesh between given social and economic groups, on the one hand, and a given party, on the other, is not close enough to answer the question of why, of all possible parties that might represent the interests of French society, these six have emerged.

Table 1   Distribution by Sex, Age, Profession, and Monthly Income of the Electorates of the Major Political Parties in 1965 and 1973 Surveys, in Percentages

Voter Characteristics	Communist 1965	Communist 1973	Socialist 1965	Socialist 1973	Radical 1965[a]	M.R.P. 1965[b]	Reformists 1973	U.N.R. 1965[c]	Indep. Repub. 1965[d]	Majority 1973
Sex										
Male	61	58	63	53	64	47	49	48	49	47
Female	39	42	37	47	36	53	51	52	51	53
Age										
21–34	33	30	27	28	25	29	27	24	32	25
35–49	32	34	28	30	26	27	33	27	29	28
50–64	23	13	27	24	32	26	22	27	25	23
65 and older	12	23	18	18	17	18	18	22	14	24
Profession of Head of Family										
Farmers	8	4	15	5	17	25	10	13	17	13
Shopkeepers, businessmen	5	5	6	6	14	9	8	11	9	8
Liberal professions, upper white-collar workers	2	3	4	7	4	4	20	5	7	13
Employees, average white-collar workers	17	15	19	21	18	14	23	20	17	16
Blue-collar workers	51	52	33	35	25	25	19	27	31	22
Without profession	17	21	23	26	22	23	20	24	17	28
Monthly Income (francs)										
Less than 500[e]	13		17		16	23		16	20	
500–799	22		22		25	20		20	20	
800–1249	32		29		28	25		26	26	
1250–1749	18		17		14	15		17	16	
More than 1750	11		9		11	8		14	11	
Nondeclared	4		6		6	9		7	7	

[a] In 1973 Radicals split, some ran as Reformists, some in coalition with Socialists.
[b] In 1973 parts of M.R.P. ran with Majority; others as Reformists.
[c] For 1973, see Majority.
[d] For 1973, see Majority.
[e] 1965, $1.00 = 5.5 francs

DATA SOURCES: *Sondages* No. 2 (1966), pp. 13–14; IFOP and SOFRES surveys cited in *Le Monde*, March 10, 1973, p. 6.

Political sociology of the parties provides only part of the explanation of why Communists, Socialists, Radicals, Christian Democrats, Independents, and Gaullists are the main political actors in France. A method that might be called political archaeology, that is, using historical research to unearth the successive strata that underlie the contemporary political system, is the approach we must take in order to understand why these parties exist today and why they behave as they do. Just as the archaeologist discovers in his work that each civilization superimposes its structures on those built by previous generations, using the creations of the old society at the same time that it covers them up with its own creations, the political scientist studying the French party system discovers that the parties today represent superimposed layers of different political periods. Each party was built with the ideals and interests of a particular period, and its structure and ideology reflect the major problems and conflicts of the moment of its founding. Parties created at different stages of French political development represent, therefore, different kinds of concerns. For this reason the conventional presentation of parties, which strings them on a single Left-Right axis (as above, where we listed Communist to Independent Republican), is misleading for it mistakenly suggests that these parties have different answers to the same set of questions. Not only the answers, but the questions or issues to which each party is oriented are different. Only an excavation down to the origins of the party and an exploration of its historical role and meaning can determine the issues around which the party is organized.

The parties, however, do not *only* reflect the problems on which they were founded, for in order to survive in a changing political environment, they have had to confront new issues and new demands. In some measure, of course, parties can control which issues and demands are admitted into the arenas of political decision making. Even very severe economic and social problems remain "nonissues" politically until a group is able to link the problem to other public discontents and desires that depend on authoritative decision. For example, whether or not regional inequalities become a political issue in France or simply remain an economic fact may well depend on whether one of the parties picks up the problem and translates it into political terms. While the reactions of the parties to a new problem may determine the timing of its entrance into politics and shape the way it is politically perceived by elites and the public, it is unlikely that parties can forever block the political consideration of significant problems. A party unwilling to take up a set of new demands must always consider the potential costs of having another party do so. In the fall of 1970, for example, when the Gaullists refused to respond to demands for regional organization, the Radical party made regionalization the banner of its program, and the Gaullists hurriedly "restated" their position in order not to lose too much political capital. In periods when all the parties have tacitly collaborated in excluding certain demands from politics, new parties have arisen to advance these claims. The founding of the Socialist party at the end of the nineteenth century, for example, owes much to the attempts by the existing parties to keep the demands of the working class out of the political system.

To avoid these risks and to widen the basis of their appeal, the political parties have shifted their interests and ideals in response to the demands of new times. Each party now represents both the structure and ideology of its origins and the successive layers of response to new political problems. Each major issue to which the party responds generates particular categories and party institutions and brings into the party special kinds of leaders and followers. In an "archaeological" slice into a French political party, we can identify the men and issues of different political periods, all of whom coexist in a single party organization. The programs of the present Christian Democratic party *(Centre Démocrate)*, for example, express certain values developed in the nineteenth- and early twentieth-century conflicts between Church and state, include other issues that emerged in the struggle between socialist and antisocialist forces in the early and mid-twentieth century, still other items that derive from the European orientation of the Christian Democrats in the early postwar period, onto all of which are added the political choices of this group during the Gaullist governments of the past decade. To each of these layers is attached a particular set of political personnel and a certain part of the Christian Democratic electorate.

The process of political change in the parties is one of accretion and erosion, not one of radical elimination. The layers below do not disappear but shape the topography of the layers on the surface. The men who entered a party thirty years ago to defend particular values are aging, and their influence and power are gradually declining; but during their long reign they will have stamped both the party institutions and the new generation of party men in their mold. The Christian Democrats, despite the virtual identity between their views on matters of current politics and the views of other political groups, cannot, or rather, choose not, to merge with other groups, because Christian Democracy remains different from even those parties whose current choices it shares. *What* are different are the men, the constituents, the institutions, the political instincts, and the political categories built up over the years of organizing around the issues of different periods.

Many conflicts of interests and ideals have shaped the behavior of French political parties. Three of these conflicts, however, have had such a massive impact on French politics in general and on the values and orientations of the parties in particular that the political crises that generated them must be discussed at some length.

The Crisis of the National Community: The Church-State Conflict

The appearance of mass political parties in France in the first decade of the twentieth century coincided with the crystallization of political conflicts around the issue of relations between the French state and the Catholic church. In the years in which party organizations were developing a mass base, the dominant political elites were lining up on the side of Church or state. The laws up for decision in Parliament, the pressures from citizens, the passions of the press—all these political forces pushed the naissant parties to focus on the issues that involved the role of the Catholic church in the state. The political parties were polarized into two camps: a Left camp of the supporters of a secular *(laïque)* France and a Right camp of the partisans of a Catholic traditional France. For most Frenchmen, Left and Right came to mean anticlerical and clerical.

When new problems arose in politics, they were looked at through glasses tinted by the colors of this particular battle. The passions and ideas, alliances and enmities generated by the alignment of party politics on the Church-state crisis continued to orient the political understanding of Frenchmen long after the moment of acute crisis had passed. We shall discuss later why the French system is so slow to generate new ideas and political alliances; why, in this particular case, clericalism and anticlericalism remain powerful organizing concepts in French politics, even when the passion and substance have evaporated from the issue that once gave the concepts their meaning. Here we intend only to emphasize that, despite public apathy about the one remaining significant issue of public policy in the Church-state area—the question of state subsidies to and control of Church-operated schools—party divisions based on the Church-state controversy persist and structure the political behavior of Frenchmen.

Today, some sixty-five years after the parliamentary decision to separate Church and state was supposed to have "solved" the problem, the division between Left and Right voters in many regions of France continues to be the same as the division between those who send their children to public schools and those who send their children to Church schools. In Finistère, a department in western France, for example, the correlation coefficient between the proportion of children in Catholic schools and Right votes is .791. Even when party labels and attachments change, the political attitudes expressed may remain the same. For example, in large parts of central France, the Left electorate switched its vote after the war from the Radical and the Socialist parties to the Communist party, but apparently the political meaning of the vote remained the same: anticlericalism. Even in regions where other political conflicts and alliances have replaced Church-state as the dominant axis of party struggle, the Church-state categories continue to account for a diminishing but still significant part of the vote.

What have been the consequences of the organization of French politics on an axis of conflict whose poles were set by the Church-state issue? First, the weight of this issue has contributed to the ideological character of French political life. As was pointed out before, parties that care more about defending ideal values like the ones central to the Church-state crisis —faith or reason, tradition or science, moral order or moral improvement —will be parties unwilling to seek out compromises. Ideological politics generates inflexible stances by the parties, not only because of the indivisible nature of the goals that are pursued but also because of the high emotions that the issues evoke. What issue of pragmatic, interest-based politics can arouse passions as intense as those of the Frenchmen who felt, in one camp, that attending public schools endangered the religious salvation of their children and, in the other camp, that all chances for political community and moral progress depended on each little citizen's receiving an equal, identical, hence public education?

And once such feelings are created by politics, how can men so bitterly opposed on one issue shift alliances when other issues, secondary by their definition to the dominant conflict, are raised? The second consequence, indeed, of the organization of political life on the Church-state axis was the freezing of party alignments and, in general, the paralysis and stagnation of the party system. Within the camp of the clerical Right there have always been groups that believed that private property and the market economy should be replaced by an economic system based on different social values that would better protect the right of all classes to a decent living and to participation in the decisions that affect their working lives. These "socialist" groups within the Catholic camp, however, have not been able to get together with elements within the anticlerical Left who share their views on economic matters, any more than Left-wingers with conservative property views have been able to ally with those on the Right with the same economic ideas. In both cases what divides Left and Right has mattered more than the issues on which groups within the camps agree, and so, despite temporary and unstable alliances across the boundaries of Left and Right, there has been no fundamental reform of party alignments. In 1965, for example, when Gaston Defferre, a conservative Socialist, tried to form a federation of the M.R.P. (Popular Republican Movement), the Socialists, and the Radicals, three parties representing constituencies with similar or overlapping social and economic interests and with moderate political programs, the proposed alliance foundered on old ideological obstacles. In 1972 Radicals led by Jean-Jacques Servan-Schreiber and Christian Democrats led by Jean Lecanuet united in the Reformist group. But whether the group can keep its two constituent elements together remains in doubt, for even during the election the different orientations of Servan-Schreiber and Lecanuet seriously strained the alliance.

The third major consequence of the organization of the parties along the Church-state axis of conflict has been the difficulty of inserting economic and social demands into the political process. Parties set up for the expression of the ideological values centered on secularism and religion are poor instruments for the aggregation and defense of economic interests. An interest group that wished to promote its demands in the parliamentary arena found parties oriented by ideas that had little to do with social and economic concerns. An agricultural group in the thirties, for example, when looking for a party to support its demands for higher food prices, found that the party system provided only left-wing and right-wing, that is, anticlerical and Catholic, parties and that choosing one or the other of them immediately classed the interest group in the camp of Left or Right. Thereupon the group lost whichever of its members belonged to the opposite electoral camp, without any guarantee that the party it chose would or could promote the group's demands.

In no political system can interest groups support a party with any absolute assurance that if the party wins power the group's demand will become policy. But in France the interest group's weighing of the potential risks and benefits of supporting a party dipped far towards the side of costs. Until the Fifth Republic, French governments were coalitions of various parties, in which no single party could impose its program. Moreover, the economic and social items in party programs were likely to have low priority. The interest group might well find that the party on which it had banked furthered ideological demands at the expense of satisfaction of social and economic demands.

Confronted with the inadequacy of the parties for identifying, organizing, and presenting economic and social demands in the arenas of political decision, some groups sought access to power outside the party framework. Interest groups tried to work directly with the state bureaucracy; others tried to establish corporative associations that could satisfy the needs of members without resort to the state; still others used violent tactics in order to force their demands into the political process. These attempts to bypass the parties produced successes that were generally directly proportional to the specificity of the group's demands and to the restricted nature of the group's clientele. A wheat producers' group whose members had large farms specializing in a single crop and whose only demand was for higher wheat prices might successfully pursue its demand, even without a party to back it up. On the other hand, an agricultural group representing owners of both large and small farms of various kinds and having a variety of demands for price supports and state assistance to "improve the lot of the peasant class" was unlikely to obtain satisfaction, because the diversity of the situations it tried to defend required a reconciliation and aggregation of interests beyond the capacity of an interest group.

Which political functions can be handled by interest groups and which can be managed only by political parties varies from country to country. But in France it is clear that the ideological character of the parties has made them such poor instruments of interest aggregation that interest groups have been forced to take on tasks that only a party could manage successfully. As one result of this, certain social and economic categories have been poorly defended in politics. Another consequence historically has been the organization of new parties in order to promote interests that existing parties ignored.

The Crisis of Socialism: Class Against Class Conflict

Among the social groups whose interests were systematically excluded from the political arena by the division of the parties into a republican, secular Left and a traditional Catholic Right was the working class. The economic, social, and political demands of the growing work force employed in industry were demands that neither Left nor Right at the turn of the century undertook to translate into projects for public action. The unwillingness of the political parties to incorporate the demands of the working class reflected in large measure the bourgeois composition of the political elites of both Left and Right parties and their broad consensus on preserving the social and economic status quo. The social consensus of the political elites provided a stable foundation for the political system, so that, despite ideological disagreements on political authority, all groups rallied to the defense of traditional social and economic institutions and supported only changes that could be accommodated within the social status quo.

To explain why the parties excluded the demands of the working class, it is not enough to show that the elites of all parties, Left and Right, were drawn from bourgeois society. In Britain, for example, the evolution of the Conservative party shows that a party based on traditional elites can incorporate the demands of other social classes and respond by adaptation to new problems. The inability of the French political parties to recognize and include working-class social and economic demands was the result not only of the conservatism of the political elites but also of the kind of politics that had developed during the Third Republic. The structuring of partisan conflict and of the parties themselves by the issues of republicanism, the Church, education, and the legacy of the Revolution of 1789 had created political categories with which it was virtually impossible to identify, let alone organize to meet, problems caused by social and economic needs and change. The struggle to introduce these demands into the political system produced new party organizations and a new axis of conflict, whose poles were the interests and values defended, on one end, by the propertied classes and, on the other, by the industrial proletariat.

The conflicts over the organization of production and the distribution of the rewards of production which divided these two camps became crystallized in a confrontation between the Socialist party (or parties) and the opponents of socialism. This conflict, like the crisis of political authority expressed in the Church-state conflict, had its origins in the nineteenth century. Indeed, its outlines can be traced in some of the later phases of the Revolution of 1789. Despite the active and increasingly autonomous role of industrial workers in the revolutionary movements of 1848 and 1871, however, the development of working-class political organizations was slow. Until the end of the nineteenth century, socialist and working-class groups were intellectual circles or workers' mutual assistance societies, with small followings and, often, short lives. The lengthy maturation of the working-class movement reflected the slow pace of French industrialization and the predominance in the industrial, as well as commercial and artisanal, sectors of small-scale family enterprises in which trade-union organization was difficult. The variety of industrial structures was matched by a great diversity of working-class statuses, situations, and attitudes, and this, too, inhibited the growth of mass organization. The fierce political repression following the Paris Commune of 1871, in which the revolutionary leaders were killed or sent into exile, further retarded the development of working-class political organizations.

The French Workers' party *(Parti Ouvrier Français)*, organized in the last decade of the nineteenth century, was the first French party focusing on working-class demands that mobilized a mass following. This party differed from the other parties of Left and Right in three important respects. Unlike the traditional parties, whose organizational structures were thinly developed and, indeed, barely existed except at election times, the French Workers' party created an organizational network that made possible continuous party activity engaging the energies of supporters at all levels of the group. In contrast to the other parties, which made little effort to recruit members and whose typical members were local notables interested in winning elections, the new workers' party had a high ratio of members to electors. Sixty percent of its members were industrial workers. Finally, unlike the other parties, whose doctrines were statements of position on the legitimacy of the republican state, the workers' party declared its adherence to Marxism and announced that the battles it would fight would be those of the working class, for whom the old political categories no longer defined the terms of political commitment.

For this party and for the unified Socialist party, which in 1905 absorbed it along with other socialist factions, it was often difficult to reconcile defending the working class, and the working class alone, with defending the republican, secular political values also held by socialists. The Socialist party came on the political scene at a time when it was already occupied by other actors and when another political drama was already being acted out. Today as at its founding, the great question for the socialist movement is its relationship to these other political actors. Unable to wipe the slate clean and to write their own terms for partisan conflict, the socialists have had to operate in a political world they did not make. In simplest form, the debate among socialists has revolved about the question of whether socialists should remain bystanders in political quarrels that do not directly affect the interests of workers as workers or whether socialists should actively line up with the republican Left, since workers are citizens as well as workers and citizens have an interest in preserving a particular kind of political regime.

The question was not an abstract one, but a matter of practical politics. Should socialists run candidates in legislative elections, particularly when this meant appealing for votes to other sectors of the population than workers? When a Socialist candidate came in after another Left candidate on the first round of balloting, should the Socialist candidate stay in the race on the run-off ballot at the risk of splitting the vote of the Left and letting the Right win? What part should the Socialist deputy play in Parliament? Should he support projects of the nonsocialist Left? or vote for a nonsocialist Left government? or accept office in a Left government? On each of these questions the socialist movement was torn by bitter conflicts between those who believed that the political system could evolve toward socialism through reforms and those who argued that the ruling classes would never peacefully relinquish power and so the state would have to be captured in a revolution.

The reformers, like the great socialist leader Jean Jaurès, believed that the socialist society they desired would emerge from a long process of historical evolution. The political traditions and accomplishments of the French Revolution and of the republican, secular Left through the nineteenth century would be extended into the economy and society, and the idea of participatory democracy would be widened to include the working class. These socialists saw themselves as an integral part of the Left and as its most advanced wing. They conceived their role as two-fold: first, to represent and defend the proletariat and, second, to ally with, encourage, and prod all that was progressive in France in order to speed up the process of change. These socialists therefore advocated a wide participation in parliamentary politics and a general policy of support to the nonsocialist Left in all matters except those where the interests of workers were directly at stake. They kept "republican discipline": In elections they withdrew after the first ballot in favor of the Left candidate most likely to win; in Parliament they voted for Left governments.

In opposition to the strategy of "republican discipline" other socialists advocated a strategy of nonalliance with the bourgeois Left, a "class against class" strategy, in the phrase of the Communist leader Maurice

Thorez. These were socialists who refused to align themselves along the axis of conflict of the traditional Left and Right and who defined Left–Right as the distinction ·between the working class and the bourgeoisie. The categories that provided their guidelines for political action were those generated by the battle for socialism, not by the battle for "bourgeois" political democracy. These socialists (and the Communists after the founding of the Communist party in 1920) broke with republican discipline and maintained their candidates alongside other Left candidates in run-off elections so that working-class interests could be expressed.

Even the staunchest advocates of class discipline against republican discipline could not always avoid lining up on old battlegrounds and allying with nonsocialist Left groups in support of republican values. As the threats of Nazism abroad and the extreme Right at home grew through the thirties, the Communist party shifted and began to urge an alliance among all Left parties to defend democratic liberties. To achieve this "Popular Front," the Communists loyally observed republican discipline in the 1936 elections and supported the Left government elected by the new legislature. Again during the period of wartime resistance to the Germans, the Communists found it politically desirable and necessary to broaden their alliances beyond the boundaries indicated by the terms of class struggle to fight a battle that they defined in national and liberal terms. To build a "national front" to win the war and restore the French republic and national independence, the Communists looked even beyond alliance with the Left to the Catholics. The Communist poet Louis Aragon dedicated to two fallen Resistance heroes, a Communist and a Catholic, a poem memorializing the single cause of the soldier who believes in heaven and the soldier who does not: "Only a madman would think of his quarrels in the heart of a common battle."

In periods other than those of national crisis the Communist party has sometimes found it expedient either to behave as the most extreme part of a Left camp defined by old republican categories and to ally with all Left parties or to present itself as the pivot of class alliance against bourgeois parties and to ally with socialist Left parties. Each of these two strategies is a departure from the strict class against class strategy by which the Communists define their party as the sole representative of the proletariat and as the ally of no other party. Whichever of these three political strategies is in force determines the election policy of the party, its willingness to negotiate joint action with the Socialist party and the non-Marxist Left, and its nationalist or internationalist orientation. The Socialist party is similarly torn between the imperatives of republican discipline and class against class struggle. The burning issues before the Socialist party in the past decade—whether to ally with Communists or Radicals, whether to merge the party in a broad Left federation—all reflect this tension. The Radical party, too, is torn by the contradictory implications of different political goals: By their republicanism they are pulled toward alliance with the Socialists (and potentially with the Communists); by their conservative economic interests, toward alliance with the Center parties.

The political alignments that emerged in conflicts over economic and social values have not replaced those that developed during the crisis over Church-state relations. One system of political institutions and political categories has been superimposed on another but has not supplanted it. There is, indeed, not only a competitive but also a symbiotic relationship between the two traditions; each derives a measure of strength and influence from the other. The Communist party, for example, enrolls as members not only Frenchmen who see the party as the political arm of the proletariat in the struggle against the bourgeoisie but also those who see the party as the most advanced sector of the Left and, hence, as the legitimate heir of the Jacobin revolutionary tradition. The Radicals appeal not only to members of the middle class but also to those voters of all classes for whom anticlericalism remains an important issue. This crosscutting of issues explains in part why all parties recruit a significant proportion of their voters from all classes (see Table 1). It also helps to account for the resilience of the old ideologies. The parties breathe life into the old political categories by their efforts to appeal to the widest likely constituency. Thus the Radicals try to keep anticlericalism alive because it secures them a part of the electorate that they would probably lose if elections were battled out on economic and social policy alone.

The Crisis of Government: Majority-Opposition Conflict

To these two political strata—the forces mobilized around the Church-state issue and around the socialism-antisocialism question—with their characteristic values and quarrels, pairs of allies and enemies, the Fifth Republic has added a third layer of political forces. The alignment of political parties in the Fifth Republic has increasingly taken place along an axis of conflict, at one pole of which is the majority party, the Gaullist Union of Democrats for the Republic, with the Independent Republicans and several Center groups gravitating around it; at the other pole is a collection of Left and Center parties, having in common only their nonparticipation in the governmental majority. The emergence of a majority camp and an opposition camp may be the single most important political development of the Fifth Republic: one that might fundamentally alter the characteristic patterns of power and representation in French national politics.

If two stable and coherent political coalitions emerge, one majority, the other opposition, it might presage the disappearance from French politics of the features that have resulted from a multiparty system with a high degree of ideological strife. In the Third and Fourth Republics governments were short-lived coalitions of different parties, drawn from a reservoir of potential governmental parties. Excluded from this pool were the parties of the Left and Right extremes, which formed a permanent opposition whose rejection of the political system was so comprehensive that their conditions for participating in power amounted to nothing less than a transformation of the regime. Alongside the permanent opposition parties and often collaborating with them to bring down governments was the temporary opposition: parties "eligible" for government but not included in the current line-up of ministers. When a government fell, its successor was formed by members of parties that had not participated in the last government and by members of the last government who had jumped off the bandwagon at an opportune moment for climbing onto the next one. The absence of a clear distinction between governmental and opposition parties strongly contributed to the instability of government, because at any time a government might be undermined by having its own members prepare to join the successor government. Just as important, it never was clear just which parties would replace the parties in power if they were voted out. By mixing the functions of government and opposition, neither could be effectively performed. The apparent opportunism of the ruling parties, the absence of clear political alternatives, and the string of short-lived governments all fostered a public cynicism and apathy about government that further undermined the efficacy of the state.

The polarization of the parties into a majority and an opposition would affect the prospects of governments in several ways. First, the existence of stable majority and opposition coalitions would mean that the political composition of governments would be decided in most cases directly by the results of the legislative elections, instead of by negotiations among the parties after the elections. The government would thus be strengthened by a direct popular mandate. At the same time, the opposition would be encouraged to present alternative sets of policies to the electorate, for each of the two groups competing in the election would present itself as a possible government. Second, the hands of government would be strengthened with respect to its own members by the hardening of the distinction between government and opposition parties. The parties that participate in government by a stable majority coalition have virtually no incentives to sabotage the government, for they have little or no chance of participating in the successor government that would be formed by the opposition. Party discipline is thus strengthened. Just as British Labour party M.P.s know that in voting against their government they risk bringing the Conservatives in, so the Gaullist deputies have been restrained in their criticism of government by the risk of helping the opposition to power. Such a constraint on the members of the governmental coalition is operative only when the defectors cannot hope to join the opposition government and only when the threat of the opposition's taking power is a credible one.

Not only the task of governing but also that of organizing opposition to government would be facilitated by a realignment of parties into majority and opposition camps. The existence of a solid majority has incited the parties outside the governmental coalition to coordinate their strategies with respect to the majority and even to try to unite their organizations. Where the previous party system rewarded with power those parties capable of maximum flexibility with regard to their allies, the new system forces the opposition parties to form stable alliances if they are to have any chance at all of participating in government. The access to power now runs along a route whose itinerary forces parties to contest elections that they can win only if they consolidate forces. Not only the run-off ballot in legislative elections but also, since 1962, the direct popular election of the President of the republic has provided incentives for the parties of the opposition to unite.

There have been four major attempts during the Fifth Republic to unite opposition parties. In 1965 Gaston Defferre tried to create a federation of the Socialists, Radicals, and M.R.P. but failed because of the traditional ideological issues. The same year, Socialists, Radicals, and several of the new political clubs allied in the Federation of the Democratic Socialist Left to support a single Left candidate, François Mitterand, against de Gaulle in the presidential election. The Federation subsequently tried to unite its three constituent groups in a single party, and in the 1967 legislative elections ran a single Federation candidate in each district. But the tensions between those parts of the Federation that wanted alliance with the Communists and those that wanted to move toward the Center finally came to a head in 1968 and the Federation fell apart. The next significant step toward creating a united Left opposition was the 1972 agreement of the Communists, Socialists, and a minority of Radicals on a joint electoral strategy for 1973 and a platform, the *Common Program*. The most dramatic of the reforms advocated in the *Common Program* is nationalization of the largest French firms. For the 1973 legislative elections, the parties agreed that in each district on the second ballot only one Left candidate —the one who had the highest tally on the first round—would remain in the race. The parties were in fact remarkably successful in disciplining their electors to vote for the single candidate, though some Socialist electors refused to transfer their votes to Communists. Together the parties of the *Common Program* polled 46 percent of the vote. As this is being written, the Communists and Socialists are discussing the future of the alliance with the prospect of the 1976 presidential race ahead. Finally, the creation in 1972 of the Reformist group, with Radicals and parts of the old M.R.P., represents a significant effort to build a unified center opposition.

The question of whether these new alliances will succeed is part of the more fundamental issue of the conditions under which the majority-opposition axis of conflict might come to structure partisan conflict in France. One obvious factor in the emergence of the majority-opposition axis is the strength of a single majority party, the Gaullist Union of Democrats for the Republic. In all the legislatures of the Fifth Republic, the Gaullist party has been able to control the majority. In the 1958, 1962, and 1967 Assemblies they needed the support of their regular allies, the left-Gaullists and the Independent Republicans; in the 1968 legislature, for the first time in French party history, they won an absolute majority of the seats. In 1973, the U.D.R. lost the absolute majority, but together with its allies, the Independent Republicans and Centrists, it still commands a legislative majority and remains "the majority within the majority."

Never before has a French government been able to rely on a parliamentary majority based on a single party. Never before has being in government provided the occupiers of power with so many opportunities for strengthening their party. These opportunities are the product of both the changed structure of government and administration and of the new tasks of the state. The enlarged role of the presidency in the political system means that when President and parliamentary majority are of the same party (as they have been throughout the Fifth Republic), that party has access to the political resources controlled not only by the Parliament but also by the executive and administration. The growing intervention of the state in society and the economy has increased the number of decisions about the allocation of resources that are made within the bureaucracy and has shifted power from Parliament to the administration. When a deputy, for example, tries to find funds for school construction in his district, he no longer presents his demand in Parliament but must convince the experts in the planning divisions of the bureaucracy. Small shopkeepers resentful of the encroachments of supermarkets seek redress—most recently in the form of a special tax on supermarkets—from the Finance Ministry. Peasant organizations that once lobbied in Parliament for tariff legislation and subsidies now must apply to administrative commissions that regulate agricultural markets.

In consequence, control of the bureaucracy is more than ever before the key to control of the resources distributed by the political system; and the majority party, by its relationship to the presidency as well as its parliamentary rule, has privileged access to the bureaucracy. The mayor of a poor mining town expressed the growing sentiment that majority deputies bring in more for their districts than opposition deputies do when he said, "I don't care whom we elect from this area as long as he's in the majority so we can get funds." U.D.R. candidates promise the voters in electoral campaigns that they can "do more" for the district than the opposition, and in fact they can. The rewards of politics are, in sum, increasingly distributed in a way that supports the "majoritarian phenomenon."

On the side of the opposition the prospects for party unification are more uncertain. Even if the ideological disputes of the past should fade in face of the united majority, there is one obstacle to Left unity that is unlikely to disappear in the near future—the Communist party. The Communist party is "not a party like the others." Its internal structure, policies, and relationship to the Soviet Union are as many reasons why it is virtually impossible that the Communist party would agree to any fusion of its organization with other Left parties. At the same time, these factors explain the reticence of many of the party members and electors of the non-Communist Left to go beyond temporary alliances at election time to any coherent program for common action with the Communist party. The adoption of a *Common Program* before the 1973 elections was the high point in efforts of the Socialists and Communists to form a unified opposition camp, but whether this will survive remains in question.

Yet the Left cannot simply circumvent the Communist party in projects for organizing the opposition. The Communist party is the largest party on the Left and wins a fifth to a quarter of the votes, a bloc second in size only to the Gaullist electorate. Indeed in the 1969 presidential election the candidates of the non-Communist Left parties received a total of only 9.8 percent of the vote, while the Communist candidate won 21.5 percent. This suggested that the Communist party, as the largest party of the opposition, might be in the best position to profit from an alignment of party politics along the majority-opposition axis. If, instead of using their votes to choose the party that best expresses their ideological preferences, French electors increasingly use their ballots to express support for the government or opposition to it, then the party that offers the most powerful opposition may be the winner. The Communist party candidate can claim to "do more" in opposition for many of the same reasons that the Gaullist candidates can promise to "do more" in government: because of the size of the party, the discipline of its members, and its control over other powerful sectors of society (in the case of the Communist party, for example, over a substantial sector of the labor movement).

The crystallization of party politics around the poles of majority and opposition camps might lead to a merger of Left parties, but it might alternatively produce a consolidation of the Left around the Communist party. The strong comeback of the Socialist party in the 1973 legislative elections in which it won almost as many votes as the Communist party suggests that this latter possibility is not at all inevitable. On the other hand, the emergence of the Communist party as the dominant or single opposition party cannot be ruled out, and this eventuality would make prediction about France's future even more difficult. In other states where the political parties alternate in government and opposition, the programs of the parties are more remarkable for their similarities than their differences. If the

Conservatives replace Labour in power, the Republicans replace the Democrats, or the Social Democrats replace the Christian Democrats, certain policies may change, but no fundamental transformation of the state or of its programs is likely. If the opposition party were the Communist party, as is not unlikely in France, the same condition would not obtain. Is a regular alternation in power of majority and opposition parties possible when the dominant opposition force is an antisystem party? Is the simplification of party politics into majority and opposition desirable if it means that the only alternative to the government is the Communist party? Or is the assumption that the strengthening of the Communist party would have destabilizing effects on the political system an assumption that is itself a product of the old ideological party politics? The Communist party has operated outside and against the political system in the past, but will it continue to do so in the future? Or might the role of opposition encourage the forces within the Communist party that tend to make it a party "like the others," a party willing to accept the rules of the political game, which imply the continued existence and competition of other parties, and willing to bring about the changes it desires within the constitutional framework.

The Parties

The future of the party system in large measure depends, as the preceding discussion suggests, on the parties' capacity for adaptation and innovation. It is no simple matter to assess the possibilities of change within a given party. Who in 1969 could have foreseen that a dynamic, ambitious leader would be able to revivify the almost moribund Radicals? Who now can predict whether the proposed reforms will in fact change the party and attract new members and voters or whether, like so many times in the past, the reformers will be defeated or absorbed? The evolution of the parties, however, is also determined by more permanent factors than the emergence of charismatic leaders or the impact of catastrophic political events. The historical development of a party, the social and economic composition of its leaders and followers, the procedures and institutions it has created to govern itself and those it uses to make policy, the regional bases of the party's power, the pattern of its influence in other organizations and sectors of society—these factors and others we will suggest in describing the state of French parties in 1973 are the factors that shape the party's future. They are, at the same time, "shapable" by the party leadership. In sum, to describe a party is to specify the factors that by their persistence, weight, and inertia are in the process of creating the party's future. It is, at the same time, to recognize that men can shape and reform their institutions. As Marx said, men make their own history, but within limits.

The following discussion of the major political forces should suggest both the possibilities and the limits that condition the development of the parties in France.

The Communist Party

The Communist party operates both within the political system and outside and against it: this is what is meant by the phrase that the Communist party is not a party like the others. On the one hand, the party performs important functions for the stability of the political system, legitimating the state by its participation in it and integrating into the political process those social groups that once were isolated and excluded from politics.[1] Since its founding in 1920, the party has shifted from a revolutionary conception of its relationship to the state, which implied total rejection of the system and no alliances with other political forces, to a conception of its political role as one of defending working-class interests and democratic liberties within the constitutional framework. This evolution is neither complete nor unidirectional: The party as a revolutionary organization and the party as opposition critic are conceptions that coexist within the Communist party and within the minds of the electorate.

In its role of "tribune of the people," the Communist party has made the defense of the working classes the principal object of its activities in politics. In fact, the Communist party has extended its support not only to industrial workers but to virtually all groups whose interests have suffered from the industrialization and modernization of French society—to the victims of capitalism, according to the diagnosis of Marxism. A 1966 survey suggests that for most Frenchmen the "tribune function" of the Communist party is its defining characteristic. Forty-one percent of those interviewed saw the party as above all the party of the workers, in contrast to 17 percent who defined it as the largest force on the Left, 7 percent who defined it as a party seeking revolution, and 27 percent who described it as the party of the discontented. The role of tribune is compatible with a large measure of acceptance of the values espoused both by those in power and by the non-Communist opposition. The Communist party has since 1934 affirmed its allegiance to the patriotic ideals of the French republican tradition. Indeed, in recent years various statements by the party suggest that it may have accepted the values of political stability and strength central to the Gaullist conception of the Constitution of the Fifth Republic. At the very least, the party's opposition to the institutional arrangements of the Fifth Republic has been greatly reduced. And in negotia-

---

[1]This interpretation draws on that of Georges Lavau, "Le Parti communiste dans le système politique français," in F. Bon et al., Le Communisme en France (Paris: Colin, 1969).

tions with other Left parties the Communist party has agreed to maintain the essential features of the constitutional framework and to work within it to develop a "real democracy."

The manner in which the Communist party pursues its goals in politics, like the definition of the goals themselves, has contributed to the legitimation of the very political system that at other times and in other ways has been the object of the party's attack. The Communist party sets a high premium on electoral victory and, with more success than any other party, encourages its party members and electors to participate actively in electoral campaigns. Communists participate in government at all levels: as mayors and municipal councillors, as members of departmental councils and of regional development commissions (C.O.D.E.R.), and nationally as deputies and senators. Whatever the purposes and intentions of the Communists, their active political participation in the system has had the *effect* of institutionalizing and legitimating the structures of government. By enmeshing Communist officials and electors in a network of choices among alternatives possible in the current regime and by involving them in activities within political institutions, the party in fact strengthens the political system—perhaps unintentionally, as Georges Lavau points out, but inevitably. The party's participation in the electoral process, the responsible and prudent way in which its members exercise public authority wherever they hold office, and the party's willingness to negotiate alliances with other parties are all fundamental indications of the extent to which the party now conceives its role as one of bringing about change by working within the system in alliance with other political groups. No evidence better illustrates this point than the party's response to the student uprising and the workers' strikes of May–June 1968. The party not only made no effort to exploit the political situation and come to power but, on the contrary, deployed its energies and its cadres in an effort to control the movement and, quite simply, to restore order. The bitterness of the student revolutionaries about the party's betrayal as well as the legendary outburst of a factory owner who, when his establishment was occupied by Maoists, exclaimed that only the Communist party could save him, both testify to the measure of integration of the party within the political system.

In three critical respects, however, the party has not accommodated itself to the system and continues to maintain structures and policies that challenge the legitimacy of the state. First, the relationship of the French Communist party to the Soviet Union, while no longer the virtually automatic subservience of Stalinist years, remains one in which the national policies and goals of the French party can be and are overruled in the interest of defending the national policies and goals of the Soviet party. In the case of the Soviet invasion of Czechoslovakia, for example, although the French Communist party at first publicly condemned the invasion, it eventually lined up with the Soviet Union in agreeing that the matter should not be discussed at a meeting of the various Communist parties. The domestic costs to the party were very high: intensification of tensions within the party between liberal and conservative elements and an embittering of the party's relations with potential allies that left the party back in the political ghetto from which it had been slowly emerging. The party's willingness to incur these costs is a dramatic example of the virtually uncritical approval it bestows on the policies, institutions, and politics of the Soviet Union and the East European Communist states. The special attachment of the Communist party to the Soviet state raises suspicions about whether, if the Communists came into power, they might prefer Soviet interests to French interests. At the very least, the actions of the Communist party create enough ambiguity on this score to make this one of the principal obstacles to alliance with the Left and a stumbling-block for electors who might otherwise vote Communist.

Second, the organization of the French Communist party continues to be shaped by other imperatives than those of operating successfully within the political system. The secrecy with which the party veils its proceedings, the very limited scope of democratic procedures in the internal governance of the party, and the restriction of possibilities for members to express dissent or organize within the party to change it—all these features of party organization suggest that the party has not given up its revolutionary aspirations. The Leninist structures of the party and its rules of discipline seem more suited to a goal of capturing the system than of winning power within it. For example, despite the party's active participation in elections, it continues to support and indeed to prefer organizing members in cells at their place of work, rather than in their neighborhoods, although neighborhood organization would be more consistent with the goal of winning power through elections. While the party justifies the discipline of democratic centralism and hierarchical structures as necessary for revolutionary organization, some of its critics point out, to the contrary, that the party uses its rules and institutions to stifle political initiatives that might lead to revolution. Roger Garaudy, a leading party intellectual until his expulsion for dissent on Czechoslovakia and for the "heresy" of proposing new political alliances of workers, technicians, and intellectuals, has argued that the absence of party democracy serves conservatism and not a program of revolution. But even if these critics are right about the nonrevolutionary character of the party, it is difficult to imagine that the Communist party could ever be a full participant in the state as long as the norms of its internal governance are so radically at variance with the pluralist, democratic rules it professes to support for the political community as a whole.

Finally, in the programs advocated by the party and in the criticisms it offers of the current government, there is an ambiguity about its ultimate aims that makes it impossible to see the party as one like the others, only more radical. As Georges Lavau has pointed out, the party's criticism of the government differs from that of the other parties not only in frequency and intensity but in nature, for it links its critique of particular policies and decisions to an analysis of the system as a whole: ". . . it integrates the critique of political choices into a critique of values, social structure, and economic relations. Its opposition therefore has altogether a different dimension than that of any other party."[2] In other words, the party's opposition to any single action of the government seems to imply a total rejection not only of the item under attack but of the regime and of the economic and social system on which it is based. The question then arises of what the party proposes to put in their place. The Communist projects for the future of state and society are in a state of flux, which can be interpreted either as evidence of a fundamental change in party positions or as simple tactical moves. If the Communist party came to power, would they permit other parties—and which other parties—to operate? Would they allow themselves to be voted out of office? What would be their foreign policy? What changes would they promote in the economic and social systems? The party has answered these questions many times—but not always in the same way and often with statements that leave room for doubt about the party's ultimate intentions. Such ambiguities lend credence to those willing to believe that the party has not renounced its revolutionary projects, and they reinforce the fears of even those groups on the Left willing to consider political rapprochement with the Communist party.

Members and Electors

To assess the prospects of change within any party requires knowing who votes for it and who the members are. The Communist party is no exception. Although its decisions appear to emanate from on high, in fact, like other parties, the Communists are constrained in their choice of policies by the nature of their constituency. We know too little about the political process within the party to be able to describe how these constraints operate: how pressures and interests of the members and electors are transmitted to the decision-makers. But we can look at the characteristics of the membership and electorate in order to estimate the kind of demands that the party must meet.

The voters of the French Communist party are the most faithful of all party electorates. While the votes for the other parties have fluctuated wildly in the period 1945–1973 (the M.R.P., for example, hit a peak of 23 percent of the registered voters in 1946 and fell to 6 percent in 1962), the Communist party has won over 20 percent of the registered voters in six of the ten postwar legislative elections and has never fallen below 14 percent in the other four.[3] While the Communist vote suffered a sharp

---

[2] *Ibid.,* p. 57.

[3] Jean Ranger, "L'Evolution du vote communiste en France depuis 1945," in Bon, *op. cit.,* p. 212.

decline in the first elections of the Fifth Republic, its successes in 1967 and 1973 legislative elections and in the presidential election of 1969 suggest that the party has recovered though not risen above its Fourth Republic level. This continuity reflects two stable phenomena: the geographic concentration of the Communist vote in three regional "bastions," north of Paris, the Center, and Provence, where the long, solid implantation of the party has buffered the Communist electorate against the impact of Gaullism; and the fidelity of the individual Communist voter, who changes his vote less often than the typical voter of any other party.

The imperviousness of the Communist party vote to changes in the fortunes of the international Communist movement and in domestic politics may reflect still another factor: that Communist voters see politics as class conflict and consider their votes primarily as instruments for affecting the balance of social and economic power. One-third of the working-class votes Communist, and half of the Communist voters call themselves members of the working class—although only 46 percent of them would be so defined by objective criteria. In fact a Communist voter is more likely than any other voter to define himself in terms of class.[4] But the immunity of the Communist voter to change is relative and perhaps wearing off: In the 1958 elections that confirmed the position of General de Gaulle and established the Fifth Republic one-third of the Communist electorate defected to vote in the new regime.

The subjective class definitions of the Communist voter are reinforced by party policies, which give highest priority to winning working-class voters and members. In this effort the party has been increasingly successful, for the proportion of workers in the Communist electorate has risen from 37 percent in 1948 to 52 percent in 1973.[5] This evolution parallels the growth of the blue-collar population within the nation, as has the rise within the party of the numbers of white-collar workers and employees of the public sector. The composition of party membership has adjusted to the long-term shifts in the composition of the national population. As a further illustration of this adjustment, at the same time that the agricultural population has declined, the number of rural electors of the Communist party has also declined. In sum, the party has proved adaptable enough to weather the decline of its old constituencies and to appeal to the rising classes of the population.

More than any other French party, the Communist party is a membership organization, not only an electoral association. The party has about 300,000 dues-paying members, a number greater than the memberships of all other parties combined. The social composition of Communist party

---

[4] *Ibid.*, pp. 223–224.

[5] *Ibid.*, p. 243.

members is virtually the same as that of its electors. In contrast to the stability of the electorate, however, the membership of the party declined massively in the postwar period, and in 1966 there was only half the membership of 1947.[6] The membership has spurted again in recent years (1968–1970), so the trend may be reversed. Not only the total membership, but the individuals composing the membership have changed drastically. Only about half of the members of the party in 1966 had belonged for over a decade, showing a rapid rate of turnover. The same is true of occupants of high party office: half of the members of the central committee have joined that body since 1961.[7] In sum, the recruitment of new members and leaders and the capacity to attract votes from the classes in the population that are expanding suggest a considerable potential for change within the party at the same time that the rigid party structures make such change difficult. In 1970 for the first time, the party tried out a new style of open meeting in which the public was invited to meet and quiz a Communist leader, "face-to-face." This open give-and-take remains so far restricted to the party's contacts with nonmembers, and the more fundamental question of whether the party will reform its own internal system of authority has not yet been answered.

The Socialist Party

In contrast to the stability of the Communist electorate and membership, the non-Communist Left has experienced great fluctuations in its fortunes. Today, after the 1973 legislative elections, the non-Communist Left appears to have a bright future, for it won about as many electors as the Communists and won many of them in new regions. But what this success means for the future remains difficult to project, for only recently after bad electoral losses in 1968 and 1969 the very existence of these parties had appeared to be at stake. In a political system with a government party that controls a majority coalition in the legislature and an opposition in which the Communist party is the largest and most stable force, is there political "space" for non-Communist Left parties? Is there a place for Left parties which neither systematically reject the legitimacy of the regime, as the Communists do, nor consider themselves potential members of the government majority, as the Center does? The answer depends in great measure on the Socialist party, for whether acting alone or as a partner in alliance with Radicals and other Left groups, the Socialist

---

[6]Annie Kriegel, *Les Communistes* (Paris: Seuil, 1968), pp. 31, 37.

[7]Guy Rossi-Landi, "Le Parti communiste français: structures, composition, moyens d'action," in Bon, *op. cit.,* p. 207.

party is the pivot of all political strategies of the non-Communist Left.

The Socialist party like the Communist party draws its doctrines from the Marxist heritage. Like the Communists, the Socialists declare that political democracy and economic democracy are inseparable and that planning and nationalization of the means of production—or at least of the key sectors of the economy—are required to transform the regime into a real democracy. The path from Marxism diverges, however, once the Communists and the Socialists try to go beyond this general agreement on national control of the economy. While the Communist path from Marxism links up with the experience of the Soviet Union and the international Communist movement, the Socialist path connects and merges with the tradition of the national French Left, going back to the Jacobins of the French Revolution. The two great Socialist leaders, Jean Jaurès and Léon Blum, conceived their political lifework as a reconciliation of socialism and French national traditions. What emerged from these syntheses was a socialism based more on a new humanism than on economic materialism. This revisionist interpretation of socialism was contested within the party by the orthodox Socialists led by Guy Mollet, who argued that the fundamental social reality remained that of class struggle.

Mollet defeated Blum in the intraparty power struggles after World War II, but with the perspective of twenty-five years it is clear that revisionism has triumphed. Both in theory and in practice the Socialist party of the seventies has given up revolution as a goal. While the Communists continue to define political power in a socialist state as "the power of the working class and other parts of the working population," the Socialists explicitly reject any exercise of public power that is not based on democratic elections: Legitimate socialist authority is for them "the power of the majority expressing itself by means of universal suffrage, freed from the limitations that are imposed on it by the domination of the capitalist class." (The two definitions of power in a socialist state are from a joint communiqué of the Socialists and Communists, which sums up conversations between representatives of the two parties.)[8] While the Socialists have lost a revolutionary vision of the transformation of capitalist society and the creation of a socialist state and society, they have not replaced it with any other. The Socialists continue to call for a new society "of justice and liberty" and claim that this requires a "fundamental transformation of social structures," but what they intend to put in the place of the old social and political system remains vague. Not only do they lack a blueprint for the construction of socialist society, but also, in giving up strict Marxist categories of class analysis, they have found no other terms for the systematic analysis of the problems of French society today.

---

[8] *Le Monde,* December 12, 1970.

No area better reflects the uncertainties of the Socialists than their alliance policies. The question of whether to ally with groups to their left, principally, the Communist party, or to their right, principally, the Radicals, goes far beyond the issue of winning elections to the question of what kind of France the Socialists desire. The vagueness and uncertainties of Socialist programs are thus perfectly mirrored in the party's shifting alliances. In the course of the Fifth Republic, the Socialists have moved from an initial position of qualified support for the regime to a position of all-out opposition. Guy Mollet had ensured de Gaulle's legal return to power in 1958 by convincing a majority of the party to vote for de Gaulle's investiture as Premier, in order to avoid political crisis and a military dictatorship. The divisions within the Socialist party over de Gaulle led to the seccession of its left wing, which regrouped in a new party, the Unified Socialist party (P.S.U.).

As the Socialists shifted into total opposition to the government and elections revealed the weakness of the Left, torn by its own divisions and reduced by the electoral successes of the Gaullists, the Socialists began to move toward alliances with the other opposition groups. The Socialists joined with the Radicals and the Convention of Republican Institutions (C.I.R.) in the Federation of the Democratic Socialist Left (F.G.D.S.), and in the years 1965–1968 the divisions of the non-Communist Left seemed to have been overcome by the common desire to return to power. (See the section "The Crisis of Government: Majority-Opposition Conflict" in this chapter.) The F.G.D.S. seemed the first step toward the fusion of the Socialists and the rest of the non-Communist Left into a single party. At the same time, negotiations between F.G.D.S. leaders and the Communists on a common political strategy against the Gaullists and on electoral arrangements to reduce the competition among Left candidates succeeded so well that the 1967 legislative elections increased Left strength in the National Assembly by half. The unity of the Left seemed closer than ever before.

Two political crises coincided to shatter this perspective: the events of May 1968 and the Soviet invasion of Czechoslovakia in August 1968. The differing responses of the Left parties to the student and worker strikes and governmental crisis of May–June divided the Federation internally. Czechoslovakia revived the non-Communist Left's fears that neither the Soviet Union nor the relation of the French Communists to the Soviet Union had fundamentally changed, and negotiations between these two parts of the Left collapsed. From all the debris of shattered hopes for Left unity, one new institution emerged: a reformed Socialist party. The balance of power within the party had shifted to younger men less marked by old quarrels and more open to working with social groups and parties that lie outside the traditional Socialist camp. The 1969 congress changed the party name from S.F.I.O. (French Section of the International) to Socialist party, and Guy Mollet was replaced as party secretary. Several groups from the C.I.R.

joined the Socialist party, and two years later one of these new recruits, François Mitterand, became party secretary. The party resumed negotiations with the Communists and in June 1972, with the prospect of legislative elections ahead, they signed an agreement on a common program. For the first time, Socialists and Communists went beyond electoral strategies and spelled out the reforms they would enact if they had a majority in the Assembly. The electoral gains of the Socialists in 1973 showed that the Socialists had at least as much as the Communists to gain from their alliance, but the shifts in the bases of Socialist support suggested that part of the traditional Socialist electorate was frightened off and voted for Centrists. Between now and the presidential election of 1976 the most important question the Socialists have to resolve is how to continue their relations with the Communists. Here the problem is to weigh the costs in terms of potential (second-ballot) Centrist votes for maintaining anything beyond an electoral deal with the Communists against the potential gains in political momentum from pursuing a common political and legislative strategy based on the platform of the *Common Program*.

Members and Electors

The problems of reconstructing and widening the Socialist electorate and party membership are serious ones. Between 1946 and 1958 the Socialists lost two-thirds of their members and three-fifths of their Assembly seats. In its old regional strongholds the Socialist party found itself contested and often supplanted by Communists, and increasingly Socialist candidates faced stiff competition from Gaullists. In the 1973 legislative elections, it became clear that the sources of support for Socialists were shifting. The Socialist electorate, like the U.D.R. electorate, is now more evenly distributed over the entire nation. At the same time that the Socialists are losing strength in the old strongholds of the North and Center they have begun to win votes in areas where they had traditionally been very weak, in Brittany, for example, where they moved from 9 percent of the vote in 1967 to 17 percent in 1973. The Socialists made a good showing in 1973 in certain Catholic areas, where the Left-Right cleavage has coincided with lines drawn over the church-state issue. The new success of the Socialists in these departments suggests a loosening up of the Catholic electorate, and this will be one of the most important points to watch in the future.

Rebuilding the party has been a major concern for the new Socialist leadership, for the S.F.I.O. had failed to recruit new members and the membership had become disproportionately old. A 1969 study of Socialists in Isère, one of the most modern French departments, found that only 28 percent of party members had joined since 1958, and that 61 percent of the members were over fifty.[9] The occupational distribution of Socialist party members was also a very skewed one, with many Socialists employed in government jobs. The national reform of the party has apparently been accompanied at least in some areas by grass-roots reform, and there are signs of a new vitality in local party life. Nevertheless, party organization remains a weak point for the Socialists.

The Radical Party

The Radical party, founded in 1901, was the first modern French political party. The first Radicals counted in their numbers men who had been the founding fathers of the Third Republic, and the history of the Radical party is inextricably linked to that of the Third Republic. The triumphal moments of the republic were the highwater marks of the Radicals, and after the debacle of 1940 the Radicals were never again to recover the strength that had been theirs in the first third of the century. Discredited by their part in the defeat of France and the fall of the Third Republic, the Radicals were sullied again in the regard of public opinion by their participation in the Fourth Republic. The elaborate parliamentary negotiations and rituals that produced and destroyed governments seemed proof to the public of the incoherence and incompetence of the old parties in the face of political crisis. And although greatly reduced in numbers and torn by internal divisions, the Radicals had come to play a critical role in the Fourth Republic. With the appearance of large permanent opposition groups—the Communists and the *Rassemblement du peuple français* (R.P.F.)—the parties that formed the governmental coalitions came increasingly to rely on the support of the small but pivotal group of Radical deputies. It was a Radical Premier, Pierre Mendès-France, who extricated France from Indochina; and conservative Radicals, like André Marie and Henri Queille, bailed the system out when combinations of parties and men from the major groups failed to produce governments that could get parliamentary approval.

The decline of the Radical party is attributable not only to its experiences in power but also to its inability—or unwillingness—to adapt the party program to contemporary problems. The Radicals' long advocacy of republicanism and anticlericalism seemed less and less relevant to generations for whom the burning questions of the Third Republic were settled matters. Even the Radicals appeared to lose interest in the old issues—some of them voted for state subsidies to Church schools—but the party

---

[9] André Bernard and Gisèle Leblanc, "Le Parti socialiste SFIO dans l'Isère," *Revue française de science politique* (June 1970).

did not develop any new platforms. The most serious attempt to reform the party was the work of Mendès-France in the mid-fifties, but he failed to rally the majority of the party to his ideas and was finally expelled. Even during the period of alliance with the Socialists and the Convention of Republican Institutions in the Federation of the Democratic Socialist Left, the Radicals hung on to their old doctrines and party structures. When the Federation collapsed, the Radicals emerged weakened but essentially unchanged. As the latest of the would-be reformers of the Radical party, Jean-Jacques Servan-Schreiber, has commented,

> Since the end of World War II, the substance of politics has shifted, . . . to what politics is about today: economic and social matters. Our times are demanding in that very area where Radicalism has never really developed its convictions, where its ideas are vague, its attitude ambiguous and often weak.

Servan-Schreiber's plan to reform the Radical party dates to the fall of 1969, when he was elected secretary general of the party and given the mandate to prepare a new party program. The document that he drew up had a dramatic impact on public opinion as well as on the party membership, for it attacked and proposed radical solutions for some of the sacred tenets of French society. The debate over the platform centered on two propositions: to control the rights of heirs to manage property they inherit by limiting the rights of inheritance and to break down the bureaucratic structures of an overcentralized state by creating regional governments and giving them rights of decision in matters once reserved to the national government. The "attack on property" implied in the limitation of inheritance rights stirred up such bitter controversy in the party that Servan-Schreiber's proposal was first watered-down, then put on the shelf politically. The arguments for decentralization, on the other hand, immediately elicited support from a wide range of individuals and groups. The defeat of the 1969 constitutional amendment on regional organization had left the advocates of regionalization in disarray, and the case for decentralization that Servan-Schreiber argued in the course of his electoral campaign for the National Assembly rallied many outside the Radical party who supported regional organization.

Four years later these issues with which Servan-Schreiber had tried to reform the Radical party had been pushed into the back wings of the party platform, and Servan-Schreiber was staking the party's future on an alliance with the wing of the old Christian Democratic party that was not part of the government majority. Before the 1973 legislative elections Servan-Schreiber and Jean Lecanuet, the leader of the Centrists outside the majority, agreed to merge in a new group, the Reformists (*Reformateurs*). Although some of the Radicals defected to ally with the Socialists, the new Reformist group was relatively successful in the election and picked up votes in regions where the Socialists had once been strong and in some areas where the Gaullists had won in 1968. For the Reformists the main issue is how to survive as a group. From the beginning Lecanuet and Servan-Schreiber had different orientations toward the government, and these differences almost exploded the alliance between the two rounds of balloting in 1973 as Lecanuet argued for siding with the U.D.R. against the Socialists and Communists and Servan-Schreiber argued for defeating U.D.R. candidates. Although the center has once again held, the fundamental question remains of what role a small party like the Radicals, with or without other centrist allies, can play in a political system whose central axis is the conflict between a governmental coalition and an opposition based on the Communists and Socialists.

Union of Democrats for the Republic

The U.D.R. (or U.N.R. as it was first called) was born in October 1958, a few days after a national referendum had given an overwhelming majority to the Constitution of the Fifth Republic. Like the *Rassemblement du peuple français* (R.P.F.) and the Social Republicans, the Gaullist parties of the Fourth Republic, the U.D.R. was formed to support the actions and policies of Charles de Gaulle. These parties all had the same point of departure, the arrival in London in June 1940 of the first groups of Frenchmen to respond to General de Gaulle's radio appeals to refuse to acknowledge the defeat of France and to continue the war against Germany. The original supporters of de Gaulle—*les compagnons*—have formed the hard core of all the postwar Gaullist parties, but their small numbers have been enormously swelled by later recruits: those who joined de Gaulle during the course of the war; those who came aboard in the R.P.F. period (1947– 1953); and, the largest contingent of all, those who became Gaullists after de Gaulle came to power in 1958.

Diverse, even contradictory, motivations made men Gaullists, but for virtually all of them, joining the party or voting for it involved a commitment to the personal authority of General de Gaulle. Leadership is always an important element in a party's appeal, but the difference that Mollet made for the Socialists, Waldeck Rochet or Thorez for the Communists, or even Servan-Schreiber for the Radicals is not only quantitatively but qualitatively different from the significance of de Gaulle for the U.D.R. Political scientists may quarrel over whether de Gaulle was a true charismatic leader, but it is indisputable that in de Gaulle's relationship to his voters and party members there was a powerful emotional component that cannot be reduced to interest or utility or constitutional legitimacy. The paternalism of an authoritarian leader may elicit the same kind of trust from the people that de Gaulle received from the French, but de Gaulle to the French was not the figure of a loving father. He was the symbol of an austere and demanding civic virtue. The trust that Gaullist followers invested in their leader evoked their active participation in his purposes, not the passivity of the subjects of a traditional authoritarian ruler. Voters and party members who accepted de Gaulle's identification of himself with France and who believed that he had a superior understanding of what the public interest required were politically changed or energized by these beliefs, though the swings in de Gaulle's popularity and electorate show that changes wrought by charisma are not always lasting.

So closely has the existence of the U.D.R. been linked to the person of de Gaulle that his retirement from the political scene in April 1969 and his death in November 1970 have raised the question of the party's long-term survival. The problem of the future of the party "after de Gaulle" has indeed haunted the U.D.R. from its early years. Gaullists feared—and others hoped—that the party's hold on the electorate was only a reflection of popular support for de Gaulle and that once he withdrew from politics, the voters would return to their old political attachments. The leader of the Christian Democrats in 1964 expressed a commonly held opinion when he described the Gaullist regime as linked to the existence of a single man and predicted that the Gaullists could not survive de Gaulle:

> The majority in Parliament is only a shadow, projected onto the electorate, of a power established at the summit, which exists in complete autonomy . . . The parliamentary majority is a group condemned to dispersal as soon as the top no longer maintains it.

Not only the party's appeal to the electorate but also the cohesion of the party itself depended on de Gaulle's appeal to men of very different political persuasions. De Gaulle's authority often seemed to be the only cement holding together the opposed factions of the Gaullist movement —those Gaullists who favor increased state intervention and planning in the economy and the Gaullists who want to liberalize the economy and encourage large modern enterprises; those who want to modernize French society and those who seek protection for traditional social groups; those who advocate regionalism and decentralization and those intent on preserving the power of the central state. Since de Gaulle's retirement these tensions have broken out into the open more frequently, revealing at one time the different social conceptions of President Pompidou and Prime Minister Chaban-Delmas, at another time the conflicts between "law and order" Gaullists who favor a hard line on extreme-Left political activists and liberal Gaullists who disapprove of using extraordinary police and judicial procedures. One measure of the U.D.R.'s chances for unity without de Gaulle will be Pompidou's success in containing these clashes within the party and buffering his government against the struggles for power among the different political tendencies of the Gaullist movement.

The party's dependence on de Gaulle has been one aspect of its fragility;

the weakness of party structures, the other. As Jean Charlot described the party in 1967: "It is first a team of cabinet ministers, then a central committee for selecting candidates to run in legislative elections, then the largest parliamentary group in the National Assembly and then—only last—a party."[10] After four years of Gaullist power, the party had only 50,000 members. It is hardly an exaggeration to say that the party existed only at election time. De Gaulle's political preeminence made it close to impossible for the party leadership to develop any independent authority in the political system. The party was obliged to swallow and defend each of de Gaulle's initiatives, without the possibility of advance discussion. The U.N.R. deputies with good reason were called the "unconditionals"; they ratified government decisions on which they had little influence. The massive U.D.R. losses in the 1973 legislative elections with the subsequent loss of the U.D.R. parliamentary majority seem to have produced a new restiveness and demands for more autonomy and for a more important role in decision making from the U.D.R. deputies.

The central question before the U.D.R. since de Gaulle's departure remains what mix of fidelity to Gaullist principles on one hand and of *ouverture* (opening) to centrist and traditional conservative forces on the other is the best strategy for maintaining the movement in the absence of its original guide. Pompidou has not yet committed the party to one or the other option: he retained Pierre Messmer, an orthodox Gaullist, as prime minister after the 1973 legislative elections at the same time that he made overtures to groups outside the majority. There is no reason to believe that this tension will soon be resolved, for the incentives for keeping both options, however contradictory, alive are powerful.

Members and Electors

What is problematic in the future of the U.D.R. is not only its dependence on the Gaullist legacy and its underdeveloped party structure, but also the ambiguity of its politics. One factor in this that has already been mentioned is the great diversity of political tendencies within the U.D.R. In a country where political parties maintain a high degree of ideological homogeneity at least among members, what is the future of a party whose members are economic liberals and planners, Jacobins and Girondins, nationalists and Europeans? The political strategy of the party leadership after de Gaulle seems in fact to be increasing the heterogeneity of the party, for in the effort to extend U.D.R. power on the local level, the party has coopted local politicians to run on U.D.R. lists in the municipal elections. These new party members come from the traditional parties and have none of the experiences in the Gaullist movement that provided the first

---

[10]Jean Charlot, *L' U.N.R.* (Paris: Colin, 1967), p. 23.

generation of U.D.R. members with a common outlook on politics.

If one turns from the party membership to look at the U.D.R. electorate, still other questions arise about the political base of the party. The Gaullist electorate was basically the electorate of the old Catholic Right parties plus some large urban centers. By and large, the gains of the U.D.R. were at the expense of the Center or Right, though in 1968 the Gaullists picked up some seats that the Left had won in 1967. [11] The 1973 elections marked an important shift in the bases of support for the Gaullists, for the U.D.R. has become stronger south of the Loire while losing electors in the Paris area and in the original Gaullist bastions of the North and East. As the bases of Gaullist strength spread out more evenly over the entire country, the party's center of gravity has shifted to central and southern France and to more rural, petit bourgeois, and traditional interests. The sociological composition of the party has altered and there are increasing proportions of women, of old people, and of farmers voting for the majority while the proportions of men, of people under fifty, of professionals, of workers, and of inhabitants of large cities voting for the majority decline.[12]

Is the U.D.R. then only the old Right, galvanized and unified by General de Gaulle? Or has the U.D.R. taken electors from the Right to make a new party—neither Left nor Right but majoritarian and governmental? Has the alignment of politics along a majority-opposition axis of conflict created a party geared not to the representation of group interests or to the expression of ideology but to producing and supporting a government? If so, the U.D.R. may be the expression of a fundamental reorganization of the French party system. What appear to be its weaknesses in comparison with the other parties may in fact be structural differences between a party that conceives its role in terms of winning elections and governing and a party that conceives its role in terms of a coherent ideology. For example, the relatively low members-to-electors ratio of the U.D.R. may not be a sign of weakness but, on the contrary, evidence that the U.D.R. is a new kind of party organization—a party of electors—in a political arena where the traditional actors have been parties based either on notables (Radicals, Independent Republicans) or on party workers and mass memberships (Socialists, Communists).[13] The Democratic and Republican parties in the United States and the Labour and Conservative parties in Britain are examples of parties of electors based on broad, general communities of values, rather than on agreement on precise doctrines. They are open to men from different milieus and with diverse stakes in political participation.

---

[11] François Goguel, "Les élections législatives des 23 et 30 juin 1968," *Revue française de science politique* (October 1968), p. 839.

[12] *Le Point*, March 13, 1973, p. 33.

[13] Jean Charlot, *Le Phénomène gaulliste* (Paris: Fayard, 1970), pp. 63 ff.

What is the evidence for considering the U.D.R. as the dominant party of a new majority-opposition party system? First, the U.D.R. pulls its electors from all groups in French society, in proportions about the same as the proportion of the group in the population. No French party relies on a single class for its voters, but the U.D.R. reflects more faithfully than any other party the diversity of the French population. The U.D.R. claim to represent the nation—to be equally available to all electors—has some foundation in the composition of its electorate. This claim runs counter to the goal of the old parties, which tried to mobilize particular classes of the population and in whose electorates those classes are therefore "over-represented."

This U.D.R. strategy has been rewarded with electoral success. From November 1958 to March 1967 the Gaullists doubled their electorate. In the legislative elections after the May–June 1968 events, one out of three voters cast a ballot for a Gaullist. This second kind of evidence of the majoritarian, governmental character of the U.D.R. is strengthened by the fact that the U.D.R. legislative electorate is rather distinct from de Gaulle's presidential electorate. The legislative elections of 1967 and 1968 showed that the voters casting ballots for the U.D.R. were not the same as those who voted for de Gaulle himself, although there was much overlap between the two groups. Indeed the U.D.R. electorate was independent enough of de Gaulle's electorate to survive when the latter disintegrated. In the April 1969 referendum the electorate turned down a proposal on which de Gaulle had staked his political office and then proceeded (June 15, 1969) to elect Georges Pompidou President with the same majority that had been supporting U.D.R. legislative majorities.

Finally, the pattern of alliances that the U.D.R. has concluded with other parties supports the case for treating the U.D.R. as the typical party of a majoritarian party system, rather than as a weak version of the parties of the old multiparty system. The party alliances that formed the basis of the governments of the Third and Fourth Republics were fragile and short-lived creations. Typically, the parties that were the pivots of government—the Radicals in the Third Republic, the Socialists in the Fourth—were elected with support from one set of allies and then in Parliament formed governments with other groups of allies. The Radicals of the Third Republic, for example, typically got themselves elected with help from the Socialists and even the Communists to their left and formed governments with Centrists and conservatives to their right. The electorate did not get to choose between alternative governmental coalitions but only between parties representing different ideologies and interests. The alliances of the U.D.R., in contrast, have created a true governmental coalition.

The "contract of the majority," in Valérie Giscard d'Estaing's phrase, which links the Independent Republicans to the U.D.R., is an alliance that differs greatly from the party alliances of the past. At critical moments for the government the U.D.R. has always been able to count on Independent Republican support: in 1965 when de Gaulle was opposed in the presidential election by a Centrist candidate (Jean Lecanuet); in May 1968 when the life of the regime was at stake; in April 1969 when the great majority of Independent Republican deputies supported de Gaulle in the regional referendum; in June 1969 when they backed Pompidou for President against the Centrist Alain Poher. In legislative elections the group has negotiated electoral agreements with the U.D.R. so that Independent Republican and U.D.R. candidates do not compete in the same districts (the arrangement of 1967) or at least step down in each other's favor on the second round of balloting (the 1968 arrangement). For the first time, then, the U.D.R. and the Independent Republicans present themselves to the voters as a government. The Center may be retracing the route of the Independents, with the 1969 split between Centrists who supported Poher and those who lined up for Pompidou and with the subsequent entry into the government of the Pompidou supporters. The composition of the government in spring 1973 reflected a coalition of U.D.R., Independent Republicans, and Centrists that elected the President, that fought the 1973 legislative elections together, and that will in all likelihood remain allied for the next round of presidential elections in 1976.

The Center: Democratic Center and Progress and Modern Democracy

The Center groups of the Fifth Republic are the heirs of the Popular Republican Movement (M.R.P.), the Christian Democratic party of the Fourth Republic, but the legacy has been greatly diminished by the claims that rival heirs have successfully pressed for the votes of the old Catholic Right. The Popular Republican Movement was one of the three great political parties of the early postwar period (the other two having been the Socialists and the Communists). The founding of the Gaullist party and the revival of traditional Right groups and of the Radicals all drew on the reservoir of conservative voters who had voted M.R.P. in the immediate aftermath of the war, when the parties of the traditional Catholic, clerical Right were absent from the political scene. At the same time that the M.R.P. was losing voters and members to the new Right parties it lost its Left wing as well, for the predominance of the right in the national leadership rapidly disillusioned the progressive Catholics who had hoped to transform the M.R.P. into a socialist party. The advent of the Fifth Republic in 1958 completed the debacle: The M.R.P., which had had 169 deputies in the 1946 National Assembly, had only 64 in the first Assembly of the Fifth Republic.

The decline of the M.R.P. continued in the Fifth Republic, and by the early sixties the party organization was virtually moribund. The survivors have now gathered in two groups. The Democratic Center *(Centre Démocrate)* was formed from the groups that supported the 1965 presidential candidacy of the former M.R.P. leader Jean Lecanuet. Despite Lecanuet's reasonably good showing in the presidential election, the Democratic Center proved no more successful than the M.R.P. had been in stemming the shift of Right voters to the U.D.R., and the number of deputies elected from this group continued to decline. Too small to form an independent parliamentary group, the Democratic Center deputies in 1967 joined with deputies from the National Center of Independents and Peasants and an assortment of Republican and Radical deputies to form a single Center parliamentary group: Progress and Modern Democracy.

The tensions between the Democratic Center led by Lecanuet and the parliamentary group Progress and Modern Democracy led by Duhamel have now gone beyond intraparty rivalry. Each of the two groups pursues an independent strategy with regard to the Gaullist majority. During Pompidou's campaign for the presidency in 1969, he proclaimed his intention to "open" the majority to other political forces. The first to respond to this "opening" were the leaders of Progress and Modern Democracy, who supported Pompidou against a Centrist presidential candidate. Despite rumblings in the U.D.R., where devoted partisans of de Gaulle accused Pompidou of having sold out the Gaullist legacy, Pompidou kept his promise of broadening the basis of the governmental majority and gave three ministries to Progress and Modern Democracy deputies. The Progress and Modern Democracy group has thus become part of the majority, alongside the U.D.R. and the Independent Republicans, while Lecanuet and the Democratic Center remain in opposition and fought the last legislative elections as allies of the Radicals in the new Reformist group.

What distinguishes the Center from the other groups in the majority? According to Jacques Duhamel, the Center's leader, the difference between his group and the U.D.R. is "something undefinable, yet essential. A certain way of acting, and a guarantee of what I would call tolerance." The "undefinable" difference is certainly nourished by the separate histories of the Catholic Center party and of the Gaullists. But in the final analysis, the refusal of the Center to merge with the U.D.R. seems to have more to do with the political advantages that the Center hopes to secure by serving as a pivotal, and autonomous, group within the majority than with any profound political differences between the Center and the U.D.R. Political groups close in doctrine to the U.D.R. now have a clear interest in joining the majority; but the structure of political incentives does not yet provide a clear advantage to those groups who throw off their organizational independence to join the U.D.R. As long as the Center retains important local bases of power and as long as the U.D.R. still sees advantage in extending its base of support by coopting groups as well as appealing to individual electors, the Center like the Independent Republicans will probably continue to remain independent partners within the majority coalition.

The Independents: Republican and Peasant

The advent of the Fifth Republic in 1958 brought the Independents and Peasants into the National Assembly in force, with a number of deputies second only to the Gaullists. The National Center of Independents and Peasants was formed to regroup moderates and conservatives and was one of the most important political groups of the Fourth Republic. The success of the Independents in maintaining and increasing their strength in Parliament in the 1958 elections when all other parties suffered important losses to the Gaullists seemed to augur well for the future of the group. Indeed, in the early years of the Gaullist republic the Gaullist party seemed so fragile an organizational creature that the Independents could reasonably hope to win a lion's share of the electoral benefits of a conservative regime. Once de Gaulle had resolved the Algerian crisis, which had brought the Gaullists to power, those conservative forces which were more deeply entrenched in local politics might well inherit the kingdom.

These hopes gradually faded as the Gaullist party showed its strength and disagreements broke out between de Gaulle and the conservatives. In the first years of the Fifth Republic relations between the government and the Independents and Peasants had been good: the Independents supported the government in Parliament, and the most prominent member of their group, Antoine Pinay, served as Finance Minister from 1958 to 1960. After 1960, however, as the government shifted its policies in Algeria toward independence and defined economic orientations that disadvantaged traditional sectors of the economy, the political support of the Independents became more problematic. The parliamentary support of the Independents and Peasants deputies became increasingly less dependable. Finally, in 1962, a majority of them lined up against the government in a vote of confidence on the issue of the election of the President of the republic by direct popular vote. The pro-Gaullist minority split off and formed a separate parliamentary group, the Independent Republicans. Led by Giscard d'Estaing, this group has become the regular, permanent ally of the U.D.R. With its growth from thirty-three deputies in 1962 to sixty-two deputies in 1968, it now constitutes a significant part of the majority. While the fortunes of the Independent Republicans soared, the National Center of Independents and Peasants declined rapidly on the national level, though its members continue to control a significant amount of power on the local level.

The Independent Republicans are a party in the old conservative pattern, based on networks of local notables whose formal organizational commitments are loose and casual: "no membership, no party card, no organized recruitment." In fact, it was four years after the 1962 split before the Independent Republican parliamentary group established a national organization. Most of the political activity of the Independent Republicans is still concentrated not in the national organization or its regional sections but in a network of "Futures and Realities" clubs, sponsored by the Independent Republicans. The party has attracted much of the old conservative clientele, but at the same time it has attempted to carve out a distinctive constituency in the new middle class by describing itself as the party of progress, dynamism, youth, and technological innovation. Its economic liberalism is a new theme on the French Right, one calculated to bring into the party the managers and upper-level employees of the modern industrial sector of the economy. Even if the party succeeds in broadening its electoral base, the fate of the Independent Republicans, like that of the other small parties, depends on the major parties. In the last analysis, the future of the Independent Republicans remains linked to the future of the Gaullist majority.

Four

The Changing Politics of Policy Making

France like other modern industrial states has experienced major changes in the process of policy making over the last thirty years. The relative power and influence of the groups and institutions that have been described in earlier chapters have been significantly redistributed, and the changes in the French political system from 1952 to 1973 have been far greater than any comparison of the formal constitutional powers of institutions would suggest. The roles that Parliament, President, the bureaucracy, political parties, and interest groups play in policy making have altered in ways that are critical for the process and output of politics.

These changes are in part the product of the new tasks the state has undertaken in the management and development of society and economy. To consider only the vast extension of the state's role in the economy, one recent study found nine goals that have become the objects of economic policy in European states:

> ... Price stability, a satisfactory balance of external payments, full employment, fairer distribution of income and wealth, adequate provision of social goods, a substantial rate of growth of GNP, balanced development of the country's regions, restriction of the growth of money incomes to that of productivity, and sufficient competition between firms and equal competitive conditions.[1]

[1]Malcolm MacLennan, Murray Forsyth, and Geoffrey Denton, *Economic Planning and Policies in Britain, France and Germany* (New York: Praeger, 1968), p. 26.

If such an inventory of goals of the economic policies of European industrial states had been drawn up before World War II, only one of the objectives would have been included: managing the balance of payments. Certain of the other items were occasional objects of political concern: States tried to provide or encouraged private industry to provide the infrastructure necessary for economic growth; in periods of economic crisis states tried to maintain price and employment levels; occasional efforts were made to aid backward regions. But by and large these goals were the object of only sporadic state action, and the policies formulated to attain them were short-term and piecemeal, based neither on overall objectives for the economy nor on coherent strategies. It was only after the war that the economic goals listed above—or some combination of them—became the regular operative objectives of state policy. As a result, the policy-making institutions of the state had to be reorganized to make it possible to achieve these new purposes.

The second source of innovation in the institutions and processes of policy making has been changes in the conceptions of tasks already performed by the state. Problems once regarded as political, in the sense of involving choices between competing sets of values, have come to be considered and treated as administrative and technical; at the same time, problems that were once seen as administrative matters have acquired political saliency. Some observers of European politics suggest that there is a long-term shift in the content of the politics of developed societies away from the divisive issues of ideological politics and toward issues in which technical competence, special knowledge, and the adjustment of material interests are more salient than value conflicts. From the mid-fifties to the mid-sixties this "end-of-ideology" theory seemed quite a convincing explanation, for the politics of both Europe and America were geared to problems that generated little ideological heat. With the reappearance in the past few years of profound conflicts over the purposes of state action, political values, and social structure, it has become clear that the end-of-ideology theory was only a partial and incomplete explanation of trends in industrial societies. At the same time that certain problems were being depoliticized, others were becoming political. The organization of higher education, for example, once a matter of almost purely administrative concern, has become a highly charged and politicized question in most European states. Political groups now regard the values at stake in the reorganization of the university as crucial to their conception of the legitimate relationship between state and society. The transfer of problems between the sphere of politics and the sphere of administration has thus moved in both directions. The rate of circulation between the two spheres has been greatly accelerated in modern states. It is this rapid transformation of the content of politics, rather than the end of politics or its radicalization, that best describes what is happening in European states. With these changes have come changes in the personnel and methods of decision making.

Strategies of Reform

The new tasks of the state and the changing conceptions of political issues have been two major sources of strain and tension for traditional policy-making institutions in France. The inadequacy of a decision-making process developed in the nineteenth and early twentieth centuries for dealing with the issues of postwar France has provoked many and diverse problems, which no single institutional reform could remedy. The French have tried to adapt the policy-making process by using three different strategies of institutional reform: transforming old institutions by bringing in new blood and creating new rules; creating new institutions alongside of and often in competition with the existing ones; and transferring the power of decision from political to administrative elites.

Attempts to bring about change by reworking old institutions are subject to familiar pitfalls, and the French reforms that have followed this first strategy have not often been successful. The values and personal interests that become attached to a given set of institutional arrangements create resistance to innovation within an organization and make it difficult to change established patterns of behavior. For example, to modify the authoritarian aspects of the French public school system, the Ministry of Education might order school principals to meet with parents and students to discuss the curriculum. But the principal's job expectations, his sense of social prestige, and his feelings about what is right in a school have become so inextricably connected to a certain way of performing his job and dealing with others in the system that such a directive would probably not have much impact.

There are two approaches that would make it likely that the school principals would try to change the system within which they work. One would be to provide incentives by rewarding principals who implement such changes and penalizing those who persist in the old ways. This would require, of course, that "someone" check up on each principal and that this person have authority to administer rewards and penalties according to the principal's performance. This "someone" in the French system can only be central authority, for to institute any other system of controls would require serious modification of the distribution of power between the central state and local authorities. In other words, power is distributed in such a way in France today that only the center can exercise effective controls. The effectiveness of reform measures that require the people already in place to obey new rules thus depends on the effectiveness of centralization. It is easy, however, to imagine the kinds of reforms that can never be carried out if they need the supervision of the central administration. The reform to democratize the school system suggested in the example above would be vitiated in its very principle if implementation required an inspector from the ministry to check on the exercise of local autonomy. The only "controllers" who could in fact assure that the principal shared his power with other participants in the local system would be local controllers, but centralization does not allow this in France.

The second way to get the principals to change the system would be to replace the principals with new ones who had been educated in the spirit of a more democratic school system. Reforming institutions by infusing them with new blood was in fact the idea behind one of the most important efforts at innovation in postwar France: the creation in 1945 of a National School of Administration, E.N.A. *(Ecole Nationale d'Administration)*. Until then, the higher civil servants were predominantly men who had graduated from a few private universities or from law schools. Their education had provided them with essentially legalistic interpretations of the problems the state confronted, and it had left them poorly prepared to understand the complexities of economic and social policy. The institutions in which they had studied recruited students almost exclusively from the bourgeoisie, and this, as well as the private character of the institutions, predisposed many of the graduates toward a rather unsympathetic view of any extensive state intervention in the economy and society. E.N.A. was founded in order to develop a class of top-level civil servants who would be both committed to an active public sector and competent to manage it. The graduates of E.N.A. were to be the main reservoir for all top posts in the administration: the ministries, the state banks and industries, the diplomatic service, the prefectoral service, and the administrative courts *(Conseil d'Etat)*. The new school was supposed to provide all higher civil servants with a common general education in the subjects relevant to the needs of a modern state: economics, sociology, political science. Book learning was to be supplemented by periods of apprenticeship in various public institutions. And the recruitment of the top civil service was to be broadened by an entrance examination system that would open E.N.A. up to students of diverse class origins. (As it turned out, E.N.A., like the schools that preceded it, draws its students almost exclusively from the Parisian bourgeoisie.)

The result of restricting entry to the higher civil service to E.N.A. graduates has been to introduce important changes into the operation of the state bureaucracy. The mentalities of the old-style bureaucrats and of the E.N.A. graduates were so different that in the school's first years of existence its graduates met hostility and resistance in their assigned positions. The social science training of the E.N.A. graduates gave them not only new methods but also new conceptions of the role of the state, and it was this difference in values as much as any differences in skills that set off the young bureaucrats from the old. The E.N.A. men succeeded in imposing their methods and values on the bureaucracy because of numbers—by 1969, 1800 higher civil servants had passed through E.N.A.—and because the old E.N.A. graduates were continuously reinforced by the new classes arriving each year in the bureaucracy.

One of the problems of trying to change an old institution by bringing in new blood is that the system often absorbs the new men and socializes them in the old ways. Would-be reformers find that they can be successful in an institution only by conforming to the norms of the system; thus they are swallowed up by the very institutions they are supposed to change. A good example of this was provided by the Parliament of the Fourth Republic. After the Liberation a generation of men with little or no previous parliamentary experience was elected to Parliament, and they brought with them new political aspirations, values, and the experience of working in the Resistance with men of different political beliefs. Despite this background, after a few years the new men found themselves involved in the same parliamentary game that had paralyzed the Third Republic. It became clear that the new deputies had been socialized by the old system. E.N.A., on the contrary, succeeds because it injects a new class of graduates into the bureaucracy each year, thus ensuring that the top levels of the administration will eventually be controlled by its men and reinforcing the commitment of E.N.A. graduates already in the system by surrounding them with other E.N.A. alumni.

The contrast between the cases of the Fourth Republic deputies and E.N.A. shows both the possibilities and the limitations of bringing about change in a system by introducing persons with new ideas and values. It works well only when a continuous flow of the new men pours into the institution—a one shot injection of new blood is hardly likely to dilute the strength of the old values and practices enough. In industrial societies schools are virtually the only institutions that can reproduce a constant supply of men with given values and skills. This means that the strategy of reform that depends on introducing new men into institutions requires an educational system already transformed by the values that are to be introduced into the bureaucracy. This is one profound reason for the central place of education in political conflicts in France today. In the organization of schools and universities and in their curriculums and procedures, all political groups in France perceive values that will mold the content and process of politics.

The second approach that has been tried in France to reform the methods and institutions of political decision making is the creation of new institutions, sometimes to replace the old ones, far more frequently to coexist with them. No case better exemplifies the possibilities of this strategy than the General Planning Commissariat, established in 1946 alongside the Ministry of Economy and Finance. While the Ministry of

Finance continued to perform the traditional economic functions of the state—raising and collecting taxes, preparing the annual budget, supervising the accounts of the public sector—the new Planning Commissariat was entrusted with responsibility for defining and achieving many of the new economic goals of the state. As suggested above, these new goals required long-term projection of the needs and resources of the country and coherent plans of action for attaining them. Whether it was the state's concern with achieving a certain rate of economic growth, the desire to relocate industries in order to promote a more even distribution of economic activities across national territory, or the selection of economic targets requiring transformation of certain industries, it was clear that the traditional personnel and structures of the Ministry of Finance would not be able to handle the new tasks. The General Planning Commissariat was given the job of projecting needs and resources, relating them to rates of economic growth, and specifying the changes in supply factors, in the production process, and in demand that would be necessary to reach given economic objectives. These economic projections were drawn up in five-year national plans. The Planning Commissariat was responsible not only for developing the plans but also for involving in their preparation the economic actors on whose decisions the success of the plan depended. The Planning Commissariat organized commissions in which industrialists, trade unionists, representatives of agriculture, commerce, consumers, and others deliberated with the planners on national goals and means to reach them. By broadening participation in the elaboration of the plan to include the economic decision-makers themselves, the planners were able to gauge the climate of the economy and, at the same time, to provide business and labor with information about the state's intentions and about the evolution of the economy. Communication and information facilitated a voluntary coordination of the economic choices of thousands of private decision-makers and made it possible to develop the national economy in particular directions without authoritative controls. The plan objectives were binding on the economic decisions of the public sector, but the plan could only encourage (by subsidies and other aids) and could not force private industry to carry out the plan. The delicate negotiations between private and public sectors and among different interests within the private sector and the conceptual problems of specifying economic objectives for a five-year period and of relating the goal of economic growth to goals of price and wage stability or favorable balance of payments are among the difficult tasks that the Planning Commissariat has undertaken. Such tasks would be more difficult for an organization like the Ministry of Finance, working within a tradition of bureaucratic secrecy, compartmentalization of activities, and suspiciousness of direct contacts with the public and constrained by the intellectual formation and values of its personnel.

New institutions are, however, no universal panacea. The Planning

Commissariat is a small organization and so the problems of staffing it are not major. When, however, the state creates new institutions that require large numbers of personnel, the difficulty of finding men with the skills and perspectives needed for the new institutions is a serious obstacle to change. For example, one of the reasons for the failure of the regional councils (C.O.D.E.R.) was that their members were drawn exclusively from established local elites and retained their loyalties to the organizations from which they came. Another problem new institutions face is coexistence with other groups. The Planning Commissariat, for example, has been involved in the kind of competitive relationship with the Ministry of Finance in which each institution has increased its power and influence often at the expense of the other.

For the political system as a whole, this competition among institutions may be highly desirable, for it provides flexibility and the organizational possibility of innovation. Different kinds of institutions generate different policies, and the presence of competitive institutions increases the chances that the public and the political decision-makers will be offered alternative policies from among which to choose. The overlap of institutional responsibilities also makes it more likely that when the executive changes course, he will be able to have his new policy carried out by the bureaucracy. For example, the governments of the Fifth Republic set a higher priority on price and wage stability and on maintaining a favorable balance of payments than the Fourth Republic governments, which had on the whole chosen rapid economic expansion even at the expense of inflation and foreign indebtedness. This shift in economic goals was accompanied by— and facilitated by—a shift in the relative power of the branches of the bureaucracy in which economic policy is developed. The Ministry of Finance has recovered the position of unchallenged predominance that had been contested by the Planning Commissariat during the Fourth Republic. The Planning Commissariat is now obliged to accept goals quite different from those it would itself propose and, indeed, to adapt to a political situation in which planning has declined in importance as a policy-making process. The availability of both the Ministry of Finance and the Planning Commissariat allows a freedom of action and choice to the executive that would be far more difficult to obtain were he dependent on a single economic agency.

Politicians or Technocrats?

The third strategy of reform has been to transfer the power of decision from politicians to bureaucrats with special expertise, the "technocrats." In this context, the most useful distinction is between decision-makers whose access to power is determined by election, the politicians, and decision-makers, the technocrats, whose route to power is the acquisition of certain skills or, more precisely, certain diplomas. The paths to power for a French politician have changed over time. There are two classical patterns: the path of the local notable, who starts as mayor or municipal councillor in his commune, then is elected to the departmental council, and finally seeks election as deputy; and the path of the party man, whose political career takes place within the organization of a political party and who is chosen by the party to run in a district as a representative of the party, not as a local son. In the Fifth Republic, a third pattern has evolved. Someone who exercises national power by virtue of his technical skills goes back and seeks election, presenting himself to the electorate not as the best informed representative of local interests nor as the representative of particular political conceptions associated with a party, but as a man who, because of his national power position, can "do more" for the solution of local problems than any local son or party man could. These three routes to power, despite divergences, all converge on a single point: election.

Winning elections requires the mastering of certain skills and the development of certain qualities. Politicians must be able to translate public issues into terms the average citizen can understand. In part this means that the politician has to be able to relate national concerns to private, local stakes. The Normandy farmer may not understand or care much about the fate of the Atlantic alliance, the future of the Commonwealth, or supranational or federal political structures for Europe—all questions at stake in the admission of Britain to the Common Market—unless politicians explain that each of these questions involves matters that are of direct personal concern to his livelihood and community. It was indeed because politicians had succeeded in convincing the peasant electorate that the Common Market was the solution to its economic problems that de Gaulle's threats to paralyze the Common Market in order to stop supranational projects turned peasant electors who had previously voted for de Gaulle to rival presidential candidates (1965). Likewise, someone whose power depends on winning votes is apt to be more sensitive to the local fallout from national decisions than the technocrat, who does not have to confront the public in face-to-face relationships. The social impact of national policy and the reactions of the public are factors that usually weigh heavily in the calculations of those who exercise power by virtue of elections. Such persons are more likely to consider individual and social costs than are men who reach power by other routes.

There are fewer points of access to the road to power for a technocrat than for a politician, and only those who have attended one of the *grandes écoles* (literally, the great schools) have a significant chance of rising to the top. Indeed as Jean Meynaud has pointed out, the most economic description of a French technocrat is a graduate of E.N.A. or *Ecole Polytechnique* (which educates engineers and scientists). The diplomatic service, the most important ministries, the state banks and industries of the public sector, and the other *grands corps* of the state are recruited almost exclusively from among the E.N.A. and the *Ecole Polytechnique* graduates.[2] Not only are the top jobs in the bureaucracy filled by the graduates of these schools but also, particularly since the advent of the Fifth Republic in 1958, these technocrats sit in the top levels of government. Charles Debbasch in his study of the role of the bureaucrat in the Fifth Republic *(The Rule of the Bureaucracy)* reports an item in a local newspaper with a revealing error. The article reads: "Mr. X has returned to Cogolin for vacation. We know that he is a student at E.N.A., a school that prepares its students to become, among other things, prefects, *ministers,* etc. We wish this brilliant student a good vacation."[3] [Italics added.] The reporter's mistake in thinking that the National School of Administration turned out cabinet ministers is understandable. In the first governments of the Fifth Republic, 40 percent of the ministers were technocrats, not politicians. In the first ten years of the regime, six ministers were graduates of E.N.A., four of *Ecole Normale Supérieure* (which prepares university teachers), and three of *Ecole Polytechnique.*[4] Though the number of nonpolitician ministers has declined in subsequent governments, the number of technocrats in the top staff jobs of ministerial cabinets remains very high. In the Third Republic the ministers usually chose other politicians to serve on their staffs. Technocrats began to appear on the staffs of the Fourth Republic ministers, and in the Fifth Republic they have come to have a virtual monopoly of these posts.

Though the shift of power from politicians to technocrats began in the Fourth Republic, it is under the Fifth Republic that this change in the cast of political decision-makers has been most dramatic. The numbers of bureaucrats exercising functions previously exercised by men who had been elected to office has greatly increased. The issue is not, however, one of numbers alone, but of the relative influence of politicians and technocrats in the process of policy making. It would be impossible to design an index of influence that would allow us to sum up the respective powers of the two groups in the political system as a whole, for there is no common denominator of power that would enable a researcher to match the increased power of an elected official (the President) in foreign-policy decisions against the increased power of the technocrats in economic matters. In most areas of policy, with the exception of defense and foreign policy, case studies of decisions made fifteen years ago and today suggest that the power of the technocrats has increased relative to that of the politicians.

---

[2]Jean Meynaud, *La Technocratie* (Paris: Payot, 1964).

[3]Charles Debbasch, *L'Administration au pouvoir* (Paris: Calmann-Lévy, 1969), p. 91.

[4]*Ibid.,* pp. 50, 57.

If the politicians' route to power develops certain qualities and skills, the technocrats' route rewards certain kinds of competence. The process of recruitment for the *grandes écoles* selects persons who can meet high standards of intellectual accomplishment and who share the cultural norms of the Parisian upper-middle class. The student from working-class or peasant origins who makes it into E.N.A. is a very rare case; the student from the provinces is almost as uncommon. The education that students receive in E.N.A. and the *Ecole Polytechnique* develops a world view quite different from that of the politician, for it presents the standards of rationality and growth as the highest priorities of state policy. For technocrats even more than for politicians, who are obliged to meet their provincial constituents regularly and to deal with their problems, Paris and the central government are the hub of the political universe. The technocrat identifies the central state with the public interest and tends to see local objections to national decisions as motivated only by private, selfish, or parochial interests. The technocrat's education has taught him that the public interest is best served by rational, coherent policy making, and so he is likely to regard processes of negotiation and compromise among interests with a certain contempt. The technocrat who works in the provinces sees himself as the emissary of the center, and it is unusual for him to develop loyalties to any local institutions.

One of the new themes of opposition parties in France today is that the state has been taken over by technocrats who disregard the human aspects of politics and try to impose policies that are perhaps economically justifiable but which have social costs that are not taken into consideration. Like some Americans who see the United States as controlled by a military-industrial elite which is politically irresponsible—that is, unchecked by popular election and insensitive to human and social needs—the French critics of technocratic power argue that rule by technocratic elites has resulted in a virtual disenfranchisement of their population.

The rise to power of the technocrats is only one part of a more general phenomenon: the transfer of policy making from arenas of power in which politicians and political criteria are dominant to arenas of power in which technocrats and technical criteria are decisive. How can we explain this shift in French politics? In part the answers lie in factors that attained their most developed form under the Fifth Republic, but whose origins preceded it. The changes in the tasks of the state and in political beliefs and values enhanced the role of the technocrats. Even when the knowledge required to tackle one of the state's new tasks was not of a highly technical nature, the presumption was established that, in whatever concerned the economy, there was a "best solution" and an expert was the man to find it. As one French politician put it, "there are not ten best ways to collect garbage." This remark is striking for Americans, whose experiences in local government suggest that there is no best way to collect garbage, only ways with different costs and benefits for different social and political groups. In other words, in France it was not only and perhaps not primarily *what* the state tried to accomplish that led to the triumph of technocrats over politicians, but *how* the state and the major political groups in the nation defined the problems and the methods to resolve them. Despite signs of rising public resentment against technocratic power and of frustrated aspirations to participate, the notion still prevails in France that for a broad range of economic, social, and political matters, only a person with the special education of a technocrat is competent to make decisions.

A second major factor that has contributed to the shift of policy making from political arenas to technocratic arenas is the Constitution of the Fifth Republic. As Chapter 2 described, the constitution specifies the subject matter on which the Parliament may legislate, thus limiting the powers of Parliament and increasing those of the government, which may act by decrees on any subject not specifically assigned to the Parliament. This distinction between the domain of law, in which Parliament legislates, and the residual domain of regulation, in which the government is free to act, has removed a vast number of decisions from the arena of policy making in which politicians dominate and has transferred them to the bureaucracy. Two other provisions of the constitution have had the same effect. One is the clause enabling the government to request that Parliament allow it to act by ordinance on matters that ordinarily are the subject of laws. The Parliament, for example, authorized the government to issue ordinances on the control of various "social diseases": alcoholism, homosexuality, and prostitution. According to the constitution, such ordinances should return before the Parliament for a vote. In fact, frequently the government has either not presented the ordinances to Parliament or has presented them after such long delay that the principle of parliamentary review and control has been subverted.

Finally, even when a bill is passed by Parliament, the government and bureaucracy often have wide scope for modifying the bill's provisions or delaying the bill for an indefinite period. Though Parliament determines the basic framework of legislation on national defense, local government, education, property law, and social security, the government determines the details of the legislation. This gives the government great latitude, which it frequently exercises in directions quite independent of the legislature's intentions. When, for example, the Parliament passed a law in December 1967 legalizing and regulating the dissemination of birth-control information, the government delayed fourteen months before issuing any measures that would enable the law to go into effect, despite the law's explicit requirement that the government act within six months. Four years later, many of the law's most important provisions were still dead letters, because of the government's failure to act. There are many similar cases. Parliament passed a law on health insurance for self-employed persons in the middle of 1966 that was to go into effect in January 1967. Two years passed, and, as a wave of protest arose from shopkeepers and professionals affected by the legislation, it became clear that the government was not going to apply the law. Indeed, the government returned to Parliament with a new project, significantly modifying the law already passed but never applied, and this modified bill finally went into effect in January 1971. Although the constitution gives Parliament the right to decide basic principles of social security, the government was able to use its right to draw up the enabling clauses as a device to stall for four years. One can only conclude that the bureaucrats, not the deputies, were in the long run the decision-makers.[5]

Many of the problems that have been transferred from Parliament to the government involve political decisions, in the sense that the criteria by which they will be decided are only secondarily technical and are above all related to interests and values. In the example above regarding health insurance for the self-employed, the ministry took four years not to work out the technical details of implementation but to reach a political arrangement among the interest groups. But decisions removed from Parliament to the government—even political ones—will be made by men who are not themselves politicians. As described above, a minister's top advisors and the higher civil servants in the permanent administration of the ministry have both followed the same career pattern: through the *grandes écoles* and not through elections.

Policy Making in the Fifth Republic: The Cases of Agriculture and Labor

Both the locus and the personnel of the policy-making process have undergone major changes in France in the past two decades. Though some of these changes antedate the Fifth Republic, the impetus provided by the new constitution and by the massive influx of technocratic personnel into the top levels of government make it reasonable to consider 1958 a watershed. We have described above some of the most significant changes in the political system and how they were brought about. What remains to be considered is the difference these changes in the process of policy making have made in the output of the political system. The most useful way to approach this problem is to take an area in which the state has intervened regularly and to examine the policies produced by two different systems of decision making. The two areas we have selected— agriculture and labor—have been problematic for the governments of both the Fourth and Fifth Republics. Legislation in both areas affects a significant

---

[5] *Le Monde,* August 13, 1971.

proportion of the working population and arouses the activity of powerful interest groups. In these areas, unlike foreign policy or defense decisions, a broad range of different political groups and institutions—parties, interest groups, Parliament, prime minister and government, President—are involved, and no single force is decisive.

In the Third and Fourth Republics the fundamental decisions on agriculture were made in Parliament. The conception of the state's role in agriculture that most political groups shared was primarily social and political and only secondarily economic. The state intervened in the agricultural sector primarily to maintain a large peasant population in the countryside. The political stability of France was believed to depend on keeping a balance between rural and urban worlds, and the countryside was the reservoir of the conservative electors that counterbalanced the socialist workers of the cities. As industrialization gradually shifted this balance, the political elites tried to maintain the rural-urban equilibrium by advantaging rural electors through malapportionment of legislative seats and by devising an agricultural policy that would preserve the traditional countryside. The political elites realized that agriculture needed to be modernized enough to survive in an industrial economy. Therefore various technological improvements, like fertilizers and machines, were introduced, and organizations such as purchasing cooperatives and farm banking and loan associations that would make the peasantry less dependent on the city were encouraged. At the same time, the modernization of the countryside could not be allowed to go too far, for any substantial increases in productivity would require transformation of farm structures and ultimately a decrease in the farm population.

What resulted from this conception of the goals of agricultural policy was a patchwork quilt of subsidies, credits, piecemeal reforms, and political crumbs, tossed out to districts largely in function of the electoral needs of the deputies of the area and the strength of a few agricultural interest groups representing the large producers. Even the general farm legislation of the Fourth Republic was not based on any long-term plan for the development of agriculture or on any deliberate set of choices about the internal restructuring of the countryside. The great agricultural bill of the Fourth Republic was one providing that the prices of all major agricultural commodities be hitched to an index of industrial prices (indexation). This bill exemplified all the weaknesses of agricultural policy in the Third and Fourth Republics. It did not consider the impact of across-the-board price increases on the development of the agricultural economy. (Should the state be encouraging surplus crops as well as the crops of which Frenchmen were consuming greater quantities?) It did not attempt to deal with the more profound problems of the countryside on which prices had only a marginal effect. (What difference would higher prices make to a peasant who farmed only ten acres and whose yields were low? What solutions would transform unproductive agricultural structures—the real cause of poverty in the countryside?) Finally, like so many other pieces of agricultural legislation of the Third and Fourth Republics, the law on *indexation* did not take into account the impact of these decisions on the general economy. (Would inflation result from generalizing all price increases through the chain of escalator clauses?)

The role of the bureaucracy in the conception and execution of agricultural policy was jealously limited by the deputies, for control over agricultural policy represented both the ammunition for elections and the essential instrument for preserving their electorates. Moreover, given the aims of the state in the agricultural sector, the decisions involved turned on political rather than technical criteria, so the bureaucrat's special expertise was not critical. The locus of agricultural policy making, then, was Parliament, and this had important consequences both for the kinds of policies that the system could produce and for the political forces and interest groups that participated in the development of policy. The concentration of agricultural decision making in Parliament advantaged certain types of agricultural organizations and certain groups of producers and supported the development of particular kinds of linkages between the countryside and the state.

The election of peasant deputies provides one example of how the structures of policy making determine the way groups organize to defend their interests in politics. When Parliament was the locus of decisions on agriculture, candidates who ran for election on peasant lists might convince the rural electors that sending "one of their own" to Parliament might bring back state aid to the district. If it is Parliament that decides who gets what from the state, it is clear that would-be recipients should find ways of getting their representatives into Parliament. At one point during the Fourth Republic this simple logic propelled forty-seven deputies elected on peasant platforms into Parliament. Just as important, the deputies who came from agricultural constituencies, having been elected as Socialists or Radicals or on some other party list, organized themselves once they reached Parliament into an agricultural parliamentary group *(amicale agricole parlementaire).* These so-called study groups of deputies representing particular interests had no formal constitutional status, but they were nonetheless among the most important forces in the political system. It was within the agricultural parliamentary group of deputies drawn from almost all the parties, rather than within the individual parties, that essential decisions on agricultural policy were debated. A hundred deputies belonged to the agricultural group in the last years of the Fourth Republic, and at several critical junctures the group had a significant part in overthrowing governments.

Agricultural interest groups, too, organized in ways that reflected the predominant role of the Parliament in policy making. The most important agricultural organization of the Fourth Republic was the F.N.S.E.A. *(Fédér-ation National des Syndicats d'Exploitants Agricoles),* a federation with branches in every department and a national membership of almost a million in 1953. Although the strongest agricultural producers had organized specialized interest groups to defend their crops—this was the case for wheat, wine, and sugar beet growers—the great majority of farmers were represented only by the F.N.S.E.A. Why should this all-purpose farm organization, rather than specialized interest groups, have provided the major link between the countryside and the state? The answer is a complicated one, for many factors contributed to the predominance of the F.N.S.E.A. It is clear, however, from the decline of the F.N.S.E.A. in the Fifth Republic that one important aspect was the parliamentary setting in which agricultural decisions were made. The F.N.S.E.A. was able to arrange compromises among a large number of diverse and contradictory agricultural interests and to present a platform to the Parliament that it could call, without challenge from any other agricultural organization, the demands of the countryside. In other words, the F.N.S.E.A. performed a function for Parliament that neither the political parties nor the Parliament itself could perform very well. Since the political parties were aligned on ideological positions that were largely irrelevant to the problems of the countryside, they were poor instruments for the aggregation of economic interests. Parliament itself was badly organized for the integration of diverse interests into a single policy, and the agricultural parliamentary group only partially filled the need for institutions to organize the terms of debate over agricultural problems. Thus the F.N.S.E.A. served an essential function of mediation between various rural interests and Parliament in presenting a list of demands that focused political discussion. That the F.N.S.E.A. did not perform this function very well did not matter much as long as the only aims of the state were to produce discrete bits of assorted assistance to the countryside.

The Fifth Republic dismantled this system in which the goals of state policy, the organization of interests, and parliamentary power were mutually reinforcing elements. One of the first acts of the new government was to repeal *indexation* because of its effects on the general economy, and Michel Debré soon gave notice to the political elites that the government would not pursue a traditional agricultural policy based on prices. In May 1960 Debré appeared before Parliament and presented the principles of agricultural legislation aimed essentially at reforming land structures and developing new marketing systems for agricultural goods. The Parliament passed this framework law, but before it could go into effect the government had to draw up enabling legislation. Two years after the passage of the law the government had barely begun to do so: Only four out of thirty enabling decrees envisaged had been issued. At this point, in the spring of 1962, the Minister of Agriculture, Edgard Pisani, appeared before Parliament with a proposal for a law to "complement" the 1960 legislation. It would be more accurate to describe the new bill *(loi complémentaire à la loi d'orientation agricole)* as replacing the previous bill, rather than filling it in. The new document went far beyond the previous one in proposing a program of long-range structural reforms in the countryside. The bill gave a state land agency the first option on all farmland purchases and restricted the purchase of land by persons not engaged in agriculture. It created a fund for pensions for old peasants who were willing to leave their farms so that they could be regrouped with neighboring ones in order to improve the productivity of farm structures. Job training was to be offered to young peasants who wished to leave the countryside. The bill also significantly strengthened the marketing groups that had been created by the 1960 bill, giving producers' groups the right to extend their rules to unorganized producers as well as to members. In sum, this was a coherent project for the development of the agricultural economy, one that took into account the need for reforming the internal structures of the countryside as well as the need for organizing agriculture's relations with the rest of the economy.

The new bill was drawn up by technocrats in the Ministry of Agriculture, and neither the political parties nor the national farm organizations were involved in the process.[6] Indeed, the project was leaked by the press before it had even been discussed in the Council of Ministers. The bill emerged onto the political scene at a time of violent peasant demonstrations against the government. To protest against the collapse of the artichoke market, Breton peasants had dumped 300 tons of artichokes in the streets of Saint-Pol-de-Léon; elsewhere, peasants protested against the purchase of land by people from the cities. Pressure mounted for the government to take some action to satisfy the rural population, whose demands had become embittered, first by the repeal of *indexation* and then by disappointment over the abortive 1960 legislation. The national farm organizations lined up behind the Pisani bill and announced that if Parliament did not pass it, they would call a massive strike and series of demonstrations. The project, after amendment by the Council of Ministers, was finally presented to the National Assembly on July 4, 1962. Instead of being passed to one of their six standing committees, a special commission was formed to consider it. The parliamentary session was supposed to finish on July 23, and this meant that deliberation on the bill both in committee and in the two houses was extremely rushed. As one observer noted, "The deputies and senators, already furious about having been ignored during the phase of drawing up the project, became more and

---

[6]Gaston Rimareix and Yves Tavernier, "L'Elaboration et le vote de la loi complémentaire à la loi d'orientation agricole," *Revue française de science politique* (June 1963), pp. 389–425.

more hostile to the procedure followed by the Minister and to the pressures that the agricultural organizations brought to bear on the Parliament."[7] Even the U.N.R. deputies protested about the pressures to which they were subjected and about the bureaucracy's infringement on the rights of Parliament. Finally, the Minister agreed to several amendments to critical provisions, and the bill passed. At every stage in this process the critical actor was the Minister of Agriculture. The key decisions had been made in the ministry, and though the minister was obliged to compromise on some points both in the Council of Ministers and in Parliament, the essential lines of policy remained those that had been drawn by the bureaucracy. This case, which is a typical example of policy making in the Fifth Republic, shows how greatly political practice has changed since the Fourth Republic: the bureaucracy has become the locus of decision making, and Parliament ratifies policies that it has not designed.

The shift in the locus of policy making from Parliament to the ministries has had important consequences for the other participants in the political system. In the case of agriculture, the first to profit from the new power situation was a young peasants' association, the "young Turks" of the national farmers movement, who had been advocating radical changes in agricultural policy for years. The young peasants had no allies among the established parliamentary elites, and as long as agricultural decisions were made in Parliament, they had virtually no chance of having their views influence policy. When bureaucrats became the real decision-makers, the young peasants were able to gain a hearing for their views that numbers alone would never have assured them. In part their success was due to the fact that their position was closer to the government's than that of any other agricultural group. But more generally, the young peasants' chances of success were greater in this system because as a small, well-organized group with a coherent set of demands they were better able to negotiate with the technocrats than with politicians. Correspondingly, the relative failure of the F.N.S.E.A. in dealing with the new governments was due, in part at least, to its inability to switch from a logic of persuasion, in which the terms were political, to negotiations with technocrats, who saw the countryside in economic terms.

The biggest winners in the new system, however, have been the specialized interest groups. In dealings with the government, the specialized producers' groups have profited from advantages that none of the general farm associations possess. The interest groups have experts who can discuss agricultural policy with the technocrats with the same economic competence. While the general farm associations are represented in discussions with the government by their elected officials, men who must

---

[7] *Ibid.*, p. 403.

travel in from the provinces each time they want to take up a problem with the government, the interest groups have permanent staffs in Paris, who meet regularly—both professionally and socially—with their counterparts in the bureaucracy. Indeed, the experts who work for the agricultural interest groups and the technocrats in the Ministry of Agriculture and the Planning Commissariat have often attended the same schools; their common education has given them similar outlooks on the problems of the countryside. They are likely to come from the same social milieu and to share a circle of well-placed friends and connections. The peasant leader from the provinces, who may have completed only the minimum years of schooling, has no friends in Paris, and often feels socially inferior to the men he deals with in government, belongs to another social world.

The question is not only one of men but of goals and organizations. The interest group is advantaged in its relations with the bureaucracy by the limited character of its demands and by the nature of its constituency. The representative of the wheat farmers' association can identify a given number of points in the bureaucracy where he must apply pressure in order to advance the demands of his members, and he can present a set of discrete proposals. The representative of the general farm association, on the other hand, has no obvious interlocutor short of the Minister of Agriculture, and the goals he defends are frequently of a global nature—a standard of living for peasants equal to that of other groups, for example—that cannot easily be broken down into the concrete measures the bureaucracy can manage. The general farm association was geared in its goals and organization to operating in a parliamentary arena, and it finds it difficult to adapt to the bureaucratic arena. The same is true of the relative strengths and weaknesses of the interest group and the broad, all-purpose farm organization in dealing with the institutions of the European Common Market. The shift in agricultural policy making from Paris to Brussels has reinforced the shift from politicians to bureaucrats, and in this new arena the F.N.S.E.A. finds itself unable to exploit the political resources that once weighed so heavily in the French parliamentary context.

The debate over agricultural policy was once carried out by representatives of peasant groups with deputies; today, with bureaucrats. Direct negotiation between interests and government bypasses the mediation of political party, and the institutional setting of policy making in France comes increasingly to resemble the British model. The latest change in the system, indeed, borrows directly from the British political system. In the summer of 1971 the Minister of Agriculture announced that each year the government would meet for a roundtable discussion with representatives of the major agricultural associations to discuss questions of prices, investments, markets, social security, and modernization of the agricultural economy. There are differences between the French roundtable and the British annual price review: In Britain representatives of all ministries concerned with agriculture participate, while in France only the Ministry of Agriculture was represented, despite the great importance of the Ministry of Finance for decisions made in the agricultural sector. Moreover, the British negotiations are prepared by lengthy studies, and they focus primarily on the evolution of agricultural revenues—a topic the French government refused to place on the agenda. Despite differences, the procedure has the same impact in both cases: to establish a privileged relationship between certain agricultural groups and the government (the Communist peasant movement, for example, was excluded in France) and to exclude from agricultural decisions the representatives of general political groups.

The Fifth Republic has not only supported the making of public policy by negotiation among organized interests but it has tried to generalize this mode of decision in the economy. After 1968 the government has set as one of the state's highest priorities the establishment of a *politique contractuelle* (a policy of contracts) as the mode of conflict resolution and regulation of relationships between labor and business. The *politique contractuelle* is a policy of industrial relations by negotiated settlement between labor unions and industrialists (in the private sector) or between the unions and the directors of the nationalized industries and the public services. The idea of regulating industrial relations by negotiated agreements is a relatively old one in the United States, where collective bargaining is the normal procedure for settling questions of wages, hours, working conditions, fringe benefits, and job security. In France, however, the traditions and values of both labor and business have been profoundly antagonistic to the idea. On the part of business men, there has been deep resistance to sharing power in the factory with the unions. Any system of collective bargaining requires that the union have the ability to check on the execution of the agreement, and for this the union must have a recognized status in the factory. The industrialists have been reluctant to grant this. Before 1968 unions were not allowed to hold meetings in the factories; union representatives had no right to meet with individual workers or to discuss problems with representatives of management. In many factories workers who were known to be members of the unions were harassed, and if they were found conducting union business, they faced being fired.

Despite the important political differences that divide the major French labor federations, they all share a tradition that regards with deep suspicion even the amount of collaboration with management that is implied in collective bargaining. The three largest federations of industrial workers are the *Confédération Générale du Travail* (C.G.T.), which is closely linked to the Communist party, the *Force Ouvrière* (F.O.), which has affinities to the Socialist party, and the *Confédération Française Démocratique du Travail* (C.F.D.T.), which was once a Catholic association and now is a Left-wing group whose sympathies go to the United Socialist party, the

Socialists, and the political clubs. Of the three, it is the C.G.T. that is most hostile to any system of negotiations in which labor commits itself to agreements with management. The C.G.T. has adopted the Marxist interpretation of industrial relations that sees grievances, strikes, and settlements as mere episodes in a class struggle whose ultimate purpose is to replace an industrial system based on capitalist control of the means of production by socialism. For this reason the C.G.T. and, in lesser measure, the C.F.D.T. and the F.O. are reluctant to commit themselves to any contract that implies an obligation to refrain from a strike before the expiration of the contract; the unions wish to retain their freedom to take up the class struggle at any time that appears advantageous for the cause of the workers. In the unions' view, collaborating with management in a settlement consolidates the industrial system, thus reinforcing the economic and political status quo. And in a situation where the unions have so little power to oblige managers to respect the contract, why should they commit themselves?

For very different reasons, therefore, both management and unions opposed a system of regulating industrial relations by contractual agreement. The issues that in other industrial states are decided by collective contracts are in France often decided unilaterally by management. When workers do go out on strike, the agreement that ends the strike has usually been one that management alone signs. In the public sector, before 1968 industrial relations were conducted in essentially the same fashion, except that the ultimate power of decision on questions involving the wage bill of the enterprise belonged to the Ministry of Finance, not to the management. Thus, in both private and public sectors the body of regulations governing management and labor was underdeveloped. Negotiations were regarded by all parties, not as the mechanism for reaching authoritative decisions that would bind all participants, but as one instrument among others in a basically conflictual situation.

The crisis of May–June 1968 brought to the fore factors that made management, state, and labor reconsider their opposition to regulating industrial relations by negotiations. For the managers of private industry and for the labor unions, it was the need to reestablish control in a situation where wildcat strikes, the politicization of thousands of nonunionized workers, and the establishment of plant committees outside the aegis of the unions had led to a general breakdown of the existing system of relationships between workers and managers in the plant and workers and unions. Once order was restored, the pressures on the unions and business for change were lessened, but the state had thoroughly committed itself to a reform of the industrial relations system. Already as part of the Grenelle agreement negotiated during the crisis, the state and industry had recognized the unions' rights in the factory, and one of the first major pieces of legislation in the wake of the May–June events was a law recognizing the right of union organization in all factories hiring more than fifty employees. Minister of Social Affairs Maurice Schumann, in presenting the bill to Parliament, described it as a step toward a new system of industrial relations. In suggesting that the managers should recognize the union leaders as their "natural interlocutors," he showed that the government considered the bill as a necessary element of the *politique contractuelle*.

The government's next steps were to reorganize the process of decision making in the public sector so as to make possible direct negotiations between the directors of the state firms and the unions. Until then, the directors had had very little power to negotiate agreements, because ultimate responsibility for the decision rested in the ministries. After 1968 the authority needed to run state enterprises was increasingly devolved from the ministries to the management. In the labor disputes that have since arisen in the nationalized electricity agency (E.D.F.), in the state railroads (S.N.C.F.), and other public services, the directors themselves have had substantial powers to decide questions at stake, including wages. At the same time, the government tried to encourage the unions and the directors of the public sectors to settle their grievances with contracts that both parties would sign. The state, indeed, was willing to pay dearly to achieve this result, and the contracts that E.D.F. and the S.N.C.F. offered to the unions contained significant concessions on such union demands as guaranteed increases in real wages. The government, moreover, was willing to abandon clauses in the contracts that the unions found unacceptable, the most important of which was a clause limiting the right to call strikes. The unions were initially hostile to the contracts, and the C.G.T. refused to sign the first agreements. Gradually, however, this resistance has weakened, largely because of the government's substantial concessions, but also in part because the unions themselves have an interest in negotiating agreements in which their right to participate in certain plant-level decisions is recognized. Since the fall of 1969 several dozen agreements have been signed in the public sector; some of the later ones have even received the signature of the C.G.T.

In the field of industrial relations, then, as in agriculture, the state is trying to establish a system of policy making by negotiation between organized interests and the state. Formidable obstacles still remain, for neither the trade unions nor industry have given up the values and stakes that derive from a long history of noncooperation.

Return to Politics?

In France since the Fifth Republic policy making has moved out of the political arenas of party and Parliament and into arenas where the participants are interest groups and technocrats. As the cases of agriculture and labor suggest, this is the result of replacing the traditional forms of political conflict by a process of negotiation between organized interests and government. In agriculture, negotiation between the Ministry of Agriculture and the agricultural groups replaces the defense of agricultural interests in Parliament. In the nationalized industries, negotiation between the director of the firm and the labor unions replaces a procedure in which the politicians in government decided on the wage bill for workers in the public sector. These changes in the personnel of politics, the shift in the locus of policy making, and the transformation of the process of resolving conflicts have apparently removed the flesh and blood from traditional political issues, leaving their bones to be picked over by the political parties while the real problems of the nation are resolved by interest groups and government.

Yet in the last five years there have been increasingly frequent signs of the fragility of government by collaboration of bureaucracy and organized interests. The most significant evidence in this respect has been the increase in political activity and even political violence by groups that are not represented in the circles of decision making. These groups are an extremely diverse lot. There are social categories like the small shopkeepers, whose organizations are too weak or whose demands are too opposed to governmental policy to gain a seat at the roundtables where technocrats and interest groups negotiate. For years small shopkeepers felt oppressed by official policies favoring lower price margins in commerce, increased competition, and supermarkets. Unable to find channels of political expression, the shopkeepers' dissatisfaction broke out in a wave of demonstrations and tax strikes. Government offices were besieged by angry shopkeepers, and several tax collectors were kidnapped for brief periods by a commando group inspired by Gerard Nicoud, leader of a new group that denounced the regular merchants' association for having sold out to the government. In other sectors of society, too, individuals whose firms or farms were small, poor, and less productive than the average and who saw themselves as the victims of the state's modernization policies began to break away from groups that had traditionally represented their interests to form their own organizations. In agriculture, for example, the M.O.D.E.F. *(Mouvement pour la Défense des Exploitations Familiales)*, an organization that once had had little influence beyond a few Communist strongholds, began to pick up members in poor regions all over France and to challenge the organizational monopoly of the F.N.S.E.A. The M.O.D.E.F. described its goals as defending the family farm and the small peasantry against the technocrats and big agricultural interests.

The major challenges to the state have come from groups that are badly represented by the interest groups that have access to the processes of decision in government. In part, this is because the interest groups themselves are controlled by the more prosperous and modern economic groups: it has been the wheat farmers and not the dairy farmers that dominate agricultural syndicalism; the skilled workers and not the *smigards* (workers earning the minimum legal wages) that are the main core of the labor movement. But even more important, the disaffected social groups are those that cannot be defended well by interest-group politics. What the small peasant or the small shopkeeper demands is not so much the satisfaction of particular economic grievances but a change in the fundamental political choices of the state. An interest group is a vehicle poorly suited to the expression of this kind of demand. And the political parties, which are structurally capable of mediating such demands by expressing them in alternatives to governmental policies, have not done so. The political parties' failure to perceive and organize the demands of those groups that have not been integrated into the policy processes of the Fifth Republic has had two serious consequences. Inability to locate the specific sources of stress in the political system of the Fifth Republic has contributed to the stagnation and decline of the opposition parties, which seem to cling blindly to old political issues while new ones escape their notice. At the same time, the political parties' failure to provide a channel for the expression of the political grievances of groups that are badly represented in the current political system leave such groups stranded. As one peasant leader from a poor region put it, "Between the government and us there is a great vacuum." The groups outside the system have come to feel that the only way to move or change the government is through what peasant syndicalists call "direct action": demonstrations, strikes, violent acts. In the absence of political parties able to funnel the needs and desires of social groups into the centers of political decision, dissatisfaction and grievances are bottled up in society and spill over into extralegal forms of political action.

No event better illustrates the explosive potential of the frustrations and unmet demands of groups excluded from the policy process than the abortive revolution of May–June 1968. What the massive demonstrations of students and workers showed was the system's inability to satisfy a broad range of economic, social, and political demands. Some of these reflected a desire for a vast transformation of the values of society and politics: for reducing or eliminating authority and hierarchy; for increasing participation and the possibilities for self-expression; for social equality. Perhaps no political system could satisfy such demands. In this sense it is no special limitation of the French state that it was unwilling to undertake changes that would have amounted to a revolution in values and social structure. What does reveal the weaknesses of the French political system is that even demands that could have been satisfied within the framework of the political and social status quo were not met and that it took the revolutionary movements of May–June 1968 to push through improvements in the standard of living and working conditions that might well have been obtained by normal political processes. In sum, the May–June 1968 events demonstrated the existence of widespread dissatisfaction that the policy-making processes of the first decade of the Fifth Republic were unable to meet.

Since May–June 1968, there has been a swing back toward politics as the government has ventured out of the closed arena to which only the organized interests and the technocrats had access and has reached out to the traditional political intermediaries. Within the government itself politicians are playing a more important role, and recent policy declarations on agriculture, for example, or on small commerce show increased attention to the political aspects of economic modernization. Circumstantial factors like the municipal elections may have contributed to this shift. And Pompidou's need to consolidate the Gaullist electorate in the absence of de Gaulle certainly accounts for some of the government's new interest in traditional political forces.

These shifts in the policy-making process of the Fifth Republic are too new and too tentative to permit the conclusion that major changes are at stake. The present situation is one in which several modes of decision making and, indeed, several different policies coexist in certain critical policy areas. For example, the government has allowed small shopkeepers to participate in decisions on building new supermarkets by establishing departmental commissions on which all forms of commerce are represented and giving these commissions the right to decide on accepting proposals for new supermarkets. At the same time, however, the technocrats apparently retain their rights of decision in the matter, for any request to build a supermarket that is refused by the departmental commission may be referred to a national commission in Paris, on which only representatives of the ministries sit; and this commission may accept the project even over the local rejection. The government now uses both political and technocratic criteria, personnel, and processes of decision; and though the balance has apparently shifted recently, it is too early to take the measure of the changes. Not only for students of French politics but for anyone interested in the politics of industrial societies, the outcome of this uneasy coexistence between political and bureaucratic processes of decision is a matter of great importance.

Five

Local Governments in a Centralized State

In the past decade in France, as in other advanced industrial societies, the problems of local governments have burst into national politics. Population movement from countryside to city, increased birth rates, racial tensions, the relationships between metropolis and surrounding communities, the desire of citizens to have a larger say in local political decisions—all these and many other factors have pressed with increased force on existing political structures and have produced a new awareness of the need for reform in the institutions of local government.

In France three of these factors have been particularly important. First, the years since World War II have been decades of unprecedented mobility in France. Over a six-year period (1962–1968) one out of every fifteen Frenchmen changed the region in which he lived, and an even higher proportion moved from one town to another within the same region. One part of this vast population movement can be accounted for by the shift in employment from agriculture to industry. Between 1954 and 1968 the proportion of the work force employed in agriculture dropped from 31 percent to 17 percent. Since few of the former farmers can find work in their regions that allows them to continue living on their farms, change in employment is usually accompanied by a change in residence. Western France and central France, regions with large agricultural populations and little industry, are being drained, while new residents continue to feed into the urban populations of Paris, the industrial northeast, and the southeast.

Another part of the population movement in this period was created by the decline in traditional industries—mining, shipyards, textiles—and the relocation of workers to regions of France with modern industry. Thus in the period 1962–1968 the departments of Nord and Lorraine, whose traditional industries were in crisis, lost heavily, while the departments of the Rhone-Alpes region around Grenoble and Lyons, where modern industries have developed, gained substantially.

The impact of internal migration has created different problems for growing and declining communes. The commune is the basic political unit in France; all parts of the country, rural and urban, are organized in communes. There are close to 38,000 communes; less than 10 percent are urban by French census definition, that is, have more than 2,000 inhabitants (see Table 2). As population has moved out of rural areas into cities, the proportion of small communes has increased. In 1968, 24,007 out of the 38,000 communes had fewer than 500 inhabitants, and these small towns experience increasingly greater difficulties in maintaining an infrastructure of public institutions and services with a dwindling pool of taxpayers. The case of the commune of Sacquenville, population 353, is typical. The town must provide school facilities, running water and electricity, public baths, fire-fighting equipment, road maintenance, and salaries for its municipal employees. In order to create facilities that might attract new people to settle in the commune, the town must make substantial investments. Since it cannot do so with its own already overtaxed resources, expansion depends on the town's borrowing money or obtaining subsidies from the state. Even so, Sacquenville is lucky, for it is not far from Paris, and the town can expect that if it improves public facilities and services, it will be able to draw in new residents as the Parisian population spreads out into surrounding areas. French small communes that are not

Table 2 Distribution of Communes by Population, 1968

Population	Number of Communes	Percentage of Number of Communes	Percentage of Number of Inhabitants
100,000 and over	37	0.1	19.0
30,000–100,000	160	0.4	15.5
10,000–30,000	482	1.3	15.9
5,000–10,000	642	1.7	8.6
2,000–5,000	1,938	5.1	11.5
1,000–2,000	3,618	9.6	9.7
0–1,000	30,831	81.8	19.8

DATA SOURCE: Jean de Savigny, *L'Etat contre les communes?* (Paris: Seuil, 1971), p. 187.

in the immediate vicinity of a large urban center face long-term decline, while at the same time they must try to satisfy their citizens' rising expectations with a shrinking reservoir of resources.

Cities confront another order of problem. The metropolitan areas of France have grown rapidly in the past two decades. The population of metropolitan Grenoble, for example, rose from 262,000 in 1962 to 352,000 in 1968, while in the same period Marseille's population expanded from 639,000 to 964,000 and other large cities experienced comparable rates of growth. Schools, housing, public services, transportation, cultural facilities, indeed, new districts of the city must be provided for the new residents. At the same time, the old residents pressure local governments to improve the quality of the public goods that they use. The problem for local finances that the massive influx into the cities raises is obvious; but there are other costs of rapid growth that are just as difficult to meet. The institutions of local government and administration were designed to service a much smaller population, and the new tasks strain their capacity to manage community affairs. When local administration cannot cope with the magnitude of needs that a large urban population generates, the burdens are shifted off onto national government, thus transforming the relationships between local government and the state.

The second factor contributing to the French urban crisis is the increased importance of problems that cannot be resolved by an individual commune but only at a regional level. There have always been good reasons for a French commune to cooperate with neighboring communes in the provision of such public services as schools, the bussing of school children, or the provision of running water and electricity, since "intercommunal syndicates" could provide such services at considerable savings to the individual towns. Today, however, communes find themselves faced with problems that they could not solve themselves, even if they had the money to do so. When, for example, the city of Grenoble tries to attract new industry, it must be able to count on neighboring communes to provide the housing for new workers, since there is little free land in the city proper. Grenoble must be able to guarantee the potential industrial developer that facilities will be built to house and transport the needed work force to the new enterprise. For this, Grenoble and the surrounding towns have to agree on a long-term plan for the development of the region. The same need for regional policies arises whenever a commune wishes to develop facilities whose benefits will accrue in large measure to those who live outside the commune itself but in the region. Housing as we have seen is one public good whose external economies may be as important as the values received by those within the community. Transportation systems are another public good whose benefits usually are enjoyed by people in a larger area than that covered by a single commune. Industrial development, too, requires a commune to make expenditures for infrastructure in order to reap a reward that cannot be kept within the confines of the political unit that has footed the bill. The patterns of urban expansion and of industrial growth have increased the number of public services whose impact is regional and have thus created new pressures for regional policy and for regional political action that cannot be met by any simple extension of the old "intercommunal syndicate" model of cooperation.

Along with the shifts in the national distribution of population and the emergence of regional problems, a third factor has weighed heavily in the current debate over local government in France: the growing desire for participation in local politics. In one sense, the new demands for civic participation in city government can be explained by the shifts in population out of small towns into larger cities. In a small town, the size of the population, the scale of the problems, the relative simplicity of the issues at stake, and the visibility and accessibility of the political elites facilitate political participation. Information spreads quickly in a small community and citizens are usually well-informed about the issues at stake in the town. They are, moreover, in a better position to influence political decisions than is the typical city-dweller, for in a small town most people have a good chance of knowing a local politician or of having access to one through friends and relatives. In French cities, in contrast, citizens both need more from local government and have fewer opportunities to express their needs than in the small town. The citizen of a city with a population of several hundred thousand has little chance of knowing a local politician and has difficulty in finding any channels through which he can influence political decisions. The decisions themselves are more complex and, so, are often made by technicians and bureaucrats, rather than by elected officials. The plight of a group of Grenoble citizens who unsuccessfully knocked on the doors of city officials and bureaucrats to complain that water pressure was insufficient to get water up to their fourth-floor apartments is typical. The response of these frustrated Grenoble citizens to the unresponsiveness of city government was to organize a civic reform group and to run candidates in the next municipal elections. This was a most untypical occurrence in France at the time the Grenoble civic associations began in the early 1960s, but such an organizational response is now spreading throughout France. The demand for wider participation in local politics has contributed in the past ten years to the flourishing of neighborhood committees, city-wide civic action groups—the G.A.M.s *(groupes d'action municipale)*—and to a national federation of civic groups. Though the creation on a wide scale of these new groups in the cities marks a significant change, the obstacles that in the past inhibited the growth of voluntary associations in France continue to block the expansion of these new organizations and to reduce their capacity to serve as vehicles for the participation of citizens in local politics. How to make possible wider participation in the affairs of city government remains on the agenda of unsolved problems in France.

These issues are of course not unique to France. Other industrial states are under pressure to accommodate larger urban populations and to satisfy growing demands for civic participation. French cities and regions confront difficulties that are virtually identical to those of the cities of Britain or the United States or Germany, but the political and social structures, values and expectations, and historical experiences that French, Germans, British, and Americans bring to the resolution of these problems vary greatly. The questions we wish to consider for France are, What resources does the political system offer for working out these problems, and what obstacles does it present? and How do these resources and obstacles shape policy outcomes?

Structure of Local Government

The political framework within which French cities deal with the changing needs and demands of their populations is built on three levels of government: the commune, the department, and the national government. These are the only political units in France that are governed by elected bodies and that have the right to legislate for their citizens. Other political units are only administrative entities (the cantons and arrondissements) or territorial groupings to facilitate planning (regions). The three-tier distribution of political power was fixed in its essential features by the end of the nineteenth century. The basic legislation on municipal government is a law passed in 1884, whose fundamental principles still regulate the exercise of political power at the local level. The 1884 law specified that the commune should be governed by an elected municipal council and a mayor, chosen by the municipal council. The number of members on the municipal council now varies according to the size of the commune's population, and the mode of election in municipal elections also differs according to population size. Aside from these and a few other differences that concern the relationship of the commune to the state, French communes are all organized in essentially the same way.

The mayor and municipal council deal with two kinds of decisions: decisions about how to carry out and finance services that the state requires local governments to perform and decisions about which priorities should orient policy in the sphere in which communes are free to allocate resources as they choose. Local governments are obliged by law to allocate sums in their budgets for such items as salaries of municipal employees, the upkeep of schools and town buildings, debt service, and various kinds of social assistance. These obligatory expenditures of local government are specified by national legislation. Should any municipal council fail to provide for them in its budget, the state will rewrite the local budget to include the obligatory expenses and to include tax revenues to cover them. After the municipal council has satisfied its legal obligations, it is in principle free to legislate in any sphere as it chooses, except where national law expressly prohibits local action. This seemingly wide mandate is, however, subject to two constraints, one budgetary and the other political. The state must approve the decisions of local government, and it may veto not only those local decisions that are illegal but also those that it judges unwise. If the commune wants to borrow money to finance new investments, if it adds a new tax, or even if it wishes to name a street after a man—to consider only a few examples—the state can refuse to authorize the commune to carry out its decision.

The state exercises checks over local government through the mayor, the prefect, and the departmental representatives of the ministries. The mayor is an elected official, but he is also the representative of the state at the local level. This is because the commune is not only an autonomous self-governing unit, but also the basic unit of the central-state system. As an agent of the state, the mayor is responsible for public order in the commune and for carrying out certain administrative tasks set by the state, for example, the collection of statistics. In this role of state representative at the communal level, the mayor is directly responsible to the prefect, who is his superior in the administrative hierarchy of the state. The mayor in these functions is not responsible before either the municipal council or the local citizenry.

The prefect is the representative of national government in the department. He embodies the authority of the state at the local level, and as Jean-Pierre Worms has pointed out, Frenchmen credit him with the same omnicompetence and omniscience that they expect from the state:

> . . . they feel that somehow everything depends on him. They blame him for everything that goes wrong, and it's to him they look to improve things. The logical destination of every petition or demonstration is the prefecture.[1]

When peasants in the sixties protested the level of agricultural prices set by the state, they naturally singled out the prefect as the object of their wrath; the buildings of the prefecture are the most common target of the rocks and eggs of political demonstrations. The prefect's wide-ranging powers over local government fall into two broad categories: control of the legality of local governmental decisions and review of the substance of the commune's decisions in policy areas where the commune is not bound by national legislation. The prefect examines the decisions of municipal councils to assure that they are legal and that they satisfy the

[1]Jean-Pierre Worms, "Le Préfet et ses notables," *Sociologie du travail,* 3 (1966), p. 252.

obligations that the state places on local governments. The prefect may refuse to approve a communal budget, and he has the authorization to write in any obligatory expenditures for which the council has failed to provide.

The prefect's powers extend, however, beyond controlling the legality of municipal acts. On behalf of the central government, the prefect exercises a tutelage authority over local governments. Much of the commune's legislation cannot go into effect without the prefect's approval; some communal decisions depend on prior consent of tutelage authority. As "tutor" of the commune, the prefect has wide powers. Indeed, under specified circumstances he may suspend a mayor or municipal council. These powers are rarely used, but their existence creates a system of incentives for local government in which avoiding any decision that the prefect might not approve is an important goal. As Marie-Françoise Souchon concluded from her study of two small communes,

> [T]he tutelage authority has little need of its powers. The mayors make it a point of honor to present a budget beyond reproach. The red marks [the prefect's comments] in the margin are extremely rare and mostly are notes to the effect that the matter should be taken up in a special meeting of the municipal council. If their budgets came back covered with corrections, the mayors would feel really guilty. The idea is quite unthinkable and they would never dream of presenting anything but a balanced budget.[2]

By anticipating the responses of the prefect, local officials avoid conflict with tutelary authority, but a "safe" policy of limited initiative and minimal risks may not be the best one for developing the commune.

In recent years the number of decisions that the commune may take without prior consent of tutelary authority has been increased. The Parliament voted in 1970 to eliminate the procedure that required a commune to await the approval of the prefect before putting its budget into effect. Now a commune's budget will automatically go into effect fifteen days after it has been submitted to the prefecture, on condition that the budget is balanced. The prefect's prior approval is no longer required before the municipal council can dispose of property belonging to the town or negotiate loans. These changes have, however, simplified only a tiny fraction of the administrative procedures through which the state regulates the behavior of local government. And the growing financial dependence of the commune on the state means that whatever independence the commune has won for disposing of matters within its own resources has been lost many times over in the controls and review the commune must accept

---

[2]Marie-Françoise Souchon, *Le Maire: élu local dans une société en changement* (Paris: Cujas, 1968), p. 160.

every time it receives money from the state. Jean de Savigny has spelled out what state controls mean for a commune that decides to build a new secondary school:

1. The subprefect must certify that the project fits into the state plan for school development in the area.
2. Before the commune can buy any land for the school, the regional prefect must give his consent.
3. The purchase of land must also be reviewed by the ministerial services that deal with land-use and then by a commission on buildings and architecture.
4. Technical agencies of the state control whether the project meets standard specifications.
5. The prefect, the regional prefect, and the central government review the project and grant a subsidy if the project has been written into the triennial plan of the Ministry of National Education.
6. A state bank *(Caisse des dépôts et consignations)* examines the dossier before granting a loan.
7. An accountant checks up on the mayor's statement of expenses.
8. Technical agencies of the state will check the progress of construction.
9. The same services will check the completed building.
10. The *inspection des finances* (one of the *grands corps* of the state) may review the financial aspects of the project.
11. A national administrative court *(Cour des Comptes)* may also examine the books.
12. On the request of a citizen, a judicial review of the process may be held.[3]

Although the 1970 relaxation of the prefect's authority over the commune's acquisition of land has made part of this process easier than in the past, the commune still needs the consent of the prefect and of the ministries concerned for many aspects of the project.

In principle, the prefect coordinates the activities of the representatives of the ministries operating in his department, so that the various state agencies do not work at cross-purposes. The representatives of the ministries in the departments, therefore, report not only to their own central offices back in Paris but also to the prefect, and at the point of intersection of these two hierarchies—that of the administrative system headed by the prefect and that of the ministry itself—there are frequent conflicts of influence and interest. The prefect himself belongs to two chains of authority: His superior in the administrative hierarchy is the Minister of Interior, but

---

[3] Jean de Savigny, *L'Etat contre les communes?* (Paris: Seuil, 1971), p. 187.

the prefect represents the government as a whole, not only the Ministry of Interior. The trend of recent legislation has been to strengthen the prefect's control over the ministries' activities in his department, but certain of the most important state agencies still act with great autonomy on the local scene. The state highway agency, a corps of civil engineers *(Ponts-et-Chaussées)*, is perhaps the most powerful of the state technical services operating at the local level. This agency not only draws up the plans for communal infrastructure and distributes state subsidies for public-works projects but also executes these projects and is remunerated for its services as any firm of private entrepreneurs might be. Local officials are dependent on the technical agencies of the state, like the *Ponts-et-Chaussées* or *Génie Rural* (rural engineers), and on the agricultural services for technical advice, for subsidies, and for assistance in carrying out projects.

Though the political tutelage of the prefect may be declining, the tutelage that these technical services of the state exercise over local governments is increasing. The prefect exerts pressure on the technical agencies of the state to coordinate their operations through his office, and he will in cases of conflict mediate between local governments and the ministries. Nonetheless, local officials ordinarily have to contend with the prefect and the departmental representatives of the ministries as two separate authorities, each of which controls resources critical for the commune.

The second tier of French government is the department. There are ninety-five of them, each governed by a departmental council *(conseil général)*. The department is administratively subdivided into cantons, and each canton elects one member to the departmental council. The boundaries of the cantons, like those of the departments and communes, were fixed at the time of the French Revolution and have changed little since then. The canton of Pont-l'Abbé with 23,577 people and the canton of Le Faou with 4,703 are both represented by a single member in the departmental council of Finistère. The inequalities in representation at the departmental level support the predominance of rural small-town interests, for the large urban population of a city is often bottled up in a single canton. Rural cantons far outnumber urban ones; more than half of French cantons have fewer than 10,000 inhabitants. The government now proposes to carve out 400 new cantons in urban areas, and so the urban population may be better represented in departmental government in the near future.

The departmental council, like the municipal council, has a certain number of functions that the state requires it to perform and, beyond these obligatory expenditures, a wide measure of discretion. The departmental budget supports most of the road building and repair in the department, and it contributes heavily to other improvements in departmental infrastructure. Schools, agriculture, social services, and welfare are all subsidized by the department. As in the case of the communes, the activities of the department come under the surveillance of the state. National laws forbid certain kinds of expenditures in the departments and narrowly restrict the department's initiatives in the field of taxation. As the tutelary authorities of departmental government, the Ministers of Interior and Finance and the state administrative court *(Conseil d'Etat)* exercise a control over departmental decisions that is comparable to the prefectural tutelage of the communes.

The department like the commune is both a self-governing body and an administrative level of the state. Indeed, in the case of the department, the chief executive of government is not an elected official, but the prefect. The departmental council does not choose a "governor"; this role is performed by the prefect who occupies at the departmental level the position that the mayor has in the commune. This means, at one end of the legislative process, that the prefect prepares the agenda and the budget on which the departmental council debates and votes and, at the other end of the process, that it is the prefect who is responsible for the execution of the departmental legislation. The Constitution of the Fourth Republic provided for an independent executive for departments; but the enabling legislation was never passed, and the prefect remains the chief executive of the department.

From an administrative chart it would appear that since local political authorities are under the control of the prefect, he could marshal them to whatever ends he chose, just as a general can move around the troops under his command. The reality of local politics is quite different. The powers of the prefect over local government, his access to the resources controlled by national government, and the prestige he has as representative of the state all give him great leverage on local elites, but they, in turn, control power resources that are critical to the prefect.[4] First, the success of most of the prefect's plans depends on the cooperation of other political groups, since he cannot force a commune or the department to carry out any projects beyond those required by national legislation. Two-thirds of the capital improvements expenditures of the state are spent at the local level, so that the prefect needs to work out some agreement with local elites if he wants to implement programs that will contribute to the economic development of the department. Some of the resistance he meets can be explained by the social conservatism of local notables, who are largely drawn from small-town and rural milieus. Other conflicts that hinder the implementation of his projects arise from the unwillingness of some local groups to pay the price of a benefit that will extend to a larger group. In the fall of 1971, for example, the regional prefect of the Rhone-Alpes area warned local elites of the disastrous consequences for the region of refusing to allow an oil refinery to establish a plant outside of Lyons. Two

---

[4]Worms, *op. cit.*

communes had already refused the refinery, one because of the protest of winegrowers, the other because of the outrage of nature-lovers, and now the population of the commune that had been selected as the third site seemed likely to add its refusal. In order to protect the general interest of the region, the prefect must often, as in this case, persuade local elites to support changes in their own environments. A prefect who wishes to move up in the administrative hierarchy of the state today needs to show that he is a dynamic entrepreneur for the state's social and economic goals. And to acquire the record of accomplishments that will further his career, the cooperation of local political groups is indispensable.

Even more important, the prefect needs local notables to serve as relays in his relations with the population. The traditional role of the prefect was to maintain order, to resolve conflicts, and to defend a general interest that was defined as the social and political status quo of the department. Although new and more dynamic functions have been added to this traditional political role, a prefect is still judged in Paris by how well he preserves law and order and the existing relations among social groups. Nothing is more injurious to a prefect's reputation than to lose contact with major groups in the department and to find that they refuse his mediation in conflicts. If he has maintained good relations with local notables, the prefect can rely on them to inform him of the political climate of the department, thus enabling him to act before conflicts break out into the open. When a prefect's relations with the notables are close, he can even count on them to channel political protest in ways that will minimize its damaging effects to his own reputation. In the fifties, for example, the leaders of the peasant syndical associations usually discussed arrangements for a demonstration with the prefecture, and the prefect was able to organize police forces, detour traffic, and generally arrange to avoid incidents embarrassing to state authority. The mark of the peasants' growing bitterness in the sixties was that they broke off relations with the prefect and chose forms of protest that exposed his political vulnerability. The peasant invasion of the subprefecture buildings in Morlaix in 1961 was a symbolic act that expressed the peasant leaders' refusal to continue cooperation with public authorities unless more peasant demands were satisfied.

In order to maintain good relations with the notables and thereby keep open his channels to the population, the prefect has to be willing to bend to local pressures and to meet outstanding grievances. This may require that he interpret national legislation "flexibly" and that he satisfy local demands even at the expense of national policy. The prefects, for example, usually accept the recommendations of the departmental advisory commissions on new commercial development, even though this frequently means refusing building permits to supermarkets, that is, hindering modernization of the commercial infrastructure. The prefects "pass the buck" to Paris, knowing that the Minister of Equipment will override their veto. By accepting the advice of local notables, however, the prefect prevents himself from getting involved in a conflict with local elites in which his own political capital would be expended and his capacity to serve as an arbiter among various social groups reduced.

Finally, the prefects need the local elites' support to protect them against pressures from Paris. As Worms has suggested, both the prefect and the local notables have common stakes to defend against the intervention of the state:

> It is obvious that if the prefect does not want his authority in the department to be subject to all the fluctuations in coalitions, policies, governments and regimes, he must maintain an important margin of autonomy in his dealings with the government. The need to calm the feelings of his citizens, to prevent them from "blowing up France" is a good argument for negotiating such a margin of freedom.[5]

To preserve his freedom of action vis-à-vis the central government, the prefect must be able to count on the support of the local elites, and to develop and protect this solidarity of interests, the prefect must be willing to make important concessions to local political groups. In sum, the relationships of prefect to local political elites are ones of mutual dependence. Each party needs the other; each is in some measure able to control the actions of the other.

Local Finances

The independence of local governments depends not only on the political relationships that link them to the center but, just as importantly, on their level of economic activity and on the resources available to finance activities. If one compares American towns and states with French communes

Table 3 Public Expenditures (Nonmilitary), 1967, in percentages

	United States	France
National government	34	72
States	23	–
Departments	–	8
Local governments	43	20

DATA SOURCE: Jean de Savigny, *L'Etat contre les communes?* (Paris: Seuil, 1971), p. 64.

---

[5] *Ibid.*, p. 271.

and departments, it is clear that American local governments are both more active relative to the national government and have more of their own resources with which to finance their projects than French local governments. As Table 3 indicates, the proportion of public expenditures (nonmilitary) carried out by local and state governments in the United States is double that of the federal government; in France the proportion is reversed. In both countries the growing expenses of local communities have forced them to turn to the national government for assistance in financing their plans. In France about 70 percent of local investments are financed by state subsidies and loans. (Communal budgets are divided into two sections: operating expenses and investments. Investments account for about 40 percent of the typical communal budget.)[6]

The economic dependence of the communes on the central government results from their extremely limited possibilities of financing expenditures beyond operating expenses with tax revenues. Of the taxes that local governments in France may levy on their citizens, only four taxes (familiarly known as the *"quatre vieilles"*) produce significant amounts of revenue; the others—a dog tax, a tax on hunting grounds, for example—are mostly trivial. The *quatre vieilles* date to the French Revolution and, while they have been amended and patched up over the years, there has been no reform of local taxes to permit local governments to tap selectively the potential sources of income for the community. *Who* shall be taxed and *how* the burden of taxation should be distributed among various groups in the community are questions that are out of the reach of local government. The four taxes that form the basis of local taxation are property taxes, an occupancy tax, and a tax on commercial establishments. These taxes used to be collected by the central government and were the principal source of national revenues. In 1917 when the income tax was adopted, the state ceased collecting these four taxes, but they were maintained as the basis for calculating local taxes. Essentially the process is the following: Taxable property is assessed. The state calculates what it would have collected if it were still collecting taxes on this basis. Then this fictive sum is divided by one-hundred, and the product is called the *centime*. Each commune figures out how many *centimes'* worth of tax it must collect in order to balance its budget. The *centimes* currently provide about 55 percent of local revenues.

The infinite complications of this tax system built on a no-longer existent national tax involve four essential problems. First, the property evaluations are so out-of-date that they bear little relation to the current distribution of wealth in the community. In 1959 the government decided to replace the four old taxes with new local property taxes that would no longer

---

[6]De Savigny, *op. cit.,* p. 64.

require the fiction that the central government still collected the old taxes. But to implement the new property taxes, property had to be reevaluated —a mammoth task that twelve years after the passage of the reform has still not been completed. Even after the reevaluation, when the new taxes will go into effect, the communes will still face the problem of being largely restricted to property taxes. Since the values of land and buildings are only poor reflections of the economic activities of the community, important sources of revenue remain outside the tax-reach of local governments. Even when the 1959 tax reform replaces the current system, local governments will still have only limited possibilities of redistributing the tax burden among different groups in the community. They will be able to raise (or lower) the rate of the tax (just as today they may increase the number of *centimes*).

Finally, basing communal finances on property taxes creates great inequities among regions and among communes. De Savigny has noted that as television, travel, and publicity make people aware of the goods and services that some areas have, they demand that their towns, too, provide these goods:

> . . . Citizens from rural areas or from the backward regions refuse to accept a situation in which they do not have the same facilities as their compatriots in the big cities: running water, swimming pools, blacktopped roads, tennis courts, youth centers—all the equipment or collective services that once were the privilege of certain towns and that now have become a universal demand.[7]

In order to acquire these goods, the poor communes with fewer taxable resources must tax more heavily. The highest taxes are, in fact, paid by the citizens of the poorest regions. Taxes on properties with the same value are 40 percent higher in western France than in the region around Paris.

After the *centimes,* the next major source of tax revenues for local governments is a tax on value-added (T.V.A.) collected by the national government and redistributed in part to local governments. The basis of this redistribution is as complex and involves as many legal fictions as the calculation of the *centimes.* The state gives each commune as much as it would have collected if the commune were still levying a local tax on commercial transactions—a tax that disappeared in January 1968! The replacement of the old local tax by a nationally-distributed tax has meant a loss of local autonomy. Formerly, a mayor who was enterprising enough to attract new business to his commune could hope to benefit from increased tax revenues. Today, his initiative has relatively little pay-off for the commune's finances. Both because local governments are engaging in new activities and thus need grants and loans from the central government

---

[7] *Ibid.,* p. 180.

and because a significant part of local taxation has shifted to a nationally-collected tax, local officials feel that they are losing control over the resources necessary to run their towns.

New Communes? New Regions?

Despite the rapid increase in recent years of local tax rates and despite fiscal reforms, it is clear that communes and departments are unable to finance the growing needs of their populations. The response has been for local governments to resort more and more frequently to state subsidies and loans, whenever they wish to develop new infrastructure. In consequence, local governments have become dependent on the state for their development, and political leaders at this level see the possibilities for initiative constrained by the declining pool of local resources. Their plight resembles that of local officials in other countries, but the obstacles they have to overcome in order to maintain some measure of autonomy are in certain critical respects specific to France.

One set of these obstacles we have already described: the multiplicity of tiny governmental units at the local level. The economies of scale of providing municipal services to people living in larger units as opposed to smaller units appear to be such that towns with fewer than 5,000 inhabitants are unable to satisfy efficiently the basic needs of their populations. Since 98 percent of the French communes with about half of the national population fall into this under 5,000 inhabitants' category, it is obvious that they are facing increasing difficulties in simply financing operating costs, to say nothing of financing investments. It is possible to imagine a redistribution of national wealth that would enable the smaller, poorer communes to profit from some of the financial resources of the more prosperous regions, but it is difficult to conceive of a redistribution of wealth that would allow each of the currently existing communes to develop and maintain a full panoply of municipal services at a level equal to that enjoyed by the citizens of larger communes.

One solution would be to regroup existing communes in order to form viable units of local government. In other European countries, Sweden notably, this method has been used with success to create larger communes out of a multiplicity of small governments. In France, however, the efforts of the state to encourage local mergers have to date been largely hortatory and have had little effect. By 1970 only about 2 percent of the communes had carried out such fusions with neighbors. In the fall of 1971 the government for the first time announced a series of measures intended to pressure the local elites into mergers. Departmental commissions are to be set up to recommend changes in the communal map of the department to the prefect. The prefect then refers any proposals for fusion to the municipal councils of the towns concerned. If the municipal councils do not accept the proposed merger, the prefect may call a referendum on the proposal in the commune.

Despite these new measures, it seems unlikely that there will be major changes in the communal map of France. Local notables of all parties are almost unanimously opposed to the notion of losing local political autonomy—which they perceive as the most immediate consequence of joining forces with neighboring communes. Just as important a motive for the local officials' hostility to communal mergers—though one less openly avowed—is the fear of losing political office. As a popular French saying expresses it: "My glass may be small but it's my glass *(Mon verre est petit, mais je bois de mon verre)*. The French mayor's commune may be small, but it is the only commune he has, and he is unlikely to become mayor of another one. Even Gaullist deputies registered strong protests when the Minister of Interior proposed the communal merger legislation to Parliament, and the enabling legislation that was ultimately enacted had far fewer teeth than that which had been proposed originally.

On the side of the state, the one political actor on whom the success of the entire scheme depends has many reasons to avoid energetic measures. The prefect is the man designated by the reform bill to prod local elites into action by wielding the threat of communal referendums if they fail to carry out mergers on their own. But the prefect knows well that any such threats would embroil him in bitter conflicts with local political leaders and that, in the course of such fights, his own political resources would be eroded. Since Paris still judges the prefect primarily on his ability to maintain law and order in the department and only secondarily on his success in stimulating social and economic change, the prefect's sense of self-preservation will dictate that he tread lightly, if at all, on the sensitive toes of local leaders. Finally, as Worms has pointed out in his study of French local governments, the power of the prefect depends in part on the small size and scale of the governmental units with which he deals. The prefect reigns over a sea of tiny communes, no one of which has the political or material resources to contest his rule. Were the communes reorganized into larger units, the prefect would most likely find his dealings with local leaders becoming relations between equals, just as the mayors of large cities today exercise considerably more independence in their negotiations with prefects than do the mayors of small communes. To the extent that the prefect's power position depends on the multiplicity of small communes, he is unlikely to play an active role in urging communal mergers.

Reform at the level of the department has been a major political issue in recent years in France. In 1969 de Gaulle proposed a reform in which the departments would be grouped into regions, each of which would be governed by an assembly that would exercise certain powers currently held by the departments. This proposal was linked to a reform of the Senate and was defeated in a national referendum. Despite the failure of the referendum proposition, the regional issue was far from dead. Jean-Jacques Servan-Schreiber, the head of the Radical party, launched a new political debate on regional organization in 1970, proposing a transfer of power to the region from both the central state and from the existing departments. Servan-Schreiber's proposals were enthusiastically welcomed by certain local elites, who saw in them a way of preserving local and regional autonomy by building governmental units on a scale adequate to manage the problems of a modern society. Others attacked the reform as irresponsible because it would splinter the authority of the state and create regional enclaves of power that would not be responsive to national needs.

Although the passions of the 1970 debate have abated, the fate of the departments is still on the agenda of politics. In the 1970 debate over the Servan-Schreiber proposals, Pompidou promised that the government would introduce a regional reform bill—but one that would be based on the region as a "union of departments," that is, one that would not create an autonomous level of political power. A year later, the council of ministers approved a regional reform, to be voted on by Parliament (and not by national referendum). The reforms proposed are but a pale shadow of the ideas that have been raised in the course of the long debate over regions. The powers of the new regional assemblies are to be dispensed by the central government (through the *Conseil d'Etat*), making the region dependent on the center both for its grant of authority and for its resources. There will be two deliberative assemblies in each region, one with representatives of social, economic, and cultural associations, the other with the elected officials of the departments: deputies, municipal councillors, departmental councillors. The region will have neither its own elected representatives nor its own elected executive.

Given the problems departments face not only in raising the resources necessary for economic development but also, and most important, in coordinating their activities with other departments in the same region, it is hard to understand why the government's proposals stopped so far short of creating regional political authorities with independent and representative assemblies. As long as a regional assembly is made up of the elected officials of other organizations—whether municipal councillors, departmental councillors, or deputies—and has no elected membership of its own, it is unlikely that the group will acquire a clear identity of its own. As the abortive experience of the C.O.D.E.R.s (the regional assemblies created in 1964) suggests, such officials are likely to retain their primary allegiance to the constituencies that elect them and to the institutions to which they are elected. For the regional assembly to acquire the power and authority necessary to establish the priority of regional needs over the particular needs of communes and departments, the regional representatives should identify their own political futures with the future of the region. To achieve this, representatives might be elected by constituencies whose boundaries did not coincide with the constituencies of other political institutions, or else, from the same districts a distinct set of regional representatives might be elected whose primary attachments would be to the regional assembly.

The explanation of the weakness of the proposed regional reform apparently lies, on the one hand, in the government's unwillingness to renounce the power that it derives from centralization and, on the other hand, in the local elites' reluctance to lose the power they exercise in the department to a regional authority, even though they would have a chance of increasing their net power through participation in regional government. It is striking to note that in a 1968 survey of the opinions of local elites on regional government, only about half of them felt that the region should have fiscal resources of its own. Most of them said the prefect should be the executive of the region, only 1 percent of the survey opting for direct election of the regional executive. And 67 percent declared that the departments should be maintained with all their present rights.[8] In sum, neither national political leaders nor local notables seem ready to support a significant shift of power and resources to regional political authorities. The latest proposals, like earlier efforts, are not likely to produce major changes in the distribution of power in France.

The Politics of Local Governments: Cases of Change

The analysis of the problems of communal and regional reform suggests that the behavior and attitudes of local political leaders are among the most important obstacles blocking change in local politics. The conservatism of local notables cannot be explained by their political party affiliations. Left-wing mayors seem on the average no more amenable to innovation than Right-wing mayors. Indeed, the political ideas that predispose local elites to resist change bear little relation to the traditional political ideologies of Left and Right. Insofar as the conservatism of local leaders derives from political beliefs and ideas and not merely from the desire to maintain their power by maintaining the status quo, the relevant ideology is what Mark Kesselman has called the "rhetoric of *apolitisme,*" the notion that the tasks of local government are really not political at all.[9]

---

[8]Ministre délégué auprès du Premier Ministre chargé du plan et de l'aménagement du territoire, *Résultats de la consultation sur la réforme régionale* (Paris: Imprimerie de l'Assemblée Nationale, November 25, 1968).

For most local elites, running local government is a question of *bon gestion,* good administration. As they see it, few if any of the decisions a mayor and council have to make determine the fundamental political priorities in a town. Left-wing politicians tend to think that this is because the real choices on values are made elsewhere—either by the state or by large industrial enterprises. Socialist and Communist doctrines, and Left ideologies generally, see the central government as the decisive arena of political decision and local communities as essentially dependent on forces that lie outside their control. As one Communist mayor said, "What really counts is national politics. The possibilities of municipal action are 99 percent dependent on national decisions." And the reply of a Communist deputy when asked to list the problems of his department was the same: "Local problems cannot be regulated outside the national context. The important issues—fiscal reform, democratic participation in factories—can only be treated in a national context." In sum, for the traditional Left nothing of real importance can be changed in local politics without a change in national politics. There are two implications of this premise for Left political action at the local level. The Left sees local politics as a lever with which to move national politics. In municipal elections, for example, Left parties present platforms in which local problems are linked to national issues: A typical Left program proclaims that the need for housing, schools, and roads cannot be met so long as France wastes national resources on nuclear armaments. The second consequence is that once a Left government is elected in a commune, it tends to define its tasks in much the same way that the Right would: as good city management. If the fundamental choices are beyond the reach of local officials, the best they can do is to administer well within the framework of the system. In fact, there appear to be few systematic differences between Left and Right municipalities. Even Communist town governments appear to differ little from others.

The Right comes to the same conclusions about what can be done in local government—but from very different premises. The state, in the view of the traditional Right, has invaded the proper sphere of activities of local government, draining the resources of towns, substituting itself for local officials in decisions that should have been left to local people, and drastically reducing the margin of autonomy of communal government. As a result, local officials are not able to do much: The authority for communal affairs has been transferred to the state, and the resources for local action must be begged from the center. Both Left and Right, then, starting from different ideological premises about the proper relationship of local to national politics, conclude that in the current state of affairs the only role for a local official is essentially one of a good manager. They tend to agree

---

[9]Mark Kesselman, *The Ambiguous Consensus* (New York: Knopf, 1967).

that, as the official we quoted before said, "there are not ten ways of collecting garbage" but only one best way and to concur that the job of local officials is to find that best way and to make it work.

The political conservatism of local elites is apparently linked to a particular understanding of their place in the national political system. Local officials see themselves as so dependent on the center that they feel they cannot accomplish any significant changes unless such reforms are propelled and promoted by the state. Confined by this vision to limited and traditional policies, local political leaders find their public apathetic and unavailable for any act of participation beyond voting. Indeed, local elites have no reason to seek mass participation, for the system they seek to preserve requires only the involvement of a small group of participants, drawn principally from the political parties. The sources of local conservatism are, of course, not only elite perceptions. As the preceding sections on the structures of local government and local finances have shown, the possibilities for political initiative on the local level *are* severely constrained. The realities of power and the ideologies of centralization mutually reinforce each other in France, and the passivity and resistance to change of the local elites are the product of this system.

As long as the vast majority of Frenchmen lived in small towns and the population grew very slowly, this system was a stable one. Today, under the pressure of the new demands on local governments, it is beginning to crack, and new models of local politics are appearing in France. The first and most important changes have been in the politics of large cities. The political leaders of cities have always had more autonomy than the officials of small communes. Their finances afford more room for maneuver, and the importance of their populations and resources make it impossible for prefects, or even the national government for that matter, to ignore their demands. The pressure of population growth and mobility and the demands for increased opportunities for political participation are felt with maximum force in the cities. It is here that the conservatism of local elites has begun to crumble.

The case of Grenoble is exemplary.[10] Until 1965, the city had been governed by a succession of Socialist and moderate governments, whose policies had been essentially the same, despite differences in political style and rhetoric. As the city's population grew rapidly, the political elites tried to adapt to the new situation with a series of improvised measures that were uncoordinated and that dealt with each crisis as it arose. New neighborhoods were built on the outskirts of the city without transportation or other public facilities; the city expanded without any overall plan. The

---

[10]See Suzanne Berger, Peter Gourevitch, Patrice Higonnet, and Karl Kaiser, "The Problem of Reform in France: The Political Ideas of Local Elites," *Political Science Quarterly,* 84 (September 1969), pp. 436–460.

concern of the political leaders of both Left and Right was to manage the city well, as the French saying expresses it, as a father would manage family affairs *(gestion en bon père de famille)*. For the Grenoble city fathers this meant, above all else, that the city should avoid raising taxes and incurring debts and that development and expansion should be financed by accumulated surpluses, just as the prudent family head buys with his savings and not on credit. The model of family management has been a compelling one for local elites all over France; *gestion en bon père de famille* is the operational logic of local conservatism. A local reformer from a town near Grenoble related that the proudest accomplishment of the Socialist mayor of his commune was that for a four-year period there had been no increase in the *centimes*. The local hospital was falling into ruin for lack of repairs, but the mayor who was the chairman of the hospital commission boasted that the ledgers of the hospital were in the black. With this model of political action, it is no wonder that problems accumulated in Grenoble and that governments became increasingly less able to meet new demands within the framework of the old system.

Change came from citizens organized in a civic association, the G.A.M. *(groupe d'action municipale)*, who were frustrated by their efforts to obtain satisfaction for what were originally very minimal demands. The current reform mayor of Grenoble, for example, became interested in local politics as a result of his attempts to get the city to adjust water pressure so that his upper-floor apartment would have a regular water supply. The G.A.M. drew on people with very diverse political sympathies: from Catholics to Left Socialists. What they all had in common was the belief that the traditional political parties were failing to provide programs for local political action that could mobilize the energies of wide circles of interested citizens who were finding no channels for expressing their grievances and goals. The G.A.M. provided an organizational framework, not only for individual citizens, but also for a number of neighborhood associations that had been organized over a ten year period. The G.A.M., like the neighborhood associations, refrained from taking positions on national political questions, for while its members could agree on approaches to local problems, they continued to hold very different positions on national controversies. The originality of the G.A.M., according to one of its Grenoble leaders, was to start with the daily local preoccupations of citizens and from these preoccupations to work up to an understanding of the political system as a whole. The traditional parties, he argued, start with national political doctrines and work down, whereas the G.A.M. begins on the local level and moves from local realities to the discovery of politics. In the future, he suggested, the G.A.M. members may realize that local problems cannot be resolved beyond a certain point without changes in national priorities—for example, that enough housing cannot be built if France is simultaneously trying to build a nuclear force. But for the time being, at least, a group based on common local objectives can make major changes in local government by working together in politics.

The Grenoble G.A.M. came to power in the municipal elections of 1965 and was reelected in 1971. The record of the G.A.M. mayor and town council suggests that there is far more leeway in the structure of local government than most communes have been willing to use and that a change in the values of those in power can have a significant impact on the output of local government, even in the absence of important changes in the resources available to the town or in the relationship with the state. What has the G.A.M. done that previous governments had not? First, the mayor and city council have committed themselves to long-range planning for the city. In order to make this possible, they created an urban planning commission *(agence d'urbanisme)* so that the information necessary for planning—surveys, sociological investigation, economic forecasting, feasibility studies—are directly available to the city, and the city will no longer have to rely on agencies of the national ministries to provide technical assistance for local projects. As we have seen, part of the dependence of communes on the state stems from their inability to deal with the complex problems at stake in running a city, and to the extent that the city can develop its own sources of expertise, it can liberate itself from the heavy hand of the state.

Recognition of the need to plan the future of the city had led the Grenoble reform government down another path rarely taken by their predecessors: the path of cooperation and coordination with neighboring communes. The G.A.M. government was willing to make considerable sacrifices to overcome the hesitations and suspicions of its potential partners. In order to convince the governments of the twenty-one communes of the metropolitan Grenoble area to meet regularly in a "intercommunal syndicate" that would plan the future of the region, Grenoble agreed to an equal representation in the syndicate—though Grenoble would have only as many representatives as a commune of 500 inhabitants. Grenoble, moreover, agreed to finance a major part of the expenses of an urban planning commission that would serve the entire area. The mayor considered these concessions an acceptable price to pay for obtaining one of his principal objectives: to open up new prospects for the development of the city. Since land is limited in the city proper, expansion depends on the capacity of the neighboring communes to absorb, house, school, and transport new populations. In sum, progress in this situation required coordination of Grenoble's plans with those of other towns in the area, hence a loss of independence vis-à-vis the surrounding communities. The alternatives were economic stagnation or reliance on the state to make plans for the metropolitan area. By its willingness to cooperate, even at the risk of losing autonomy, the new Grenoble government won increased power for resolving problems without recourse to the state.

Finally, the G.A.M. method of local government has given high priority to encouraging the participation of citizens. The neighborhood associations that were a constituent element in the alliance of political forces that founded the G.A.M. continue to play an active role in the politics of the new government. The G.A.M. government has experimented with various ways of encouraging citizens to participate, from diffusing more information about the issues before the town council to creating working committees on special urban problems on which representatives from civic associations as well as members of the city council sit. Members of the neighborhood associations have such good access to the mayor and the municipal council that the representatives of the traditional parties, which are the electoral allies of the G.A.M., complain about their exclusion from power and about the preference given to nonparty organizations. Grenoble, however, is far from having resolved the problem of creating enough channels for participation in the affairs of a large urban center. Despite greater information on decisions before the city council, the number of citizens attending council meetings remains small. Despite the existence of neighborhood associations in most parts of the city, the majority of the participants are middle class; the working class continues to rely on the unions and parties that have been its traditional representatives in politics.

The collapse of the old urban consensus is producing experiments in local government in cities all over France. By the end of 1970 there were 100 G.A.M.s, half of which were located in cities of over 30,000 inhabitants. This means (see Table 2) that about a third of the cities over 30,000 have a G.A.M. in operation, even if not in power; still other cities have broken out of the traditional pattern without using the G.A.M. organizational model. Statistics on the G.A.M.s, moreover, probably underestimate the extent of change in communal France, for the G.A.M. is a model that is not very useful in small communes, yet many small communes have been engaged in much the same processes of political transformation as the cities with G.A.M.s. A study of towns in the area of Grenoble showed that even in towns whose populations were stable and whose traditional economic base—mining and agriculture—was declining without replacement by more modern industries, some of the same phenomena observable in Grenoble were at work. In a mining town, for example, whose previous mayor had resisted any change that would raise the *centimes,* a coalition of conservatives and Left Socialists (P.S.U.) formed a new government. The old mayor had relied completely on the mining company, a nationalized industry, to resolve all problems of housing and employment. The reform government broke out of this dependence on the state and began to solicit new industries for the region and to raise the tax rate in order to improve the hospital and provide industrial infrastructure.

No case demonstrates better how much even a commune with a small population and limited resources can accomplish once traditionalist local ideology is abandoned than Crolles, a town of 2,000 people in the Grenoble region. Crolles is one of the poorest communes in the department of Isère. The population is mostly composed of workers and peasants. M. Jargot, the mayor of Crolles since 1953, has been the moving force behind the major changes in the commune. By his own account, the reason that Crolles has acquired more power and more independence from the state lies in the patterns of participation and communication that the commune has developed over the past two decades. Every year, the municipal council convokes the town's population to meet and debate the priorities for municipal action. When the town decided to establish an industrial zone in order to attract new industries to settle there and provide jobs, Jargot called together all the peasants in the area. After long discussions they agreed to sell some of their lands in the zone and to sell them at a fixed price. The town could then approach industries and offer them a site, without having had to purchase the land itself. At the same time, Crolles hired its own experts to draw up plans for the industrial zone. By involving all those affected by the decision in discussions and negotiations, Jargot was even able to convince a group of citizens whose taxes were disproportionately—though legally—lower than those of other citizens to make voluntary contributions to the commune.

Crolles like Grenoble has enlarged its resources by cooperation with groups outside the commune. By taking the initiative of uniting fifty-two communes in its region in a study commission, Crolles has been able to share the costs of technical expertise and economic studies for which most small communes must depend on the state. In order to raise the funds to build a community center, Crolles negotiated contracts to rent the building to various departmental groups that need occasional facilities for training programs, summer camps, and so forth. In effect, Crolles has been able to decide on and pay for a major investment by itself.

What are the limits of municipal reform? The financial resources available to the commune and the centralized system of power in which the commune must operate are, as we have seen, major obstacles to change in urban France. When the fiscal reform of 1959 at long last goes into effect, the basis of taxation in communes will be rationalized, but the tax revenues available to the communes will not be substantially increased. Neither the new legislation on communal mergers nor the new regional reform proposals are likely to alter significantly the structures of centralization. Thus at least in the immediate future even communes with reform governments are likely to come up against serious constraints on their power and independence whenever they attempt major undertakings.

Just as important as the constraints imposed by limited resources and by the system of centralization are the difficulties that the political party system poses to the transformation of local politics. French political parties continue to be oriented to issues that are by and large irrelevant to the questions at stake in modern urban centers (see Chapter 3). Church-state, socialism-antisocialism, majority-opposition realignment of national politics—these are axes of conflict with important consequences for local politics, but they do not express well the choices among values, interests, and groups that are salient today in France's cities. The coalitions that have emerged in communes that are breaking with the old patterns of local government reflect this lack of fit between the traditional political parties and the new problems of the cities: In the mining town, the reform government was based on conservatives and Left Socialists; in Grenoble, the G.A.M. allied with Socialists and progressive Catholics; in Crolles, Jargot's alliance depends on Communists and Catholics. The problem is that in many towns the lines of partisan division remain so important that a local coalition built with elements of traditional Left and Right parties is still impossible. The strength of the traditional political parties—based on the party organizations, the partisan affiliations and beliefs of the population, and the monopoly on local power held by party men—continues in many parts of France to be the major obstacle to the emergence of new coalitions at the local level.

At the same time, the eclipse of the political parties is not a solution either. Local politics in France has depended on a reservoir of political activists and interested citizenry that are mobilized by political parties, and according to local reformers, the decline of the parties has produced a general decline in political interest. Jargot, in attempting to explain the lack of political awareness among Crolles' youth, argued that it was essential to rebuild party organizations "for youth today find nothing: no structures, no traditions, nothing. Our generation inherited a Communist Party; we inherited the Church; we inherited political structures."

As individuals spend more of their lives within the walls of their own houses, watching television sets or involved in family-centered activities, where once they spent more of the day with others, in the factory, in cafes, in clubs, and at party meetings, the existence of structures that promote collective activity becomes more critical than ever before. A renewal of the values and understandings that orient French political life at the local level depends on the emergence of groups that can perform for citizens the role that the traditional parties once played in educating them for participation in national politics. The neighborhood associations and the G.A.M.s are to a certain extent developing as alternative centers of political life in the cities and are thus performing the functions of political parties. But the strength of the new local organizations depends in part on their narrow definition of political objectives. They confine their concerns to matters that lie within the city, and they interpret their task essentially as one of maximization: of the city's resources, of the efficiency of government. Despite their desire to encourage more participation, they continue to define the job of government in largely technocratic, administrative terms. When they move beyond efficiency, they rediscover the political differences that separate their members.

Finally, a reform of the political parties is needed if changes in local politics are to have a significant impact on national politics. The channels of communication—the political parties—must be cleared of the debris of past quarrels and refitted for the conflicts of interests and values of contemporary French society. Nothing is more revealing of the limits of reform at the local level than the sense of isolation and powerlessness in the national system experienced by even the most successful of the new mayors. As Jargot at Crolles concluded,

> We accomplish something at Crolles; in Grenoble they accomplish something, but there is no system to connect these developments into national politics. Parties are necessary to break out of our isolation, and in the sense that they are weaker now than twenty years ago, perhaps we have regressed. On the other hand, we have more power than ever before: power to run our communes, to direct the economic evolution of our regions, whereas in the past our power was mainly one of demanding things. Now we have the power to govern, but we have become administrators, and we are no longer political men.

Six

The Legacy and the Future

Today in French politics two problems emerge as central: conflicts over the legitimacy of the government and a crisis of relations between the state and the citizen. Both contribute to the instability of the French political system. Both derive from patterns of political development in which the choices of the elites to preserve a significant part of the past in the new political system required particular solutions to the problems of political integration. Political modernization, in sum, was achieved at the cost of building permanent sources of tension and conflict into the modern French state. Despite important changes in French politics over the past three decades, these tensions and conflicts continue to turn on the issues of legitimacy and citizenship. These two issues have recurred frequently in these pages, for they have woven a net of frustrations and contradictions in which rulers and ruled, government parties and opposition parties, bureaucrats and citizens alike find themselves caught.

The legitimacy problem—that is, the failure to obtain agreement from most citizens on which rules should regulate the distribution and exercise of political power—reflects the survival of diverse and conflicting conceptions of the purposes the state should pursue and the means it may use to reach them. These ideas have been embodied in different constitutions, and the succession of regimes since the Revolution mirrors the triumph and defeat of different ideas about the state. Still today there is strong disagreement over whether the state should be ruled by a strong President, as the constitutional practice of the Fifth Republic provides, or by an assembly

of deputies. Those who support the latter solution draw upon the constitutional traditions of the past and look forward to a political future in which
their "rules" would once again determine the organization of power. Were
it only a matter of efficiency and the rational organization of the government's business, the supporters of government by assembly might well
agree with the advocates of presidential government that the Constitution
of the Fifth Republic is best for France. But the question of the constitution
goes far beyond institutional effectiveness to the issue of who has the right
to decide what political institutions should do. Who should rule? Whose
interests should be represented, and how? What limits should regulate the
exercise of power? Each of the French constitutions has provided a different set of answers to these questions. The legitimacy of the state established by the Constitution of the Fifth Republic is challenged, however, not
only by Frenchmen attached to the values and institutions expressed in
past constitutions, but also by groups of Frenchmen like the Communist
party, for example, who reject old constitutional traditions and demand a
radical change in the rules governing the distribution and exercise of
political power in the nation.

In all nations there are conflicts over the *content* of state policy. In
France, however, the absence of consensus on the state means that not
only the substance of political decision but also the decision-making structures themselves are contested. The Communists, for example, challenge
not only the legislative proposals of the Gaullist government but also the
government's right to exist. In Britain, in contrast, no matter how bitter the
opposition to particular governmental policies, no significant group questions the government's right to make policy. Despite the angry trade-
unionist reaction against the Conservative government's plans to regulate
unions, for example, neither the unions nor the Labour party ever denied
that the government had the authority to pass and carry out such legislation. In France the line between opposition to a policy and opposition to
the regime remains blurred and unfixed. History provides many examples
of dissent over policy spilling over into a battle against the government that
ends with the fall of the regime. The Fifth Republic, indeed, came to power
as a result of opposition to the Algerian policies of the previous governments that escalated into a revolt against the government itself. What
makes French politics unstable and French governments weak is not so
much the inability of various groups to agree on policy as their inability to
agree on who has the right to make policy or on how the rulers should be
changed.

The second major problem of modern French politics is the crisis of
relations between citizens and the state. The legitimacy problem describes
a situation in which a certain part of the nation refuses to recognize the
legitimacy of the government. But in France even those citizens who do
acknowledge the legitimacy of the regime frequently regard the state with

a mixture of cynicism, hostility, and apathy that makes them unwilling to participate beyond the act of voting or to provide much support for the personnel or institutions of politics. The state is frequently perceived as a distant and foreign force; it can be cajoled for favors, but not fundamentally redirected to new ends; it can be captured but not controlled. The feelings of inefficacy and cynicism reflect the citizen's belief that there is no way to make his voice heard.

Objectively, an individual citizen in any country is relatively powerless to change the course of government in a direction of his choosing. In France, however, the citizen's sense of impotence is magnified by the weakness of the intermediaries that might assist the individual in his efforts to reach the state. The problem is not only one of perceptions and attitudes. Political parties, interest groups, and civic associations do exist in France, but they have developed in ways that make them ineffective at linking the needs and desires of individuals and localities into national politics. There is a vicious circle at work here: intermediary associations are weak because citizens do not support them; citizens refuse their participation because of the inadequacy of the organizations available to them. Today in France major reforms are proposed to transform the structures of politics. Parties and voluntary associations, local and regional governments are in a state of ferment and change. Where this change will lead, whether it will go anywhere at all or simply be absorbed by the old system, depends on how the relationship of citizen to state is modified. The central question here, as in any analysis of the prospects of political reform in France, must be whether the French can find new solutions to the old problems of building a political community.

Appendixes

CONSTITUTION OF FRANCE
October 4, 1958, as amended June 4, 1960, November 6, 1962,
December 30, 1963

PREAMBLE

The French people hereby solemnly proclaims its attachment to the Rights of Man and the principles of national sovereignty as defined by the Declaration of 1789, reaffirmed and complemented by the Preamble of the Constitution of 1946.

By virtue of these principles and that of the free determination of peoples, the Republic hereby offers to the Overseas Territories that express the desire to adhere to them, new institutions based on the common ideal of liberty, equality and fraternity and conceived with a view to their democratic evolution.

Art. 1. The Republic and the peoples of the Overseas Territories who, by an act of free determination, adopt the present Constitution thereby institute a Community.

The Community shall be based on the equality and the solidarity of the peoples composing it.

TITLE I ON SOVEREIGNTY

Art. 2. France is a Republic, indivisible, secular, democratic and social. It shall ensure the equality of all citizens before the law, without distinction of origin, race or religion. It shall respect all beliefs.

The national emblem is the tricolor flag, blue, white and red.

The national anthem is the "Marseillaise."

The motto of the Republic is "Liberty, Equality, Fraternity."

Its principle is government of the people, by the people and for the people.

Art. 3. National sovereignty belongs to the people, which shall exercise this sovereignty through its representatives and by means of referendums.

No section of the people, nor any individual, may attribute to themselves or himself the exercise thereof.

Suffrage may be direct or indirect under the conditions stipulated by the Constitution. It shall always be universal, equal and secret.

All French citizens of both sexes who have reached their majority and who enjoy civil and political rights may vote under the conditions to be determined by law.

Art. 4. Political parties and groups shall be instrumental in the expression of the suffrage. They shall be formed freely and shall carry on their activities freely. They must respect the principles of national sovereignty and democracy.

TITLE II   THE PRESIDENT OF THE REPUBLIC

Art. 5. The President of the Republic shall see that the Constitution is respected. He shall ensure, by his arbitration, the regular functioning of the governmental authorities, as well as the continuance of the State.

He shall be the guarantor of national independence, of the integrity of the territory, and of respect for Community agreements and treaties.

Art. 6. The President of the Republic shall be elected for seven years by direct universal suffrage.

The procedures implementing the present article shall be determined by an organic law.

Art. 7. The President of the Republic shall be elected by an absolute majority of the votes cast. If this is not obtained on the first ballot, there shall be a second ballot on the second Sunday following. Only the two candidates who have received the greatest number of votes on the first ballot shall present themselves, taking into account the possible withdrawal of more favored candidates.

The voting shall begin at the summons of the Government.

The election of the new President shall take place twenty days at the least and thirty-five days at the most before the expiration of the powers of the President in office.

In the event that the Presidency of the Republic has been vacated, for any cause whatsoever, or impeded in its functioning as officially noted by the Constitutional Council, to which the matter has been referred by the Government, and which shall rule by an absolute majority of its members, the functions of the President of the Republic, with the exception of those provided for by the Articles 11 and 12 below, shall be temporarily exercised by the President of the Senate and, if the latter is in his turn impeded in the exercise of these functions, by the Government.

In the case of a vacancy, or when the impediment is declared definitive by the Constitutional Council, the voting for the election of a new President shall take place, except in case of *force majeure* officially noted by the Constitutional Council, twenty days at the least and thirty-five days at the most after the beginning of the vacancy or the declaration of the definitive character of the impediment.

There may be no application of either Articles 49 and 50 or of Article 89 of the Constitution during the vacancy of the Presidency of the

Republic or during the period that elapses between the declaration of the definitive character of the impediment of the President of the Republic and the election of his successor.

Art. 8.   The President of the Republic shall appoint the Premier. He shall terminate the functions of the Premier when the latter presents the resignation of the Government.

On the proposal of the Premier, he shall appoint the other members of the Government and shall terminate their functions.

Art. 9.   The President of the Republic shall preside over the Council of Ministers.

Art. 10.   The President of the Republic shall promulgate the laws within fifteen days following the transmission to the Government of the finally adopted law.

He may, before the expiration of this time limit, ask Parliament for a reconsideration of the law or of certain of its articles. This reconsideration may not be refused.

Art. 11.   The President of the Republic, on the proposal of the Government during Parliamentary sessions, or on joint motion of the two assemblies, published in the *Journal Officiel,* may submit to a referendum any bill dealing with the organization of the governmental authorities, entailing approval of a Community agreement, or providing for authorization to ratify a treaty that, without being contrary to the Constitution, might affect the functioning of existing institutions.

When the referendum decides in favor of the bill, the President of the Republic shall promulgate it within the time limit stipulated in the preceding article.

Art. 12.   The President of the Republic may, after consultation with the Premier and the Presidents of the Assemblies, declare the dissolution of the National Assembly.

General elections shall take place twenty days at the least and forty days at the most after the dissolution.

The National Assembly shall convene by right on the second Thursday following its election. If this meeting takes place between the periods provided for ordinary sessions, a session shall, by right, be held for a fifteen-day period.

There may be no further dissolution within a year following these elections.

Art. 13.   The President of the Republic shall sign the ordinances and decrees decided upon in the Council of Ministers.

He shall make appointments to the civil and military posts of the State.

Councillors of State, the Grand Chancellor of the Legion of Honor, Ambassadors and Envoys Extraordinary, Master Councillors of the Audit Office, Prefects, representatives of the Government in the Overseas Territories, general officers, Rectors of Academies (regional divisions of the public educational system) and directors of central administrations shall be appointed in meetings of the Council of Ministers.

An organic law shall determine the other posts to be filled in meetings of the Council of Ministers, as well as the conditions under which the power of the President of the Republic to make appointments to office may be delegated by him and exercised in his name.

Art. 14.   The President of the Republic shall accredit Ambassadors and Envoys Extraordinary to foreign powers; foreign Ambassadors and envoys Extraordinary shall be accredited to him.

Art. 15.   The President of the Republic shall be Commander of the Armed Forces. He shall preside over the higher councils and committees of national defense.

Art. 16.   When the institutions of the Republic, the independence of the nation, the integrity of its territory or the fulfilment of its international commitments are threatened in a grave and immediate manner and when the regular functioning of the constitutional governmental authorities is interrupted, the President of the Republic shall take the measures commanded by these circumstances, after official consultation with the Premier, the Presidents of the assemblies and the Constitutional Council.

He shall inform the nation of these measures in a message.

These measures must be prompted by the desire to ensure to the constitutional governmental authorities, in the shortest possible time, the means of fulfilling their assigned functions. The Constitutional Council shall be consulted with regard to such measures.

Parliament shall meet by right.

The National Assembly may not be dissolved during the exercise of emergency powers by the President.

Art. 17.   The President of the Republic shall have the right of pardon.

Art. 18.   The President of the Republic shall communicate with the two Assemblies of Parliament by means of messages, which he shall cause to be read, and which shall not be followed by any debate.

Between sessions, Parliament shall be convened especially for this purpose.

Art. 19. The acts of the President of the Republic, other than those provided for under Articles 8 (first paragraph), 11, 12, 16, 18, 54, 56 and 61, shall be countersigned by the Premier and, should circumstances so require, by the appropriate ministers.

TITLE III THE GOVERNMENT

Art. 20. The Government shall determine and direct the policy of the Nation.

It shall have at its disposal the administration and the Armed Forces.

It shall be responsible to Parliament under the conditions and according to the procedures stipulated in Articles 49 and 50.

Art. 21. The Premier shall direct the operation of the Government. He shall be responsible for national defense. He shall ensure the execution of the laws. Subject to the provisions of Article 13, he shall have regulatory powers and shall make appointments to civil and military posts.

He may delegate certain of his powers to the ministers.

He shall replace, should the occasion arise, the President of the Republic as chairman of the councils and committees provided for under Article 15.

He may, in exceptional instances, replace him as chairman of a meeting of the Council of Ministers by virtue of an explicit delegation and for a specific agenda.

Art. 22. The acts of the Premier shall be countersigned, when circumstances so require, by the ministers responsible for their execution.

Art. 23. The office of member of the Government shall be incompatible with the exercise of any Parliamentary mandate, with the holding of any office at the national level in business, professional or labor organizations, and with any public employment or professional activity.

An organic law shall determine the conditions under which the holders of such mandates, functions or employments shall be replaced.

The replacement of members of Parliament shall take place in accordance with the provisions of Article 25.

TITLE IV THE PARLIAMENT

Art. 24. The Parliament shall comprise the National Assembly and the Senate.

The deputies to the National Assembly shall be elected by direct suffrage.

The Senate shall be elected by indirect suffrage. It shall ensure the representation of the territorial units of the Republic. Frenchmen living outside France shall be represented in the Senate.

Art. 25. An organic law shall determine the term for which each Assembly is elected, the number of its members, their emoluments, the conditions of eligibility and ineligibility and the offices incompatible with membership in the assemblies.

It shall likewise determine the conditions under which, in the case of a vacancy in either Assembly, persons shall be elected to replace the deputy or senator whose seat has been vacated until the holding of new complete or partial elections to the Assembly concerned.

Art. 26. No member of Parliament may be prosecuted, sought, arrested, detained or tried as a result of the opinions or votes expressed by him in the exercise of his functions.

No member of Parliament may, during Parliamentary sessions, be prosecuted or arrested for criminal or minor offenses without the authorization of the Assembly of which he is a member except in the case of *flagrante delicto.*

When Parliament is not in session, no member of Parliament may be arrested without the authorization of the Secretariat of the Assembly of which he is a member, except in the case of *flagrante delicto,* of authorized prosecution or of final conviction.

The detention or prosecution of a member of Parliament shall be suspended if the Assembly of which he is a member so demands.

Art. 27. All binding instructions upon members of Parliament shall be null and void.

The right to vote of the members of Parliament shall be personal.

An organic law may, under exceptional circumstances, authorize the delegation of a vote. In this case, no member may be delegated more than one vote.

Art. 28. Parliament shall convene, by right, in two ordinary sessions a year.

The first session shall begin on October 2; it shall last eighty days.

The second session shall open on April 2; it may not last longer than ninety days.

If October 2 or April 2 is a holiday, the session shall begin on the first working day following.

Art. 29. Parliament shall convene in extraordinary session at the request of the Premier, or of the majority of the members comprising the National Assembly, to consider a specific agenda.

When an extraordinary session is held at the request of the members of the National Assembly, the closure decree shall take effect as soon as the Parliament has exhausted the agenda for which it was called, and at the latest twelve days from the date of its meeting.

Only the Premier may ask for a new session before the end of the month following the closure decree.

Art. 30. Apart from cases in which Parliament meets by right, extraordinary sessions shall be opened and closed by decree of the President of the Republic.

Art. 31. The members of the Government shall have access to the two assemblies. They shall be heard when they so request.

They may call for the assistance of Commissioners of the Government.

Art. 32. The President of the National Assembly shall be elected for the duration of the legislature. The President of the Senate shall be elected after each partial re-election of the Senate.

Art. 33. The meetings of the two Assemblies shall be public. An *in extenso* report of the debates shall be published in the *Journal Officiel.*

Each Assembly may sit in secret committee at the request of the Premier or of one tenth of its members.

TITLE V   ON RELATIONS BETWEEN PARLIAMENT AND THE GOVERNMENT
Art. 34. All laws shall be passed by Parliament.

Laws shall establish the regulations concerning:

–civil rights and the fundamental guarantees granted to the citizens for the exercise of their public liberties; the obligations imposed by the national defense upon the persons and property of citizens;

–nationality, status and legal capacity of persons, marriage contracts, inheritance and gifts;

–determination of crimes and misdemeanors as well as the penalties imposed therefor; criminal procedure; amnesty; the creation of new juridical systems and the status of magistrates;

–the basis, the rate and the methods of collecting taxes of all types; the issuance of currency.

Laws shall likewise determine the regulations concerning:

–the electoral system of the Parliamentary assemblies and the local assemblies;

–the establishment of categories of public institutions;

–the fundamental guarantees granted to civil and military personnel employed by the State;

–the nationalization of enterprises and the transfer of the property of enterprises from the public to the private sector.

Laws shall determine the fundamental principles of:

–the general organization of national defense;

–the free administration of local communities, the extent of their jurisdiction and their resources;

–education;

–property rights, civil and commercial obligations;

–legislation pertaining to employment, unions and social security.

The financial laws shall determine the financial resources and obligations of the State under the conditions and with the reservations to be provided for by an organic law.

Laws pertaining to national planning shall determine the objectives of the economic and social action of the State.

The provisions of the present article may be developed in detail and amplified by an organic law.

Art. 35.   Parliament shall authorize the declaration of war.

Art. 36.   Martial law shall be decreed in a meeting of the Council of Ministers.
Its prorogation beyond twelve days may be authorized only by Parliament.

Art. 37.   Matters other than those that fall within the domain of law shall be of a regulatory character.

Legislative texts concerning these matters may be modified by decrees issued after consultation with the Council of State. Those legislative texts which may be passed after the present Constitution has become operative shall be modified by decree, only if the Constitutional Council has stated that they have a regulatory character as defined in the preceding paragraph.

Art. 38.   The Government may, in order to carry out its program, ask Parliament to authorize it, for a limited period, to take through ordinances measures that are normally within the domain of law.

The ordinances shall be enacted in meetings of the Council of Ministers after consultation with the Council of State. They shall come into force upon their publication, but shall become null and void if the bill for their ratification is not submitted to Parliament before the date set by the enabling act.

At the expiration of the time limit referred to in the first paragraph of the present article, the ordinances may be modified only by law in those matters which are within the legislative domain.

Art. 39.   The Premier and the members of Parliament alike shall have the right to initiate legislation.

Government bills shall be discussed in the Council of Ministers after consultation with the Council of State and shall be filed with the Secretariat of one of the two assemblies. Finance bills shall be submitted first to the National Assembly.

Art. 40.   Bills and amendments introduced by members of Parliament shall not be considered when their adoption would have as a consequence either a diminution of public financial resources, or the creation or increase of public expenditures.

Art. 41.   If it appears in the course of the legislative procedure that a Parliamentary bill or an amendment is not within the domain of law or is contrary to a delegation of authority granted by virtue of Article 38, the Government may declare its inadmissibility.

In case of disagreement between the Government and the President of the Assembly concerned, the Constitutional Council, upon the request of either party, shall rule within a time limit of eight days.

Art. 42.   The discussion of Government bills shall pertain, in the first Assembly to which they have been referred, to the text presented by the Government.

An Assembly, given a text passed by the other assembly, shall deliberate on the text that is transmitted to it.

Art. 43.   Government and Parliamentary bills shall, at the request of the Government or of the Assembly concerned, be sent for study to committees especially designated for this purpose.

Government and Parliamentary bills for which such a request has not been made shall be sent to one of the permanent committees, the number of which shall be limited to six in each Assembly.

Art. 44.   Members of Parliament and of the Government shall have the right of amendment.

After the opening of the debate, the Government may oppose the examination of any amendment which has not previously been submitted to committee.

If the Government so requests, the Assembly concerned shall decide, by a single vote, on all or part of the text under discussion, retaining only the amendments proposed or accepted by the Government.

Art. 45.   Every Government or Parliamentary bill shall be examined successively in the two Assemblies of Parliament with a view to the adoption of an identical text.

When, as a result of disagreement between the two Assemblies, it has become impossible to adopt a Government or Parliamentary bill after two readings by each Assembly, or, if the Government has declared the matter urgent, after a single reading by each of them, the Premier shall have the right to have a joint committee meet, composed of an equal number from both Assemblies and instructed to offer for consideration a text on the matters still under discussion.

The text prepared by the joint committee may be submitted by the Government for approval of the two Assemblies. No amendment shall be admissible except by agreement with the Government.

If the joint committee fails to approve a common text, or if this text is not adopted under the conditions set forth in the preceding paragraph, the Government may, after a new reading by the National Assembly and by the Senate, ask the National Assembly to rule definitively. In this case, the National Assembly may reconsider either the text prepared by the joint committee or the last text adopted by the National Assembly, modified, when circumstances so require, by one or several of the amendments adopted by the Senate.

Art. 46.   The laws that the Constitution characterizes as organic shall be passed and amended under the following conditions:

A Government or Parliamentary bill shall be submitted to the deliberation and to the vote of the first Assembly to which it is submitted only at the expiration of a period of fifteen days following its introduction.

The procedure of Article 45 shall be applicable. Nevertheless, lacking an agreement between the two assemblies, the text may be adopted by the National Assembly on final reading only by an absolute majority of its members.

The organic laws relative to the Senate must be passed in the same manner by the two Assemblies.

Organic laws may be promulgated only after a declaration by the Constitutional Council on their constitutionality.

Art. 47.   Parliament shall pass finance bills under the conditions to be stipulated by an organic law.

Should the National Assembly fail to reach a decision on first reading within a time limit of forty days after a bill has been filed, the Government shall refer it to the Senate, which must rule within a time limit of fifteen days. The procedure set forth in Article 15 shall then be followed.

Should Parliament fail to reach a decision within a time limit of seventy days, the provisions of the bill may be enforced by ordinance.

Should the finance bill establishing the resources and expenditures of a fiscal year not be filed in time for it to be promulgated before the beginning of that fiscal year, the Government shall immediately request

Parliament for the authorization to collect the taxes and shall make available by decree the funds needed to meet the Government commitments already voted.

The time limits stipulated in the present article shall be suspended when Parliament is not in session.

The Audit Office shall assist Parliament and the Government in supervising the implementation of the finance laws.

Art. 48.   The discussion of the bills filed or agreed upon by the Government shall have priority on the agenda of the Assemblies in the order set by the Government.

One meeting a week shall be reserved, by priority, for questions asked by members of Parliament and for answers by the Government.

Art. 49.   The Premier, after deliberation by the Council of Ministers, may pledge the responsibility of the Government to the National Assembly with regard to the program of the Government, or with regard to a declaration of general policy, as the case may be.

The National Assembly may question the responsibility of the Government by the vote of a motion of censure. Such a motion shall be admissible only if it is signed by at least one tenth of the members of the National Assembly. The vote may only take place forty-eight hours after the motion has been filed; the only votes counted shall be those favorable to the motion of censure, which may be adopted only by a majority of the members comprising the Assembly. Should the motion of censure be rejected, its signatories may not introduce another motion in the course of the same session, except in the case provided for in the paragraph below.

The Premier may, after deliberation by the Council of Ministers, pledge the Government's responsibility to the National Assembly on the vote of a text. In this case, the text shall be considered as adopted, unless a motion of censure, filed in the succeeding twenty-four hours, is voted under the conditions laid down in the previous paragraph.

The Premier shall be entitled to ask the Senate for approval of a general policy declaration.

Art. 50.   When the National Assembly adopts a motion of censure, or when it disapproves the program or a declaration of general policy of the Government, the Premier must submit the resignation of the Government to the President of the Republic.

Art. 51.   The closure of ordinary or extraordinary sessions shall by right be delayed, should the occasion arise, in order to permit the application of the provisions of Article 49.

TITLE VI   ON TREATIES AND INTERNATIONAL AGREEMENTS

Art. 52.   The President of the Republic shall negotiate and ratify treaties.

He shall be informed of all negotiations leading to the conclusion of an international agreement not subject to ratification.

Art. 53.   Peace treaties, commercial treaties, treaties or agreements relative to international organization, those that imply a commitment for the finances of the State, those that modify provisions of a legislative nature, those relative to the status of persons, those that call for the cession, exchange or addition of territory may be ratified or approved only by a law.

They shall go into effect only after having been ratified or approved.

No cession, no exchange, no addition of territory shall be valid without the consent of the populations concerned.

Art. 54.   If the Constitutional Council, the matter having been referred to it by the President of the Republic, by the Premier, or by the President of one or the other Assembly, shall declare that an international commitment contains a clause contrary to the Constitution, the authorization to ratify or approve this commitment may be given only after amendment of the Constitution.

Art. 55.   Treaties or agreements duly ratified or approved shall, upon their publication, have an authority superior to that of laws, subject, for each agreement or treaty, to its application by the other party.

TITLE VII   THE CONSTITUTIONAL COUNCIL

Art. 56.   The Constitutional Council shall consist of nine members, whose term of office shall last nine years and shall not be renewable. One third of the membership of the Constitutional Council shall be renewed every three years. Three of its members shall be appointed by the President of the Republic, three by the President of the National Assembly, three by the President of the Senate.

In addition to the nine members provided for above, former Presidents of the Republic shall be members *ex officio* for life of the Constitutional Council.

The President shall be appointed by the President of the Republic. He shall have the deciding vote in case of a tie.

Art. 57.   The office of member of the Constitutional Council shall be incompatible with that of minister or member of Parliament. Other incompatibilities shall be determined by an organic law.

Art. 58.   The Constitutional Council shall ensure the regularity of the election of the President of the Republic.

It shall examine complaints and shall announce the results of the vote.

Art. 59. The Constitutional Council shall rule, in the case of disagreement, on the regularity of the election of deputies and senators.

Art. 60. The Constitutional Council shall ensure the regularity of referendum procedures and shall announce the results thereof.

Art. 61. Organic laws, before their promulgation, and regulations of the Parliamentary Assemblies, before they come into application, must be submitted to the Constitutional Council, which shall rule on their constitutionality.

To the same end, laws may be submitted to the Constitutional Council, before their promulgation, by the President of the Republic, the Premier or the President of one or the other Assembly.

In the cases provided for by the two preceding paragraphs, the Constitutional Council must make its ruling within a time limit of one month. Nevertheless, at the request of the Government, in case of emergency, this period shall be reduced to eight days.

In these same cases, referral to the Constitutional Council shall suspend the time limit for promulgation.

Art. 62. A provision declared unconstitutional may not be promulgated or implemented.

The decisions of the Constitutional Council may not be appealed to any jurisdiction whatsoever. They must be recognized by the governmental authorities and by all administrative and juridical authorities.

Art. 63. An organic law shall determine the rules of organization and functioning of the Constitutional Council, the procedure to be followed before it, and in particular the periods of time allowed for laying disputes before it.

TITLE VIII   ON JUDICIAL AUTHORITY

Art. 64. The President of the Republic shall be the guarantor of the independence of the judicial authority.

He shall be assisted by the High Council of the Judiciary.

An organic law shall determine the status of magistrates.

Magistrates may not be removed from office.

Art. 65. The High Council of the Judiciary shall be presided over by the President of the Republic. The Minister of Justice shall be its Vice President *ex officio*. He may preside in place of the President of the Republic.

The High Council shall, in addition, include nine members appointed by the President of the Republic in conformity with the conditions to be determined by an organic law.

The High Council of the Judiciary shall present nominations for judges of the Court of Cassation (Supreme Court of Appeal) and for First Presidents of Courts of Appeal. It shall give its opinion, under the conditions to be determined by an organic law, on proposals of the Minister of Justice relative to the nomination of the other judges. It shall be consulted on questions of pardon under conditions to be determined by an organic law.

The High Council of the Judiciary shall act as a disciplinary council for judges. In such cases, it shall be presided over by the First President of the Court of Cassation.

Art. 66.   No one may be arbitrarily detained.

The judicial authority, guardian of individual liberty, shall ensure respect for this principle under the conditions stipulated by law.

TITLE IX   THE HIGH COURT OF JUSTICE

Art. 67.   A High Court of Justice shall be instituted.

It shall be composed of members of Parliament elected, in equal number, by the National Assembly and the Senate after each general or partial election to these Assemblies. It shall elect its President from among its members.

An organic law shall determine the composition of the High Court, its rules, and also the procedure to be followed before it.

Art. 68.   The President of the Republic shall not be held accountable for actions performed in the exercise of his office except in the case of high treason. He may be indicted only by the two Assemblies ruling by identical vote in open balloting and by an absolute majority of the members of said Assemblies. He shall be tried by the High Court of Justice.

The members of the Government shall be criminally liable for actions performed in the exercise of their office and deemed to be crimes or misdemeanors at the time they were committed. The procedure defined above shall be applied to them, as well as to their accomplices, in case of a conspiracy against the security of the State. In the cases provided for by the present paragraph, the High Court shall be bound by the definition of crimes and misdemeanors, as well as by the determination of penalties, as they are established by the criminal laws in force when the acts are committed.

TITLE X   THE ECONOMIC AND SOCIAL COUNCIL

Art. 69.   The Economic and Social Council, whenever the Government calls upon it, shall give its opinion on the Government bills, ordinances and decrees, as well as on the Parliamentary bills submitted to it.

A member of the Economic and Social Council may be designated by the latter to present, before the Parliamentary Assemblies, the opinion of the Council on the Government or Parliamentary bills that have been submitted to it.

Art. 70.   The Economic and Social Council may likewise be consulted by the Government on any problem of an economic or social character of interest to the Republic or to the Community. Any plan, or any bill dealing with a plan, of an economic or social character shall be submitted to it for its advice.

Art. 71.   The composition of the Economic and Social Council and its rules of procedure shall be determined by an organic law.

TITLE XI   ON TERRITORIAL UNITS

Art. 72.   The territorial units of the Republic are the communes, the Departments, the Overseas Territories. Other territorial units may be created by law.

These units shall be free to govern themselves through elected councils and under the conditions stipulated by law.

In the departments and the territories, the Delegate of the Government shall be responsible for the national interests, for administrative supervision, and for seeing that the laws are respected.

Art. 73.   Measures of adjustment required by the particular situation of the Overseas Departments may be taken with regard to their legislative system and administrative organization.

Art. 74.   The Overseas Territories of the Republic shall have a special organization, which takes into account their own interests within the general interests of the Republic. This organization shall be defined and modified by law after consultation with the Territorial Assembly concerned.

Art. 75.   Citizens of the Republic who do not have ordinary civil status, the only status referred to in Article 34, may keep their personal status as long as they have not renounced it.

Art. 76.   The Overseas Territories may retain their status within the Republic.

If they express the desire to do so by a decision of their Territorial Assemblies taken within the time limit set in the first paragraph of Article 91, they shall become Overseas Departments of the Republic or member States of the Community, either in groups or as single units.

TITLE XII   ON THE COMMUNITY

Art. 77.   In the Community instituted by the present Constitution, the States shall enjoy autonomy; they shall administer themselves and manage their own affairs democratically and freely.

There shall be only one citizenship in the Community.

All citizens shall be equal before the law, whatever their origin, their race and their religion. They shall have the same duties.

Art. 78.   The Community's jurisdiction shall extend over foreign policy, defense, currency, common economic and financial policy, as well as over policy on strategic raw materials.

It shall include, in addition, except in the case of specific agreements, the supervision of the tribunals, higher education, the general organization of external transportation and transportation within the Community, as well as of telecommunications.

Special agreements may create other common jurisdictions or regulate any transfer of jurisdiction from the Community to one of its members.

Art. 79.   The member States shall benefit from the provisions of Article 77 as soon as they have exercised the choice provided for in Article 76.

Until the measures required for implementation of the present title go into force, matters within the common jurisdiction shall be regulated by the Republic.

Art. 80.   The President of the Republic shall preside over and represent the Community.

The institutional organs of the Community shall be an Executive Council, a Senate and a Court of Arbitration.

Art. 81.   The member States of the Community shall participate in the election of the President according to the conditions stipulated in Article 6.

The President of the Republic, in his capacity as President of the Community, shall be represented in each State of the Community.

Art. 82.   The Executive Council of the Community shall be presided over by the President of the Community. It shall consist of the Premier of the Republic, the heads of Government of each of the member States of the Community, and the ministers responsible for the common affairs of the Community.

The Executive Council shall organize the co-operation of members of the Community at Government and administrative levels.

The organization and procedure of the Executive Council shall be determined by an organic law.

Art. 83.   The Senate of the Community shall be composed of delegates whom the Parliament of the Republic and the legislative Assemblies of the other members of the Community shall choose from among their own membership. The number of delegates of each State shall be determined according to its population and the responsibilities it assumes in the Community.

The Senate of the Community shall hold two sessions a year, which shall be opened and closed by the President of the Community and may not last longer than one month each.

The Senate of the Community, when called upon by the President of the Community, shall deliberate on the common economic and financial policy before laws on these matters are voted upon by the Parliament of the Republic and, should circumstances so require, by the legislative Assemblies of the other members of the Community.

The Senate of the Community shall examine the acts and treaties or international agreements, which are specified in Articles 35 and 53, and which commit the Community.

The Senate of the Community shall make executory decisions in the domains in which it has received delegation of power from the legislative Assemblies of the members of the Community. These decisions shall be promulgated in the same form as the law in the territory of each of the States concerned.

An organic law shall determine the composition of the Senate and its rules of procedure.

Art. 84.   A Court of Arbitration of the Community shall rule on litigation occurring among members of the Community.

Its composition and its jurisdiction shall be determined by an organic law.

Art. 85.   By derogation from the procedure provided for in Article 89, the provisions of the present title that concern the functioning of the common institutions shall be amendable by identical laws passed by the Parliament of the Republic and by the Senate of the Community.

The provisions of the present title may also be amended by agreements concluded between all the States of the Community; the new provisions shall be put into force under the conditions required by the Constitution of each State.

Art. 86.   A change of status of a member State of the Community may be requested, either by the Republic, or by a resolution of the legislative Assembly of the State concerned confirmed by a local referendum, the organization and supervision of which shall be ensured by the institutions of the Community. The procedures governing this change shall be

determined by an agreement approved by the Parliament of the Republic and the legislative Assembly concerned.

Under the same conditions, a member State of the Community may
become independent. It shall thereby cease to belong to the Community.

A member State of the Community may also, by means of agreements, become independent without thereby ceasing to belong to the
Community.

An independent State not a member of the Community may, by
means of agreements, join the Community without ceasing to be independent.

The position of these States within the Community shall be determined by agreements concluded to this end, in particular the agreements mentioned in the preceding paragraphs as well as, should the
occasion arise, the agreements provided for in the second paragraph of
Article 85.

Art. 87.   The special agreements made for the implementation of the present title
shall be approved by the Parliament of the Republic and the legislative
assembly concerned.

TITLE XIII   ON AGREEMENTS OF ASSOCIATION

Art. 88.   The Republic or the Community may make agreements with States that
wish to associate themselves with the Community in order to develop
their own civilizations.

TITLE XIV   ON AMENDMENT

Art. 89.   The initiative for amending the Constitution shall belong both to the
President of the Republic on the proposal of the Premier and to the
members of Parliament.

The Government or Parliamentary bill for amendment must be
passed by the two Assemblies in identical terms. The amendment shall
become definitive after approval by a referendum.

Nevertheless, the proposed amendment shall not be submitted to a
referendum when the President of the Republic decides to submit it to
Parliament convened in Congress; in this case, the proposed amendment shall be approved only if it is accepted by a three-fifths majority
of the votes cast. The Secretariat of the Congress shall be that of the
National Assembly.

No amendment procedure may be undertaken or followed when the
integrity of the territory is in jeopardy.

The republican form of government shall not be subject to amendment.

TITLE XV   TEMPORARY PROVISIONS

Art. 90.   The ordinary session of Parliament is suspended. The mandate of the members of the present National Assembly shall expire on the day that the Assembly elected under the present Constitution convenes.

Until this meeting, the Government alone shall have the authority to convene Parliament.

The mandate of the members of the Assembly of the French Union shall expire at the same time as the mandate of the members of the present National Assembly.

Art. 91.   The institutions of the Republic, provided for by the present Constitution, shall be established within four months after its promulgation.

This time limit shall be extended to six months for the institutions of the Community.

The powers of the President of the Republic now in office shall expire only when the results of the election provided for in Articles 6 and 7 of the present Constitution are proclaimed.

The member States of the Community shall participate in this first election under the conditions derived from their status at the date of the promulgation of the Constitution.

The established authorities shall continue to exercise their functions in these States according to the laws and regulations applicable when the Constitution becomes operative, until the authorities provided for by their new regimes are set up.

Until it is definitively constituted, the Senate shall consist of the present members of the Council of the Republic. The organic laws that determine the definitive composition of the Senate must be passed before July 31, 1959.

The powers conferred on the Constitutional Council by Articles 58 and 59 of the Constitution shall be exercised, until this Council is set up, by a committee composed of the Vice President of the Council of State, as chairman, the First President of the Court of Cassation, and the First President of the Audit Office.

The peoples of the member States of the Community shall continue to be represented in Parliament until the measures necessary to the implementation of Title XII have been put into effect.

Art. 92.   The legislative measures necessary for the setting up of the institutions and, until they are set up, for the functioning of the governmental authorities, shall be taken in meetings of the Council of Ministers, after consultation with the Council of State, in the form of ordinances having the force of law.

During the time limit set in the first paragraph of Article 91, the Government shall be authorized to determine, by ordinances having the force of law and passed in the same way, the system of elections to the assemblies provided for by the Constitution.

During the same period and under the same conditions, the Government may also adopt measures, in all matters, which it may deem necessary to the life of the nation, the protection of citizens or the safeguarding of liberties.

Appendix B   ABBREVIATIONS OF POLITICAL PARTIES AND INSTITUTIONS

Political Parties

C.D.   Centre Démocrate
           (Democratic Center)
C.I.R.   Convention des Institutions Républicains
           (Convention of Republican Institutions)
F.G.D.S.   Fédération de la Gauche Démocrate et Socialiste
           (Federation of the Democratic Socialist Left)
M.R.P.   Mouvement Républicain Populaire
           (Popular Republican Movement: Christian Democracy)
P.D.M.   Progrès et Démocratie Moderne
           (Progress and Modern Democracy)
P.S.U.   Parti Socialiste Unifié
           (Unified Socialist party)
R.I.   Républicains Indépendants
           (Independent Republicans)
R.P.F.   Rassemblement du Peuple Français
           (Rally of the French People)
S.F.I.O.   Section Française de L'internationale Ouvrière
           (French Section of Workers' International; Socialist party)
U.D.R.   Union des Démocrates pour la République
           (Union of Democrats for the Republic; earlier called UNR)
U.N.R.   Union pour la Nouvelle République
           (Union for the New Republic)

Institutions

C.F.D.T.   Confédération Française Démocratique du Travail
           (French Democratic Confederation of Labor)
C.G.T.   Confédération Générale du Travail
           (General Confederation of Labor)
C.O.D.E.R. Commission de Développement Economique Régional
           (Commission of Regional Economic Development)
E.D.F.   Electricité de France
           (French Electricity Co.)
E.E.C.   European Economic Community
E.N.A.   Ecole Nationale d'Administration
           (National School of Administration)
F.N.S.E.A. Fédération Nationale des Syndicats d'Exploitants Agricoles
           (National Federation of Farmers' Unions)
F.O.   Force Ouvrière
           (Workers' Force)

G.A.M. Groupes d'Action Municipale
(Civic Action Groups)

M.O.D.E.F. Mouvement pour la Défense des Exploitations Familiales
(Movement for the Defense of Family Farms)

S.N.C.F. Société Nationale des Chemins de Fer Française
(State Railroads)

T.V.A. Taxe sur la Valeur Ajoutée
(Tax on Value-added)

Appendix C French Legislative Election Results, 1893–1968
Percent Share of Party Vote

Year	Communists	Extreme Left	Socialists		Socialist Radicals	Radicals	Center (Moderate Republicans)	Ralliés	Nationalists	Extreme Right	Other
1893			8.5		2.4	20.5	45.3	6.5		16.8	
1898			11.3		9.6	17.9	41.5	6.9		12.8	
1902		4.1	6.3		10.1	16.8	29.7	4.6	14.2	14.1	
1906			10.0	2.3[1]	28.5	7.9	22.0[2]			29.2	0.1
1910			13.3	4.1[1]	20.1	18.4	22.5[3]			20.9	0.6
1914			16.9	3.9[4]	17.9	16.8	28.5[3]			15.6	0.4
1919			22.7		11.0	-[5]	6.0		33.4[5]	26.9	
1924	9.8		38.1				11.5		39.5		1.0
1928	11.4	0.9	18.2	4.4[4]	17.7		22.9		23.1		1.4
1932	8.4	0.9	20.7	5.3[4]	19.2		23.4		22.1		
1936	15.4		19.9	7.5[4]	14.6			42.6[6]			0.2

Year	Communists		Socialists (S.F.I.O.)	Radicals	Christian Democrats (M.R.P.)	Gaullists	Moderates (Right Independents)	Extreme Right	Other
1945	26.2		23.4	10.5	23.9		15.6		0.1
1946[14]	25.9		21.1	11.6	28.2		12.8		0.1
1946[15]	28.2		17.8	11.1	25.9		12.9		0.8
1951	26.9		14.6	10.0	12.6	21.7	14.1		
1956	25.9	1.7	15.2	13.5	11.1		14.6	13.9[7]	4.3[8]
1958	19.2	1.2	15.7	7.3	11.1	20.4	22.1	2.6	
1962	21.7	2.4	12.6	7.5	8.9	36.3[9]	9.6	0.9	

Appendix C French Legislative Election Results, 1893–1968
Percent Share of Party Vote

	Commun- ists		Socialists S.F.I.O.		Radicals	Christian Democrats (M.R.P.)	Gaullists	Moderates (Right Inde- pendents)	Extreme Right	Other
1967	22.4	2.2[10]	18.7[11]		13.4[12]		38.1	3.9	0.8	0.5
1968	20.0	4.0[10]	16.5[11]	0.6	10.3[13]		43.7	4.1	0.1	0.5

[1]Independent Socialists.
[2]Left and Moderate Republicans.
[3]Moderate Right and the Republican Federation.
[4]Socialist Republicans.
[5]Bloc National (combined Radical and Right lists).
[6]National Front.
[7]Includes the Poujadists (11.6%).
[8]Includes Social Republicans.
[9]Includes Republican Independents (Gaullists).
[10]Parti socialiste unifié.
[11]Fédération de la gauche démocrate et socialiste (F.G.D.S.).
[12]Centre démocrate.
[13]Centre progrès et démocratie moderne.
[14]June 1946.
[15]November 1946.

DATA SOURCES: Peter Campbell, *French Electoral Systems and Elections Since 1789* (Hamden: 1958); François Goguel and Alfred Grosser, *La Politique en France* (Paris: 1964); *L'Année Politique*; Georges LaChapelle, *Les Élections Législatives: Resultats Officiels*. (Paris: 1914, 1919, 1928, 1932, 1936); *Annuaire statistique de la France, 1969*.

The Statistical Appendix was prepared by Glenn A. Robinson.

Appendix D I. LEGISLATIVE ELECTIONS, 1945 TO 1973, FIRST ROUND VOTES

1. First Constituent Assembly, October 21, 1945

Percent Valid Votes

Registered voters	24 622 862	
Voting	19 657 603	
Abstentions	4 965 259	
Blank and invalid ballots	504 887	
Communists	5 024 174	26.2
Socialists	4 491 152	23.4
Radicals	2 018 665	10.5
M.R.P.	4 580 222	23.9
Conservatives	3 001 063	15.6
Others	37 440	0.1

2. Second Constituent Assembly, June 2, 1946

Registered voters	24 696 949	
Voting	20 215 200	
Abstentions	4 481 749	
Blank and invalid ballots	409 870	
Communists	5 145 325	25.9
Socialists	4 187 747	21.1
Radicals	2 299 963	11.6
M.R.P.	5 589 213	28.2
Conservatives	2 538 167	12.8
Others	44 915	0.1

3. Legislative election, November 10, 1946

Registered voters	25 083 039	
Voting	19 578 126	
Abstentions	5 504 913	
Blank and invalid ballots	361 751	
Communists	5 430 593	28.2
Socialists	3 433 901	17.8
Radicals	2 136 152	11.1
M.R.P.	4 988 609	25.9
Gaullists	585 430	3.0
Conservatives	2 487 313	12.9
Others	154 377	0.8

4. Legislative election, June 17, 1951   Percent Total of List Averages

Registered voters	24 530 523	
Voting	19 670 655	
Abstentions	4 859 869	
Blank and invalid ballots	541 231	
Communists	5 056 605	26.9
Socialists	2 744 842	14.6
Radicals	1 887 583	10.0
M.R.P.	2 369 778	12.6
R.P.F.	4 058 336	21.6
Conservatives	2 656 995	14.1

5. Legislative election, January 2, 1956

Registered Voters	26 774 899	
Voting	22 171 957	
Abstentions	4 602 942	
Blank and invalid ballots	671 167	
Communists	5 514 403	25.9
Socialists	3 247 431	15.2
Radicals	2 389 163	11.3
Other Left	1 680 672	7.8
M.R.P.	2 366 321	11.1
Conservatives	3 259 782	15.3
Poujadists	2 483 813	11.6
Extreme Right	260 749	1.2
Others	98 600	0.4

6. Legislative election, November 23, 1958   Percent Valid Votes

Registered voters	27 736 491	
Voting	20 994 797	
Abstentions	6 241 694	
Blank and invalid ballots	652 889	
Communists	3 907 763	19.2
Socialists	3 193 786	15.7
Radicals	1 503 787	7.3
Other Left	261 738	1.2
M.R.P.	2 273 281	11.1
Gaullists	4 165 453	20.4
Conservative	4 502 449	22.1
Extreme Right	533 651	2.6

7. Legislative election,
November 18, 1962

Percent Valid Votes

Registered voters	27 535 019	
Voting	18 931 733	
Abstentions	8 603 286	
Blank and invalid ballots	601 747	
Communists	3 992 431	21.7
Extreme Left	499 743	2.4
Socialists	2 319 662	12.6
Radicals	1 384 498	7.5
M.R.P.	1 635 452	8.9
Gaullists	5 847 403	31.9
Independent Republicans	798 092	4.4
Conservatives	1 742 523	9.6
Extreme Right	159 682	0.9

8. Legislative election, March 5, 1967

Registered voters	28 291 838	
Voting	22 887 151	
Abstentions	5 404 687	
Blank and invalid ballots	494 834	
Communists	5 029 808	22.4
P.S.U.	506 592	2.2
Federation of the Left	4 207 166	18.7
Gaullists	8 453 512	37.7
Gaullist dissidents	104 544	0.4
Democratic Center	3 017 447	13.4
Others	878 472	3.9
Extreme Right	194 776	0.8

9. Legislative election, June 23, 1968

Registered voters	28 171 635	
Voting	22 539 743	
Abstentions	5 631 892	
Blank and invalid ballots	401 086	
Communists	4 435 357	20.0
P.S.U.	874 212	3.9
Federation of the Left	3 654 003	16.5
Other Left	133 100	0.6
Gaullists	10 201 024	46.0
P.D.M.	2 290 165	10.3
Other Conservatives	410 699	1.8
Others	140 097	0.6

10. Legislative election,   **Percent Valid Votes**
March 4, 1973

Registered voters	30 672 952	
Voting	24 811 314	
Abstentions	5 861 638	
Blank and invalid ballots	552 264	
Communists	5 156 619	21.25
P.S.U.	810 645	3.34
Union of Democratic Socialist Left[a]	4 939 603	20.36
Other Left	314 604	1.29
Reformists	3 015 472	12.43
Union of Republicans for Progress[b]	8 364 904	34.48
Other Majority	972 623	4.00
Other Right	684 580	2.82

[a] Alliance: Socialist Party and Left Radicals.

[b] Alliance: U.D.R., Independent Republicans, Centrists.

II. REFERENDA OF FIFTH REPUBLIC

1. September 28, 1958   **Percent Valid Votes**
(Acceptance of de Gaulle's Constitution)

Registered voters	26 603 464	
Voting	22 596 850	
Abstentions	4 006 614	
Blank and invalid ballots	303 559	
Yes votes	17 668 790	79.2
No votes	4 624 511	20.7

2. January 8, 1961 (Self-determination for Algeria approved)

Registered voters	27 184 408	
Voting	20 791 246	
Abstentions	6 393 162	
Blank and invalid ballots	594 699	
Yes votes	15 200 073	75.2
No votes	4 996 474	24.7

3. April 8, 1962 (French approve Evian accords on Algerian
independence)

Registered voters	26 991 743	
Voting	20 401 906	
Abstentions	6 589 837	

Percent Valid Votes

Blank and invalid ballots	1 098 238	
Yes votes	17 508 607	90.6
No votes	1 795 061	9.3

4. **October 28, 1962 (Approval of election of President by universal suffrage)**

Registered voters	27 582 113	
Voting	21 301 816	
Abstentions	6 280 297	
Blank and invalid ballots	559 758	
Yes votes	12 809 363	61.7
No votes	7 932 695	38.2

5. **April 27, 1969 (Voters reject proposals for regions and reform of the Senate)**

Registered voters	28 655 692	
Voting	23 093 296	
Abstentions	5 562 396	
Blank and invalid ballots	635 678	
Yes votes	10 512 469	46.7
No votes	11 945 149	53.2

6. **April 23, 1972 (French accept enlargement of Common Market)**

Registered voters	29 081 036	
Voting	17 578 323	
Abstentions	11 502 713	
Blank and invalid ballots	2 067 198	
Yes votes	10 502 551	67.70
No votes	5 008 574	32.29

III. PRESIDENTIAL ELECTIONS OF FIFTH REPUBLIC, FIRST ROUND VOTES

1. **December 5, 1965**   **Percent Valid Votes**

Registered voters	28 233 167	
Voting	24 001 961	
Abstentions	4 231 206	
Blank and invalid ballots	244 292	

Percent Valid Votes

General de Gaulle	10 386 734	43.7
F. Mitterrand	7 658 792	32.2
J. Lecanuet	3 767 404	15.8
J. L. Tixier-Vignancour	1 253 958	5.2
P. Marcilhacy	413 129	1.7
M. Barbu	277 652	1.1

2. June 1, 1969

Registered voters	28 774 041	
Voting	22 492 059	
Abstentions	6 281 982	
Blank and invalid ballots	287 372	
Georges Pompidou	9 761 297	43.9
Alain Poher	5 201 133	23.4
Jacques Duclos	4 779 539	21.5
Gaston Defferre	1 127 733	5.0
Michel Rocard	814 051	3.6
Louis Ducatel	284 687	1.2
Alain Krivine	236 237	1.1

Appendix E   FRANCE: THE ECONOMIC REGIONS

Appendix F CHRONOLOGY OF IMPORTANT EVENTS, 1789–1973

1789	French Revolution begins
	Last legal barriers to free exchange within France abolished
	Decrees abolish feudal rights
1790	Civil Constitution of the Clergy
1791	Pope condemns oath of Civil Constitution
	Constitution of 1791
1792	Outbreak of war: France declares war on Austria
	Convention abolishes monarchy
1793	Louis XVI executed
	Vendée revolt
	Committee of Public Safety created
	Constitution of 1793
1794	Thermidor: Fall of Robespierre and his execution
1795	Constitution of Year III
	Convention dissolved; Directory established
1799	Coup d'état of 18 brumaire by Napoleon Bonaparte
	(November 9–10)
	Constitution of Year VIII
1802	Concordat reorganizes relations between church and state
1804	Civil Code (Napoleonic Code) promulgated
	First Empire proclaimed
1805–	
1814	European Wars
1814	Abdication of Napoleon
	Restoration of monarchy by Louis XVIII
1815	Napoleon returns and is defeated at Waterloo
	Second Restoration
	Second Peace of Paris
1830	July revolution in Paris
	Louis Phillippe abdicates
	Proclamation of universal suffrage
	Second Republic declared
	Louis Napoleon elected President of the Republic
1852	Plebiscite on Second Empire
	Louis Napoleon becomes Emperor Napoleon III
1870	War with Prussia
	France invaded
	Napoleon III surrenders at Sedan
1871	Paris Commune
1875	Third Republic established by passing of Constitutional laws
1877	President MacMahon dissolves Assembly
	Legislative elections bring republican victory

1884	Laws on local government
	Trade unions legalized
1892	Pope Leo XIII accepts Republic: *Ralliement*
1894–	
1899	The "Dreyfus affair": 1894 condemnation of Dreyfus to life imprison-ment for treason; case reopened; Zola's *J'Accuse* (1898); Dreyfus freed (1899)
1895	Confédération Génerale du Travail founded
1901	Radical party founded
1905	S.F.I.O. founded
	Law separating Church and state passed
1914–	
1919	World War I
1917	First income tax laws passed
1920	Communist party founded
1936	Electoral victory of Popular Front
1939	Start of World War II as Germany invades Poland (September 1) and France and England declare war on Germany
1940	France invaded by Germany (May)
	General de Gaulle broadcasts from London an appeal to continue the war against Germany (June 18)
	National Assembly votes full powers to Pétain (July 10)
1941	Germany invades Russia (June)
	French Communists enter into resistance
1944	Liberation of Paris
	De Gaulle heads government
1945	October referendum ends Third Republic
	First Constituent Assembly elected
1946	De Gaulle resigns
	First Constitution rejected in May referendum
	Second Constituent Assembly elected (June)
	Second Constitution accepted by referendum (October)
	First legislative elections of Fourth Republic (November)
1947	Formation of Gaullist Rassemblement du Peuple Français (R.P.F.)
	Communists leave government (May)
1951	Coal and Steel Agreement between France, Germany, Benelux and Italy
	Reform of electoral law
	Legislative elections
1954–	
1955	Government of Mendès-France
	End of Indochinese War (June–February)
1954	Start of Algerian revolt
1956	Legislative election
1957	Rome Treaties for Common Market ratified by Assembly

1958	Revolt by European settlers and Army in Algeria (May)
	Government of General de Gaulle
	Constitution of Fifth Republic accepted by referendum
	U.N.R. founded
	Gaullist victory in legislative elections; return of electoral system to single member system
	General de Gaulle elected President of the Republic
1959	Debré named Prime Minister (January)
1960	Algerian "barricades uprising" (January)
1961	Referendum ratifies de Gaulle's policy of self-determination for Algeria (January)
	Army revolt in Algeria (April)
	De Gaulle invokes Article 16
1962	Pompidou becomes Prime Minister
	Referendum ratifies Evian accords with Algeria
	Independence of Algeria (July)
	Censure of Pompidou government followed by November legislative elections.
	Referendum approves election of President of the Republic by universal suffrage (October)
1964	C.O.D.E.R. created
1965	De Gaulle reelected President in ballot run-off against François Mitterand
1967	Legislative elections
1968	May–June student strikes spread to general crisis
	Massive strikes
	De Gaulle dissolves Assembly
	New legislative elections return majority for U.N.R.
	Couve de Murville becomes Prime Minister (July)
1969	April referendum on Senate and regions
	De Gaulle resigns after the defeat
	Georges Pompidou elected President of the Republic
	Chaban-Delmas becomes Prime Minister (June)
1970	Radicals adopt Servan-Schreiber's Manifesto; reopens question of regions
	Death of de Gaulle (November)
1972	April referendum ratifies enlarging Common Market to include Great Britain, Ireland, Denmark
	Pierre Messmer becomes Prime Minister (July)
1973	Legislative elections

Select Bibliography

For the reader who wishes to investigate particular events or problems in contemporary French political life, the best starting point is the annual publication *L'Année politique* (Presses Universitaires de France), which describes in chronological order the major political (domestic and foreign), social, and economic events and decisions of the year. It also includes some important official speeches, documents, and election returns. Beyond this, one should consult *Le Monde,* probably the best French newspaper. For primary information, the basic source is the *Journal officiel de la République française,* in which the debates of the Parliament and laws, decrees, and ordinances are published. Two government agencies publish regular and occasional documents of particular interest to scholars of French politics. The *Documentation française* produces studies on various aspects of French life; the Institut National de la Statistique et des Etudes Economiques (I.N.S.E.E.) issues publications on economic problems each year which include a short volume with critical economic, demographic, and political statistics, *Tableaux de l'economie française.*

Studying French politics requires an understanding of the social and cultural context in which political phenomena are embedded. Two perceptive studies of French villages, Laurence Wylie's *Village in the Vaucluse* (New York: Harper and Row, 1965) and Edgar Morin's *The Red and the White* (New York: Pantheon, 1970), explain the values and structures of local life in ways that illuminate the national society. John Ardagh's *The*

New French Revolution (New York: Harper and Row, 1969) describes the ferment in French society over the last decade and, particularly when read together with an account of France in the immediate postwar period, such as Herbert Luethy's *France against Herself* (New York: Meridian, 1957), shows how rapid the process of modernization has been in certain sectors of French life. Michel Crozier in *The Bureaucratic Phenomenon* (Chicago: University of Chicago Press, 1964) and *La Société bloquée* (Paris: Seuil, 1970) has analyzed the obstacles to change and to participation that derive from the French style of authority and from particular cultural norms. Also valuable for understanding change in French society are chapters by Laurence Wylie and Jesse Pitts in Stanley Hoffmann et al., *In Search of France* (Cambridge: Harvard University Press, 1963).

For the history of France from the Revolution of 1789 to the Fifth Republic, there are several good overviews: Gordon Wright, *France in Modern Times, 1760 to the Present* (Chicago: Rand McNally, 1962); Alfred Cobban, *A History of Modern France*, 3 vols. (Baltimore: Penguin, 1963); and David Thomson, *Democracy in France*, 5th ed. (London: Oxford University Press, 1969). Stanley Hoffmann's essay "Paradoxes of the French Political Community" in *In Search of France* is a brilliant analysis of French politics from the Third to the Fifth Republic. On the Third Republic, Thomson, *op. cit.;* W. L. Middleton, *The French Political System* (New York: E. P. Dutton, 1933); and François Goguel, *La Politique des partis sous la troisième République* (Paris: Seuil, 1946) provide good political histories. Robert de Jouvenel, *La République des camarades* (Paris: Grasset, 1914), describes the rules of the game of Third Republic politics. On the Fourth Republic, the best study of the whole period is Philip Williams's *Crisis and Compromise: Politics in the Fourth Republic* (Garden City: Doubleday Anchor, 1960). On the founding of the Fourth Republic, see Gordon Wright, *The Reshaping of French Democracy* (New York: Harcourt, Brace, and World, 1948). On parliamentary politics in the Fourth Republic, in addition to Williams, *op. cit.,* see also the provocative argument of Nathan Leites, *On the Game of Politics in France* (Stanford: Stanford University Press, 1959), and Duncan MacRae, Jr., *Parliament, Parties and Society in France, 1946–1958* (New York: St. Martin's Press, 1967). The political history and accomplishments of the Fourth Republic are dealt with in Raymond Aron, *France: Steadfast and Changing* (Cambridge: Harvard University Press, 1960), and Jacques Fauvet, *The Cockpit of France* (London: Harvill, 1960). On the end of the Fourth Republic and birth of the Fifth, Philip Williams and Martin Harrison, *De Gaulle's Republic,* 2nd ed. (London: Longmans, 1962), should be consulted.

The origins of the Fifth Republic must be located in political projects developed by Charles de Gaulle in speeches and writings during the Fourth Republic. De Gaulle's account of his wartime role and participation in the first postwar government is contained in *The Complete War Memoirs of Charles de Gaulle* (New York: Simon and Schuster, 1968). Indeed, one might profitably go back to a statement of his political views in a book written before the war, Charles de Gaulle, *The Edge of the Sword* (New York: Criterion Books, 1960). Also on de Gaulle, see the biography by Jean Lacouture, *De Gaulle* (New York: New American Library, 1966), and two essays by Stanley Hoffmann, "De Gaulle's Memoirs: The Hero as History," *World Politics,* XIII, no. 1, and "Heroic Leadership: The Case of Modern France," in Edinger, ed., *Political Leadership in Industrialized Societies* (New York: Wiley, 1967). The incorporation of Gaullist ideas into the Constitution of the Fifth Republic has been analyzed by Nicholas Wahl in "The French Constitution of 1958: The Initial Draft and its Origins" in *American Political Science Review,* LIII, no. 2, June 1959.

On the institutional evolution of the Fifth Republic, the best source is Maurice Duverger, *Institutions politiques et droit constitutionnel,* 11th ed. (Paris: Presses Universitaires de France, 1970). Although focusing primarily on Parliament, Philip Williams, *The French Parliament, 1958– 1967* (London: Allen & Unwin, 1968), provides an excellent account of the operations of the major institutions of the Fifth Republic. Both for general analysis of French politics through recent years of the Fifth Republic and for a good selection of documents, one should read François Goguel and Alfred Grosser, *La Politique en France,* 4th ed. (Paris: Colin, 1970). An excellent overview of politics in the Fifth Republic is presented in Philip M. Williams and Martin Harrison, *Politics and Society in de Gaulle's Republic* (New York: Doubleday, 1973). The great crisis of the Fifth Republic—the student-worker strikes of May–June 1968—has been analyzed in well over a hundred books. For a sympathetic Left account of the events, read Daniel Singer, *Prelude to Revolution* (New York: Hill and Wang, 1970), and a collection of programs and tracts written by participants in the "revolution" and edited by Alain Schnapp and Pierre Vidal-Naquet, *The French Student Uprising: November 1967–June 1968* (Boston: Beacon Press, 1971). For a conservative critique of the goals of the students, see Raymond Aron, *The Elusive Revolution: Anatomy of a Student Revolt* (New York: Praeger, 1964).

On political parties and interest groups in the Fifth Republic, there has been relatively little work in English. The Communist Party has been perceptively studied in Frédéric Bon et al., *Le Communisme en France* (Paris: Colin, 1969), and Annie Kriegel, *Les Communistes* (Paris: Seuil, 1968). On the non-Communist Left, see Harvey J. Simmons, *The French Socialists in Search of a Role, 1956–1967* (Ithaca: Cornell University Press, 1970), and Frank L. Wilson, *The French Democratic Left, 1963–1969* (Stanford: Stanford University Press, 1971). On Gaullism and the U.D.R., Pierre Viansson-Ponté, *The King and His Court* (Boston: Houghton Mifflin,

1965), provides sketches of the leading figures of the regime. The leading scholar of the Gaullist party is Jean Charlot, who has written *L'Union pour la nouvelle République* (Paris: Colin, 1967) and *Le Phenomène gaulliste* (Paris: Fayard, 1970). The Right is analyzed in René Rémond, *The Right Wing in France from 1815 to de Gaulle* (Philadelphia: University of Pennsylvania, 1968). Gordon Wright describes the changes in agricultural syndicalism from Third to Fourth to Fifth Republics in *Rural Revolution in France* (Stanford: Stanford University Press, 1964); and agricultural groups in the Fifth Republic are the subject of Yves Tavernier *et al., L'Univers politique des paysans* (Paris: Colin, 1972). Business groups have been studied by Henry W. Ehrmann in *Organized Business in France* (Princeton: Princeton University Press, 1957); labor unions, by Jean-Daniel Reynaud, *Les Syndicats en France* (Paris: Colin, 1963).

There are several good studies of economic policy and planning in France. On the causes of economic growth in France after World War Two and the role of the state in promoting growth, see Jean-Jacques Carré, Paul Dubois, and Edmond Malinvaud, *La Croissance française* (Paris: Seuil, 1972). On planning, see John Hackett and Anne-Marie Hackett, *Economic Planning in France* (Cambridge: Harvard University Press, 1965); Stephen Cohen, *Modern Capitalist Planning: The French Model* (Cambridge: Harvard University Press, 1969); and Malcolm MacLennan, Murray Forsyth, and Geoffrey Denton, *Economic Planning and Policies in Britain, France and Germany* (New York: Praeger, 1968). The role of the French state in promoting the development and reorganization of industry is analyzed in John H. McArthur and Bruce R. Scott, *Industrial Planning in France* (Boston: Division of Research, Graduate School of Business Administration, Harvard University, 1969). The problems of regional policy are discussed in Kevin Allen and M. C. MacLennan, *Regional Problems and Policies in Italy and France* (Beverly Hills: Sage, 1970), and Niles Hansen, *French Regional Planning* (Bloomington: Indiana University Press, 1968). Robert Gilpin, *France in the Age of the Scientific State* (Princeton: Princeton University Press, 1968), examines obstacles to technological innovation in France and the state's policies in research and development. French educational policy is described well in Organisation for Economic Co-operation and Development, *Reviews of National Policies For Education: France* (Paris: O. E. C. D., 1971).

On local and departmental government, the two basic sources in English are Brian Chapman's *Introduction to French Local Government* (London: G. Allen, 1953) and his *The Prefects and Provincial France* (London: G. Allen, 1955). F. Ridley and J. Blondel, *Public Administration in France* (New York: Barnes and Noble, 1965), deals with the field administration of the ministries as well as local government. Mark Kesselman has studied politics in small French towns in *The Ambiguous Consensus: A Study of*

Local Government in France (New York: Knopf, 1967) and Suzanne Berger, Peter Gourevitch, Patrice Higonnet, and Karl Kaiser in "The Problem of Reform in France: The Ideas of Local Elites," *Political Science Quarterly,* LXXXIV, no. 3, September 1969, have analyzed the political ideas of groups in the large modern city of Grenoble.

Index

Index

Suzanne Berger received a B.A. from the University of Chicago and an M.A. and Ph.D. from Harvard University. She began teaching at Harvard University and is now Associate Professor in the Department of Political Science at the Massachusetts Institute of Technology. She is a member of the Center for International Studies at the Massachusetts Institute of Technology and a Research Associate of the West European Studies Center, Harvard University. She is the author of *Peasants Against Politics: Rural Organization in Brittany, 1911–1967* and of various articles on French politics.